Doing SLA Research with Implications for the Classroom

Language Learning & Language Teaching (LL&LT)

ISSN 1569-9471

The LL&LT monograph series publishes monographs, edited volumes and text books on applied and methodological issues in the field of language pedagogy. The focus of the series is on subjects such as classroom discourse and interaction; language diversity in educational settings; bilingual education; language testing and language assessment; teaching methods and teaching performance; learning trajectories in second language acquisition; and written language learning in educational settings.

For an overview of all books published in this series, please see
http://benjamins.com/catalog/lllt

Editors

Nina Spada
Ontario Institute for Studies in Education
University of Toronto

Nelleke Van Deusen-Scholl
Center for Language Study
Yale University

Volume 52

Doing SLA Research with Implications for the Classroom
Reconciling methodological demands and pedagogical applicability
Edited by Robert M. DeKeyser and Goretti Prieto Botana

Doing SLA Research with Implications for the Classroom

Reconciling methodological demands
and pedagogical applicability

Edited by

Robert M. DeKeyser
University of Maryland

Goretti Prieto Botana
University of Southern California

John Benjamins Publishing Company
Amsterdam / Philadelphia

The paper used in this publication meets the minimum requirements of the American National Standard for Information Sciences – Permanence of Paper for Printed Library Materials, ANSI z39.48-1984.

DOI 10.1075/lllt.52

Cataloging-in-Publication Data available from Library of Congress:
LCCN 2018058471 (PRINT) / 2019012792 (E-BOOK)

ISBN 978 90 272 0306 9 (HB)
ISBN 978 90 272 0307 6 (PB)
ISBN 978 90 272 6265 3 (E-BOOK)

John Benjamins Publishing Company · https://benjamins.com

Table of contents

CHAPTER 1

Current research on instructed second language learning

A bird's eye view

Robert DeKeyser and Goretti Prieto Botana
University of Maryland / University of Southern California

In this introductory chapter we provide a picture of recent research on instructed second language learning (ISLA), not about its findings, but about what questions it addresses, on what aspects of the second language, and with what methodologies. We also address some potential reasons for why ISLA research is a relatively small part of the SLA research published in the leading journals, and for why a rather small part of that ISLA research is carried out in actual classrooms. We then present a set of questions about research methodology and generalizability of results that we asked the authors of each empirical chapter in the book (Chapters 2–9) to address, and we provide a brief overview of where the various contributions fall on the spectrum from least to most instructional intervention, which in turn largely determines their answers to the questions we asked them to address.

Keywords: instructed second language acquisition, research methodology, classroom research, laboratory research

This book grew out of a 2016 AAAL colloquium on "Reconciling methodological demands and pedagogical applicability in SLA research." The goal for that colloquium was twofold: bringing together empirical studies that have clear implications for the classroom, while also providing a forum for discussing advantages and disadvantages of different methodologies for such research. The aim of this book is the same. What motivated us to organize the colloquium and edit this book is that, while one of the arguments for conducting research on second language learning is being able to formulate recommendations for second/foreign language instruction, in practice much SLA research does not deal with instruction, and more importantly, the research that does that often does not yield findings with clear implications for practice.

https://doi.org/10.1075/lllt.52.01dek

Why is this so? The reasons are many, but the most important one perhaps is the well-known dilemma between experimental control and ecological validity. Classroom research virtually never meets all the requirements for experimental research in the true sense: strict control over treatments, random assignment of groups to treatments, and random assignment of individuals to groups. Therefore, it is hard to give a clear, especially a causal, interpretation to the findings, and hence generalizability to other classrooms is questionable. Laboratory research, on the other hand, including research where the classroom itself is essentially turned into a laboratory for an hour or so, is conducted under circumstances so different from those that prevail in a regular classroom, that it is also difficult to generalize its findings to real classrooms with a high degree of confidence. We are not suggesting, of course, that we should abandon both classroom and laboratory research because of the limited generalizability of their findings. The real question is: what can we learn from each, and how, in order to establish generalizable findings that are applicable to the classroom?

In order to have a more concrete and precise picture of what the SLA literature has to offer, as represented in what are arguably the most prominent research journals in the field of SLA, we surveyed all articles published in those journals in the five-year period from mid 2012 to mid 2017. The journals are, in alphabetical order: *Applied Linguistics, Language Learning, Language Teaching Research, Second Language Research, Studies in Second Language Acquisition, TESOL Quarterly*, and *The Modern Language Journal.*

Out of the roughly 700 articles published in these journals in these five years (7 journals x 5 years x 4 issues x 5 articles on average), we identified 194 as being about instructed second language acquisition (ISLA). Housen and Pierrard defined ISLA as "any systematic attempt to enable or facilitate language learning by manipulating the mechanisms of learning and/or the conditions under which these occur" (2005, p. 2). In the same vein, Loewen defined ISLA *research* as "a theoretically and empirically based field of academic inquiry that aims to understand how the systematic manipulation of the mechanisms of learning and/or the conditions under which they occur enable or facilitate the development and acquisition of a language other than one's first" (2015, p. 2). In line with these definitions, in this book we took the term 'ISLA (research)' in a very broad sense, including not only classroom instruction, but also laboratory experiments or any other context where a treatment was given and (some of) its effects were observed. On the other hand, we did not include the small number of studies that were carried out with classroom learners, but where nothing of what happened in the classroom was a variable in the study, and the classroom learners were just a convenience sample (e.g., survey research on motivation, or correlational studies only involving individual difference variables but not outcome variables or only correlations among outcome variables).

It was not always obvious where to draw the line between classroom and laboratory research. We decided to classify studies with learners from regular classrooms who were taken to a laboratory context for a specific treatment that was separate from their regular classroom instruction as laboratory studies. On the other hand, in the few cases where intact classrooms participated in an experiment in their regular computer lab going through a treatment with the whole group, we classified the study as a classroom experiment. Studies where the treatment consisted entirely of synchronous or asynchronous computerized communication were counted as laboratory studies. Besides experiments, we also included the few studies that were observational rather than experimental in nature, i.e. where no special treatment was given to anybody, but where the regular classroom treatment and its effects were observed by the researcher.

It will come as no surprise that in the majority of the studies the target language was English ($n = 112$). The other target languages, in order of frequency, were: Spanish ($n = 23$), German ($n = 9$), Chinese ($n = 9$), French ($n = 5$), Japanese ($n = 4$), Turkish ($n = 4$), Italian ($n = 3$), Russian ($n = 3$), Latin ($n = 3$), Dutch ($n = 2$), Korean ($n = 2$), and several languages with 1 study each: Finnish, Icelandic, Indonesian, Slovak, Welsh, and Esperanto. Another 10 studies used a (semi-)artificial language in the sense of a miniature linguistic system. A few articles dealt with more than one L2; therefore, the total does not add up to exactly 194. The same applies to the other distinctions made below: totals will not always add up to 194, because sometimes a study dealt, e.g., with both vocabulary and grammar, or with both an experiment and observation.

In the 194 articles about ISLA included in our survey, a few topics stood out as having received much attention in the five years from mid 2012 to mid 2017: implicit vs. explicit learning and/or input enhancement/awareness (51 articles), corrective feedback (43), incidental versus intentional learning (13), inductive versus deductive learning (6). Many studies included individual differences, but we are not listing them separately here because the individual difference focus was usually subordinate to another focus.

It is not our intention to provide a literature review for all the topics that have been of great interest in the ISLA literature of recent years. Our focus here is on the methodological aspects of current ISLA research rather than in terms of findings. We distinguished between classroom observational studies ($n = 13$), classroom experiments ($n = 84$), and laboratory experiments ($n = 103$). It may come as a surprise to some that such a large percentage of the studies report on laboratory experiments. This type of research has definitely become more prevalent in ISLA research in recent years, for various reasons, not only because laboratory experiments provide better experimental control, but also because they tend to be easier to organize because of logistics (when no permission can be obtained to carry the experiments out in an existing classroom or when not every learner in an existing class participates), ethics (avoiding interference with existing instruction), or administrative requirements.

The number of articles reporting on classroom experiments, on the other hand, may look distressingly small from the point of view of practitioners eager for research findings that can unambiguously inform their classroom teaching. The number of studies that can be called longitudinal in any meaningful way is even much smaller: there were only a handful in our survey. Of course, the same obstacles to classroom research in general apply even more here, with the dangers of attrition (students dropping out of the study for various reasons) or contamination (some extraneous event affecting (one of the) treatment(s)) on top.

Finally, it should also be mentioned that the vast majority of studies were carried out with adult learners, usually college students. This may seem surprising, given that a great deal of language learning around the world takes place in primary and especially secondary schools nowadays. It is easily explained, however, by the notion of 'convenience sample:' very often the participants are students on the same campus where the researchers work, which not only has the advantage of proximity but may also makes it easier to obtain permission for classroom research from teachers who are colleagues.

What does the ISLA literature have to offer to those who want research that is relevant to their own classrooms then? Again, our contention is that all the forms of research illustrated and discussed in this volume have a role to play and that it is precisely the literature as a whole that can provide the best guidance for classroom practice, not any particular part of it. Observational studies can lead to correlational ones and correlational ones to semi-experimental or perhaps even experimental ones in the classroom. This is what Rosenshine and Furst (1973) called the observational-correlational-experimental loop. Many variants of this are possible, of course: observation can already include correlations, e.g., and classroom observation can lead to experimental studies in the laboratory, which can then lead to less controlled but more ecologically valid (quasi)experimental research in the classroom. The latter also have the advantage of having more face validity, which is important if the research is to appeal to practitioners who may want to try to apply the findings to their classroom, or at least test their applicability there.

The empirical studies in this volume represent the whole range: classroom observation, quasi-experimental research in regular classrooms, laboratory research with learners from regular classrooms, research conducted in a CALL environment with learners from regular classrooms, and longitudinal research on classroom learners' out-of-class writing assignments. The studies were carried out in the US, Canada, Chile, and Japan, and had English, French, or Spanish as target language. In each case the students involved were either young adults or secondary school students. Five of the empirical studies were presented in preliminary form at the 2016 AAAL meeting; the other three (Juffs, Shintani, and Bardovi-Harlig et al.) were invited afterwards.

The authors of each empirical study in this volume were asked to discuss issues of cost, ethics, participant availability, experimental control, teacher collaboration, and student motivation, on the one hand, as well as the generalizability of their findings to different kinds of educational contexts, languages, and structures, on the other hand. The overall guiding question is "What renders this research particularly relevant to classroom applications, and what are the advantages, challenges, and potential pitfalls of the methodology adopted?" All chapters follow the same general structure: (1) empirical study, (2) pedagogical implications, (3) methodological take-away points. The studies are ordered from the least to the most experimentally controlled.

At one end of the spectrum is the study by Collins and White. In their study there is no experimental treatment; they observed spontaneous language-related episodes (LREs) in three intact classes of 12-year-old Francophones learning English as a Second Language. The authors show that peer-initiated LREs and attention to grammar were more common when the teacher had provided support for such activities; they argue that in spite of the limits to the generalizability of observational research, the rich description, large database and high ecological validity enhance the relevance of the findings for L2 pedagogy. At the same time, of course, as we argued above, a study like this can inspire a quasi-experimental study in the classroom. Sato and Loewen's chapter is a good example of that, as it also shows that learners with metalinguistic preparation can handle feedback better.

Three chapters present quasi-experimental studies carried out in the classroom, with only small modifications to the treatments the students were otherwise used to. Sato and Loewen investigated the effects of two types of corrective feedback in interaction with provision or absence of metacognitive instruction about the benefits of receiving corrective feedback. They show that the metacognitive instruction enhanced the benefit of (implicit forms of) corrective feedback and argue that their seamless integration of the treatments into the regular classroom activities made it possible to combine an experimental design with minimal disturbance and hence maximal ecological validity.

The chapter by Bardovi-Harlig, Mossman, and Su represents a classroom study on the effect of instruction and materials specifically designed with the research in mind. They compared the teaching of pragmatics in English L2 through the use of teacher-developed corpus-based materials with hands-on corpus searches by the learners themselves. Their main findings, from the point of view of research methodology and the generalizability of findings, were that the working relationship with the teachers was one of the most valuable assets in their study, and that the feasibility of the use of corpora for teaching speech acts may depend on the availability of large corpora for the languages to be taught.

Shintani reports on a classroom experiment with Japanese university students learning a new and complex construction in English L2, drawing on skill acquisition theory. She explains how providing metalinguistic knowledge and systematic practice was more effective than the other treatments provided (metalinguistic knowledge only or practice only), and that such teaching and practicing of an isolated construction DOES have ecological validity in the Japanese university context. She also points out, however, that some of the other treatments and the testing format were chosen to allow for theoretically-driven comparisons and are therefore of little interest to practitioners.

The next three studies were carried out with regular classroom learners, but these students were taken out of the classroom for the duration of the study. Nassaji describes a study on the effect of corrective feedback where each learner met with a native speaker interlocutor outside the classroom four times over a four-week period for the pretest, treatment, and immediate and delayed posttests. He shows that the recasts and prompts differed in their relative effect on uptake versus learning and discusses the relevance of a laboratory study like this to the classroom.

Prieto Botana and DeKeyser present a study on the learning of two different structures in Spanish L2, with the goal of establishing the importance of explicit information. They find that explicit information is crucial when the practice conditions are not task-essential, and useful for at least some outcome variables when conditions are task-essential. They argue that the multiple exposure to the explicit information that characterized their experiment offers greater ecological validity relative to previous research, and at no cost to experimental control. They discuss the limitations that adopting a lab-oriented framework imposed on the materials for the treatment, as well as the implications this may have for classroom applicability and generalizability to other structures.

Leow, Cerezo, Caras, and Cruz also conducted an experiment with Spanish L2 under laboratory conditions, in this case exclusively providing computer-assisted instruction. They studied the learning of a complex structure under deductive and guided inductive conditions and found that guided induction did not provide the same advantages for this complex structure that it did for a simpler one in a previous study. They end by discussing advantages and challenges of using CALL in SLA research.

Finally, Juffs' study consists of an analysis of out-of-class written assignments collected from studies in an International English Program in the US, with native speakers of Arabic, Chinese, and Korean, and its purpose is entirely methodological. The chapter compares different methodologies for measuring lexical diversity, concludes that one is clearly better than the other for the kinds of text under investigation, and discusses what this implies for the 'messy data' that are typically collected in classroom research.

The book concludes with a discussion by Nina Spada of what the contributions to this volume tell us about the various aspects of ISLA research that we asked all contributors to discuss: cost, ethics, participant availability, experimental control, teacher collaboration, student motivation, and generalizability of results. She offers a compilation of questions that are investigated in the chapters of this book and that are relevant to pedagogical practice: Can L2 learners provide each other with accurate information about language? What are the effects of different types of corrective feedback on L2 learning? Does enhancing learners' awareness of language contribute to L2 development and to the process of learning? Is explicit deductive information about the L2 beneficial for learning and for what kinds of L2 knowledge? Are different types of explicit CALL instruction more effective than others? How effective are corpus-based approaches for the teaching of vocabulary and pragmatics?

These are questions that have been asked in some form or another in a considerable number of studies already, and some of these topics may (soon) be ready for meta-analysis. While replication of experiments and meta-analysis of the results is very important, it has the danger, however, of showing fairly consistent outcomes just because the studies analyzed share so many characteristics, e.g. all being quasi-experimental, all using multiple-choice tests, or all being focused on receptive skills. One could argue that a set of studies using quite diverse methodologies, such as the ones in this book, but focused on one specific question and at the same time specifically designed to look at that question from these different angles can provide a useful complement to meta-analysis, and we hope this book will contribute to such a perspective.

References

Housen, A., Pierrard, M., & Vandaele, S. (2005). Structure complexity and the efficacy of explicit grammar instruction. In A. Housen & M. Pierrard (Eds.), *Investigations in instructed second language acquisition* (pp. 235–267). Berlin: Mouton de Gruyter. https://doi.org/10.1515/9783110197372.2.235

Loewen, S. (2015). *Introduction to instructed second language acquisition*. London: Routledge.

Rosenshine, B., & Furst, N. (1973). The use of direct observation to study teaching. In R. M. W. Travers (Ed.), *Second handbook for research on teaching* (pp. 122–183). Chicago, IL: Rand McNally.

CHAPTER 2

Observing language-related episodes in intact classrooms
Context matters!

Laura Collins and Joanna White
Concordia University

Observations of spontaneous language related episodes (LREs) in actual class-rooms capture pedagogical behaviours that may affect the characteristics of LREs. In this study of 87 twelve-year old intermediate francophone EFL students in 3 intact classes, we examined the type, frequency, and resolution of 607 LREs during 20 paired/small group communicative activities (311,000-word, 55-hour corpus). Common findings across classes were the students' ability to resolve LREs and their focus on lexical issues. However, peer-initiated LREs and attention to grammar were greater in the class where the teacher highlighted task-useful language, provided self-access tools for addressing language needs, and promoted a culture of peer collaboration. Observational research presents methodological challenges and its design limits generalizability. However, the rich description, large data-base and high ecological validity enhance the relevance of the findings for L2 pedagogy.

Keywords: EFL, language-related episodes, LREs, classroom research, feedback, peer collaboration

Introduction

A study of teacher and student behaviour situated in an existing L2 classroom clearly generates findings with potential applications for L2 pedagogy. An observational design has particularly high ecological validity because it documents naturally occurring practices, as opposed to what a researcher/teacher hopes will happen when piloting an innovation, or manipulates to make happen during an experimental study. Observational research can also reveal unanticipated aspects of classroom behaviour that merit further examination. That was indeed the case with the study we report on in this chapter. The compilation of an oral interaction corpus designed

https://doi.org/10.1075/lllt.52.02col

to look at 11–12 year old EFL students' opportunities for using different features of language during typical pair/group work (Collins & White, 2014) revealed multiple instances of children *spontaneously* focusing on language issues. These learner-initiated "language related episodes" (LREs) (Swain & Lapkin, 1995) led to a new, unplanned topic of research, allowing us to address two understudied aspects in the existing literature on LREs. They are the characteristics of LREs among child L2 learners, and certain classroom factors, including pedagogical behaviour, that may influence the frequency, language focus, and resolution of these episodes. The classroom observational design also presented some challenges, notably with respect to cost, experimental control, and the impact of researcher presence on teacher/student behaviour. Although the research design limits the generalizability of the findings to other classroom contexts, the high ecological validity and rich description yielded findings of clear relevance to second language teaching.

The organization of this chapter is as follows. We begin with an explanation of LREs and a synthesis of the findings relevant to the current study, identifying the issues that we set out to address. We then describe the study, highlighting the different methodological challenges that emerged. The advantages of the observational design are presented during the interpretation and discussion of the findings. We conclude with a synthesis of the contributions and limitations of the research approach taken for understanding LREs, and point to directions for future research raised by the findings of the study.

Language-related episodes

Language-related episodes describe collaborative situations where students 'talk about the language they are producing, question their language use, or correct themselves or others' (Swain & Lapkin, 1998, p. 326).[1] They are incidental and determined by learner needs (Williams, 1999) and interests.

Two constructs are relevant to research investigating the relationship between LREs and language learning. The first, *attention*, is believed to facilitate second language learning (Schmidt, 1990, 1993), and LREs provide evidence that learners are paying attention to language. The second construct, *output*, is said to promote noticing gaps in knowledge (Gass & Mackey, 2015; Swain, 1995). LREs provide evidence

---

1.   We followed this definition of LREs. As it covers students correcting each other, we did not code student-student recasts separately. Note that Gass, Mackey, and Feldman (2005) compared classroom and laboratory student-student interactional feedback and coded negotiation for meaning, LREs, and recasts separately.

of learners' awareness of these gaps as they attempt to fill them while working collaboratively on a task. As a type of meta-talk, LREs may 'engage language learning processes' (Swain, 1998, p. 77), and they promote meta-reflection and self-regulation processes (Ortega, 2009). From a Vygotskian perspective, LREs may represent instances of actual language learning (Lantolf & Appel, 1994; Swain, 2000).

Because of their possible role in facilitating language learning, LREs have received considerable research attention across a number of different designs. These include laboratory-type settings in which participants may be drawn from existing classrooms to participate in dyadic or small group tasks (e.g. Gilabert, Baron, & Llanes, 2009; Pica, Lincoln-Porter, Paninos, & Linnell, 1996; Watanabe & Swain, 2007), computer-mediated interaction (Bueno-Alastuey, 2013; Yilmaz, 2011), and interaction in second language classrooms (e.g. Kim & McDonough, 2011; Philp, Walter, & Basturkmen, 2010; Williams, 1999). Typically, the characteristics of LREs that are reported on are language feature (lexis, grammar, pronunciation), initiator (speaker, interlocutor, teacher), and resolution. Factors studied that may influence one or more of these characteristics include task features (e.g. Dao, Iwashita, & Gatbonton, 2016; Gass, Mackey, & Ross-Feldman, 2005; Swain & Lapkin, 2001), participant characteristics, such as proficiency (e.g. Kim & McDonough, 2008; Yilmaz, 2011), and roles and relationships assumed by learners during paired/group interaction (e.g. Philp et al., 2010; Storch & Aldosari, 2012; Watanabe & Swain, 2007).

One dimension of LRE research that is understudied is learners' spontaneous attention to language during communicative (i.e. not language-focused) tasks performed with their classmates as part of their regular classroom routine. In many studies, the tasks are introduced by the researcher (e.g. Kim & McDonough, 2011; Swain & Lapkin, 2001), and while they may have pedagogical and communicative value, they are not necessarily activities typically used by the classroom teacher or taken from the syllabus in use with the students participating in the study. In addition, in these studies, there has been a disproportionate focus on dictogloss (or text reconstruction) and jigsaw tasks. While the replication of research in different contexts using the same tasks enhances the *generalizability* of findings, the *relevance* to L2 pedagogy would be further enhanced by the examination of a greater range of tasks, including tasks teachers commonly use (for example, neither dictogloss nor jigsaw tasks are typical in the primary and secondary EFL classes in the context in which we work). Among the studies that have examined LREs during activities observed in intact classes, under-researched activities have been observed, including role play, discussion (Philp et al., 2010; Tognini, Philp, & Oliver, 2010; Williams, 1999), and collaborative composition writing (Storch, 2002). However, these four studies also include interactive activities with a language focus or grammatical objective, and, with the exception of Williams (1999), who found that the frequency of LREs was greater during activities with specific language objectives, the analysis of the LREs does not distinguish between these and the communicative tasks without a language focus, in which students' spontaneous attention to language is incidental to the task.[2]

A second aspect that has not received much research attention is the use of LREs by elementary school children learning a foreign language. Learner-initiated attention to language during pair/group work has been studied primarily with adult participants (e.g. Philp et al., 2010; Springer & Collins, 2008; Williams, 1999) or young adolescents (e.g. Swain, 1998; Swain & Lapkin, 2001), who are potentially more language-focused than children. There is evidence that young children, when guided, are capable of focusing on language during meaning-focused activities (Bouffard & Sarkar, 2008; Harley, 1998; Horst, White & Bell, 2010). A small-scale study of 8 grade 6 francophone EFL children interacting in different tasks in groups of 4 demonstrated that the students were able to request and offer assistance to each other without teacher guidance (Gagné & Parks, 2013). Given the world-wide lowering of the starting age of foreign language instruction to early elementary school grades (Collins & Muñoz, 2016), including the Quebec context of our study, more research with young learners is needed to investigate the contexts in which children spontaneously talk about language during pair and group work activities planned by their teacher. What do they do when they encounter gaps in their knowledge? Do they ask their peers for help, do they offer each other help, or do they ask the teacher? Are they equally concerned about grammar, vocabulary, and pronunciation?

As we looked over our corpus of learner language produced during their pair and group work tasks (Collins & White, 2014), it became apparent that learners were focusing on form in contexts where the main focus was on meaning and where the teacher had not drawn their attention to any particular language feature while explaining the task. Although most of the task types were familiar to the students and had fluency development (practice using known language) as the main goal, learners did not hesitate to initiate LREs, correct each other, and even to provide metalinguistic information, when they or their peers were faced with a linguistic gap.

As we see in Example 1, taken from a picture description task, when Student 1 asked his partner whether to use *a* or *an* before *umbrella*, his partner supplied not only the form, but an abbreviated rule of thumb as well.

---

2. The description of the tasks may distinguish between grammar and communicative focused orientations (e.g. Tognini et al., 2010), but the actual LRE analyses do not consider this difference as a variable.

(1) S1: It's okay. He he is holding holding an umbrella. Uh he uh
     S2: Holding holding
     S1: An unnn is it an "a" umbrella or "an" umbrella?
     S2: <u>An</u> umbrella because it's a "u". What's next?

Our pair/group work corpus thus provided us a large database from which we could examine the use of LREs by children during the communicative interaction activities they experienced in their ESL classes, thereby contributing to these under-studied aspects of LREs, as outlined above. One set of research questions addressed the frequency of the LREs and their characteristics (initiator, language feature, resolution). We also coded for instances of students' self-corrections during their oral interaction with peers (i.e. not in response to assistance, either requested or volunteered from a peer). However, we have restricted our discussion in this paper to LREs that involve two or more conversational turns among two or more peers during the activities we observed. A second set of research questions considered the contextual factors of the classroom that might influence the characteristics of the LREs that the children produced.

The study

Context and participants

The observations and recordings took place in three intact classes of French-speaking grade 6 (11–12 year old) students studying English in Quebec. The three schools were in French-dominant regions of the Greater Montreal area, such that the English class was the students' primary contact with English. The language of instruction outside the English class in the rest of the school was also French. Thus, although the convention in Quebec is to refer to the classes as ESL, the context has more in common with EFL situations elsewhere in the world. Students were in the fourth month of a five-month intensive program in which they spent most of the school day (~ 4 hours) engaging in oral interaction and comprehension activities in English. They began the program with very limited knowledge of English due to the restricted exposure students in Quebec have to English in elementary school. At this point in their intensive experience they had become confident communicators, with an approximately intermediate-level proficiency in listening and speaking.[3] There were 87 students (29 per class). All three teachers were trained ESL specialists with experience in both intensive and regular ESL curricula.

---

3. For more details on different aspects of proficiency and how they develop over the course of the intensive ESL program in this context, see Collins & White (2011; 2012).

Corpus

The corpus consists of transcribed pair and small group interactions from the three classes. There were 11 observation periods: four for each of Classes One and Three, three for Class Two, which took place once a week over four consecutive weeks. Sessions lasted 60 – 90 minutes. As the teachers were fully aware of our interest in pair/group interaction, they chose the days and times for our visits in which such activities would be taking place. Prior to data collection we visited each class to explain the purpose of the study to the children and to familiarize them with the two research assistants, the recording equipment, and the experience of having their conversations recorded. A total of 17 *different* tasks were observed, with all students' interactions recorded for each task. There were thus multiple pairs/groups doing the same task at the same time. All of the recorded interaction was transcribed, yielding a corpus of 310,931 words and 55 hours of interaction. The corpus was complemented by field notes, task materials, and informal post-recording interviews with the teachers.

Identifying teachers willing to participate in the study was relatively easy, given that we were not asking them to use any activities other than what they would normally use. Moreover, we maintain good contacts with teachers through our annual presentations at the province-wide conference for ESL teachers in Quebec (SPEAQ: *Société pour le perfectionnement de l'enseignement de l'anglais langue seconde au Québec*) and through the practice teaching placements of our institution's undergraduate degree in TESL. Many intensive teachers in Quebec's elementary schools also welcome the opportunity to have visitors in their classrooms to allow students to interact with other proficient speakers of English.

One challenge we faced was the difficulty of getting all parents and some teachers to consent to video recordings of the interactions. Furthermore, as it would have been impossible to video-capture so many pairs/groups at the same time, we opted for audio recordings. These have the advantage of being less intrusive than video recordings (see Galaczi, 2008), but they do present other challenges. It was not always possible to identify who was speaking, and occasionally some speech was inaudible due to the noise generated by the interactions of other pairs/groups in close proximity. The transcription of 55 hours was both labour-intensive and costly, as it required a team of six research assistants, who worked in pairs over six months to transcribe, code, and verify each other's work. All coding categories (LRE; type of language feature; initiator and resolution) and their sub-categories were verified through a process by which a second coder randomly selected 25% of the pairs/groups for a given task and independently coded all LRE categories. The percentage agreement among the two coders for each category was then calculated. There was 92% agreement for the identification of an LRE; 100% for language feature categories; and 97% agreement for initiator and resolution categories. Any differences were resolved through discussion.

Analyses and findings

For the analyses, we included any pair or group interactive activity in which the students' primary focus was on meaning to exchange information, solve problems, plan events, and so on. We excluded language-focused activities completed in collaboration, such as worksheets on homophones, parts of speech, and vocabulary definitions.[4] A total of 20 activities were observed, which varied in length from three to forty minutes (see Table 1). The only repeated activity (within and across classes) was skit preparation; thus we recorded a total of 17 different tasks, both open (many answers possible) and closed (only one answer possible). The number and length of tasks varied across the three classes, with Class 1 typically engaging in shorter tasks than the two other classes. The tasks in Classes 1 and 3 were more varied than Class 2. The only communicative group work observed in Class 2 was a skit preparation task, a weekly event for these students.

Table 1. Summary of tasks

Class	Distribution	Task #s	Length in minutes	Type
One	pairs/groups	11	3 – 34 most: < 10	interviews about weekend activities games descriptions of people/objects discussions (general & consensus) predictions tongue twister creation
Two	groups of 5	3	14 – 21 all > 10	preparing improv
Three	pairs/groups	6	28 – 40 all > 10	discussions of books read treasure hunt game skit preparation based on a book festival planning comic strip captions

A total of 607 language-related episodes were observed (Class 1 $n = 309$; Class 2 $n = 80$; Class 3 $n = 218$), across a variety of pairs, groups, classes, and tasks.

---

4.   Four of these types of collaborative activities were observed, all in Class Two.

Frequency of LREs

Our first research question focused on the frequency of LREs. As we did not control the task type or length, the observational design presented us with the methodological challenge of comparing LREs across tasks of different lengths, both within and across classes. Following previous research in which a time metric was used (e.g. Ellis, Basturkmen, & Loewen, 2001; Williams, 1999), we calculated the total time it took for all pairs/groups to complete a given task, and divided this by the total number of LREs observed for that task, which we report as how often an LRE occurred during each task. Tables 2–4 present the findings by class. All but one of the tasks resulted in LRE episodes, with widely differing frequencies, ranging from one every 2 minutes (according to the metric we adopted), during a clothing guessing game in Class 1, to one every 36 minutes, during a game in which students read aloud scripted clues to determine which animal in a zoo the protagonists did not visit (also Class 1). The metric used also revealed that the tasks that took the longest to complete did not necessarily generate the greatest number of LREs (compare, for example, the relative infrequency of LREs during the planning of a class festival in Class 3 with the relative frequency of LREs during the consensus-seeking task in Class 1).

Table 2. Tasks and LREs: Class one

Task	LREs	Total time for all pairs/groups	LRE frequency: one every...
Weekend interview– closed	12	57 min	5 min
Weekend interview– open	9	45 min	5 min
Clothing guessing game	**122**	**290 min**	**2 min**
Past activities interview	11	77 min	7 min
Comparing favourite things	44	192 min	4 min
Creating tongue twisters	61	413 min	7 min
Directions around class	9	117 min	13 min
Directions around town game	**0**	**117 min**	**NONE**
Directions around zoo game	4	144 min	36 min
Consensus– expedition	35	100 min	3 min
Future predictions	2	28 min	14 min

Table 3. Tasks and LREs: Class two

Task	LREs	Total time for all pairs/groups	LRE frequency: one every...
Preparing improv 1	18	116 min	4 min
Preparing improv 2	3	83 min	28 min
Preparing improv 3	9	128 min	14 min

Table 4. Tasks and LREs: Class three

Task	LREs	Total time for all pairs/ groups*	LRE frequency: one every...
Book Qs & skit	39	256 min	7 min
Comics & treasure hunt	91	333 min	4 min
Festival planning	62	672 min	11 min
Reading questions	26	194 min	7 min

* Note: During our first two visits, the teacher gave the students two tasks to complete at their own pace; consequently both activities were recorded on the same file, making it difficult to determine the exact time spent on each activity for each pair/group. Consequently, the LRE analyses reported are for the two tasks combined.

Characteristics of LREs

Our second set of research questions examined (i) who initiated the LRE, (ii) the language feature that was involved, and (iii) whether the issue was resolved. As noted above, one of the challenges in coding for the LREs in the absence of video recordings or individual microphones for each student was tracking the speakers in groups of 3 or more speakers. It was always possible to identify whether the initiator of an LRE came from the speaker himself or herself, or was offered by a peer, but it was not always possible to know how many other students participated in the back and forth until an issue was resolved or abandoned.

Initiator

The initiator of an LRE could be a student requesting assistance, a peer offering unsolicited assistance, including corrective feedback, or the teacher as she was circulating, monitoring the activities. Examples (2) and (3) illustrate student and peer-initiated episodes, respectively. As Table 5 shows, almost all of the LREs were generated by the students themselves, with 64% from the original speaker and 32% initiated by a peer in response to another student's utterance.

(2) Student Initiated
    Asking for lexical item:
    S1: Is what? (pointing to an item in a picture)
    S2: Goggles. He's wearing goggles.
    S1: Google! *(laughs)*
    S2: Goggles.

(3)   Peer Initiated
      Correcting a pronoun
      S1: She–
      S2: *(laughs)* He-He
      S1: Is wearing–
      S2: He. It's a boy. %Is he%
      S1: %Oh!% She wearing
      S2: He *(laughs)*
      S1: Ha! He wearing[5]
      Note: % refers to simultaneous speech

Table 5. LRE Initiator: Whole corpus

Initiator	% of times initiated	Raw totals
Student	64	392
Peer	32	192
Teacher	4	23

Language feature

Vocabulary items accounted for the vast majority of LREs (see Table 6). Students requested and offered each other assistance with finding an appropriate word, understanding the meaning of a word, choosing between two or more words, and with the form of a word (spelling) (see examples in Table 7). LREs focused on grammar features were less frequent and involved both morphology (e.g. searching for the correct form of a past participle, part of speech, plural, or pronoun) and syntax (e.g. word order in questions, adjective/noun order, article choice). Pronunciation LREs were infrequent and tended to occur when students were trying to use unfamiliar words that they needed to describe pictures, or that they had encountered in written but not oral exposure (e.g. *parrot*; *lobster, whale*[6]).

---

5. It is interesting to note that the attention the student gave to correcting the pronoun error resulted in the dropping of the auxiliary, which was part of the original utterance!

6. We coded pronunciation LREs separately from lexical and grammatical LREs. Some researchers have coded pronunciation as a dimension of lexical LREs (e.g. Kim & McDonough, 2008; Williams, 1999) or as mechanical LREs (e.g. Storch & Aldosari, 2012).

Table 6. LRE feature: Whole corpus

Language feature	% of corpus	Raw totals
Vocabulary	80	483
Grammar	14	87
Pronunciation	6	37

Table 7. Vocabulary LREs

Word search	She's wearing a marine– how do you say [bleu marine]?
Word meaning	S1: What is insect repellement? S2: The OFF. You know, shstshhhh (spray noise) and no insect come for you.
Word choice	S1: To do a fire S2: To make uh to make S1: To do not to make
Word form (spelling)	S1: How did you write sleeve? S2: On the board! On the board!

Resolution

The LREs were resolved 81% of the time, usually without the teacher's assistance. Indeed, of all the resolved LREs, 82% were resolved by the students themselves. Sometimes students appealed to classmates in other pairs/groups, as Example 4 demonstrates. In this example, one of the pairs elsewhere in the class had asked the teacher for assistance to find the missing vocabulary item, and this information began to travel across the class from group to group.

(4) S1: And...He is holding skiers...**ski stick**
     S2: Holding...what?
     S1: Ski sticks...ski sticks
     S2: **Ski poles**
     S1: Ski
     (student from another group) No, it's a ski poles...it's a ski poles... it's not a ski stick, it's a ski poles

Successful resolution did not vary widely across language features. Table 8 shows that similar proportions of vocabulary and pronunciation issues were resolved. Resolution for vocabulary features was somewhat lower (71%), but still shows that almost three quarters of the issues related to lexis were successfully resolved.

For the comparatively few items that were not resolved, this was either because students attempted a resolution but arrived at the wrong conclusion (49% of the unresolved cases) or did not attempt a resolution, either because of lack of knowledge or motivation (51% of the unresolved cases). The attempts with wrong results and the lack of attempts were roughly comparable across grammar and vocabulary features (see Table 9).

Table 8. LRE resolution by language feature: Whole corpus

Language feature	% resolved	Raw totals
Vocabulary	71%	345
Grammar	84%	73
Pronunciation	84%	31

Table 9. Unresolved LREs by language feature: Whole corpus

LRE	Vocabulary	Grammar	Pronunciation
Attempted: wrong	52%	43%	NA*
Not attempted: unable	48%	57%	NA

* Note: There were too few instances of unresolved pronunciation features to report percentages.

Summary of frequency and characteristics of LREs

The analysis revealed similar trends across all three classes. Students initiated almost all of the focus on language, with the greatest attention given to vocabulary, and to a lesser extent, grammar. Very few LREs involved pronunciation. The children attempted to resolve almost all of the language issues on their own, and were largely successful at doing so.

There were, however, some differences across the groups in terms of the initiator of the LRE and the language feature in focus. Table 10 shows that peers initiated unsolicited assistance twice as frequently in Class 1 as in the other two classes. Students in this class also had a greater proportion of LREs involving grammar features (23% versus 5%) (see Table 11). In the next section we consider some contextual factors that may explain these findings.

Table 10. LRE initiator: Class comparison

Class	Student	Peer	Teacher
One	54%	40%	6%
Two	73%	25%	2%
Three	76%	23%	1%

Table 11. LRE language feature: Class comparison

Class	Vocabulary	Grammar	Pronunciation
One	73%	23%	4%
Two	86%	5%	9%
Three	86%	5%	9%

Contextual factors influencing the characteristics of LREs

From our field notes and interviews with the three teachers, we identified two contextual factors that may account for the differences in the nature of the LREs across the three classes. All three teachers had received training in cooperative learning as part of their professional development as ESL teachers in Quebec (e.g. Kagan, 1994). The teacher in Class 1 was a particularly strong advocate of positive interdependence. She cultivated a classroom culture of self-reliance and emphasized the individual and collective benefits of students working together. The students were organized in base groups with clearly defined roles to play within the group. Students were further trained to offer assistance to each other and had access to resources in the class that they were expected to consult (word banks, dictionaries, wall charts on different grammar points), only approaching the teacher for language problems they were not able to solve on their own. This was the class with the greater proportion of peer-initiated (unsolicited) assistance. Teacher 2 rarely had students work in pairs or groups except during the preparation of the weekly improvisation. She favoured a teacher-centred approach in which students interacted with her during whole-class activities, or worked on individual tasks on their own. Teacher 3 frequently had students work in different pairs/groups, but she expected students to use her as a resource for language issues. This may explain why students in Classes 2 and 3 were less likely to take the initiative to offer language assistance to each other.

In all three classes, the pair/group work we analyzed consisted of activities chosen for their communicative interest, not for specific language practice. However, the teacher in Class 1 frequently identified task-useful language at the beginning of an activity. For example, she provided the students with sample yes/no questions they could use when interviewing each other about their week-end activities, and she referred them to the appropriate vocabulary pages in their workbook for the verbs they might need to express their ideas. During these activities there were LREs, both student- and peer-initiated, that focused on the form of the past tense and question formation, as illustrated in Example 5

(5) S1: Do you eat pizza last weekend?
     S2: <u>Did</u> you
     S1: Did you- did
     S2: Did you- Did you eat
     S1: pizza last weekend? // *some turns later....*
     S2: Uh uh a music CD? Uh no! I didn't. Uh did you watch TV this morning?
     S1: Yes, I watch.
     S2: I <u>did!!</u>
     S1: *(whispering)* yes, I did
     S2: Yes, you did

This attention to task-useful language may explain why students in Class 1 had many more instances of grammar LREs than the students in the two other classes.

Discussion of findings

This study of three elementary school classes of francophone ESL learners in an intensive program in Quebec demonstrated that young learners initiated a focus on language during regular communicative-based activities, and that they tended to do so most frequently with vocabulary. They were also able to resolve most of the language issues they raised on their own.

The focus on lexical needs over grammar and pronunciation issues during communicative interaction is consistent with much of the previous research with adults (e.g. Kim & McDonough, 2011; Philp et al., 2010; Williams, 1999). As Williams (1999) notes, what learners tend to notice when they talk to each other is that they need words (p. 618). Philp et al. (2010) conclude that more task focus or teacher intervention may be required when non-salient grammar features are less vital to meaning (p. 262). There is indeed evidence that task type may influence the frequency of LREs (e.g. Gass et al., 2005) and that both task type and task-set up may encourage greater focus on grammar issues (Kim & McDonough, 2011; Swain & Lapkin, 2001; Yilmaz, 2001), especially when there are grammatical objectives that students are aware of (e.g. Dobao, 2012; Williams, 1999). Interactive tasks that involve writing also tend to generate larger proportions of grammar-related episodes (e.g. Swain & Lapkin, 2001; Yilmaz, 2011). There was very little writing involved in the classes we observed for this study; the only text that was produced was the tongue twister, during which students were largely focused on identifying vocabulary that started with the letter of the alphabet they had chosen to construct their short texts.[7]

---

7.   The teacher instructed students to choose a word initial letter around which they could build their tongue twister. So, for example, students created short texts about baby brown bears going to the bakery or Frank the funny fire fighter saving a French family in the forest.

As for the infrequent focus on pronunciation, Bueno-Alastuey (2013) observed in a study of computer-mediated interaction that when students share the same first language, they understand each other and are unlikely to notice pronunciation errors. Our finding that pronunciation LREs were infrequent among the francophone learners in our study is in line with this interpretation. For example, 'h' is not pronounced in French. The students in our study often omit word-initial 'h' entirely in English, resulting in errors such as *air* for *hair*, which did not give rise to LREs.

In contrast to lab-based studies, in which students interact with a researcher or another student in a separate location from their actual classroom, or experimental studies in which students engage in researcher-created tasks that may not be typical of the activities they normally do, the observation of students in their actual classes allowed us to identify classroom context factors that may influence characteristics of LREs. One is the impact of collaboration fostered by the teacher, which was associated with a greater proportion of unsolicited peer assistance. This finding is consistent with the interpretation Gagné and Parks (2013) offer for the apparent willingness of the 10-year old ESL students in their study to offer assistance to each other with language during pair/group work. They note that the teacher in the study actively promoted collaboration and self-reliance among the young students. Fernandez-Dobao (2012) noted a greater incidence of LREs with adult students who adopted a more collaborative orientation to the completion of a picture-prompted narrative task (the initiator of the LRE is not reported); Lesser (2004) also reported more LREs among collaborative partners than those in which one partner dominated the interaction.

However, a learner-centered approach may not in itself be sufficient for students to generate attention to language and offer assistance on their own. Williams (1999), for example, found that adult students across proficiency levels had a preference for addressing the teacher for their language-related issues, despite the teacher's initiatives to encourage students to rely on each other for assistance. She also found that the lower proficiency students did not generate many LREs, and she wondered if this was simply because it was too difficult for them to do so. In the current study, we observed two additional factors that may have contributed to the spontaneous occurrence of LREs and their frequent resolution. The approach of Teacher One to task set up, in which task-useful language drew students' attention to these features in their own communication attempts and those of their peers, was associated with a greater incidence of grammar-related language issues in this class than the other two classes. Kim and McDonough (2011) also found a greater incidence of LREs and their resolution when a teacher included some pre-task modelling of key language for the task at hand. Another factor was the access to resources that allowed these low-intermediate students to take responsibility for addressing their language needs as they arose, rather than relying on their teacher for help.

It is also important to underscore that the students in these classes are very familiar with each other: they spend full school days together over the course of a year, and many have been in the same school together for several years. This familiarity may have influenced their ease with asking for and offering assistance to each other with language-related issues, as has been observed with adults (Philp et al., 2010). The sustained time spent together in school (including time on the playground) is in contrast to most of the research with adult students. In addition, in lab-based studies of interaction, the pairs may be formed from different classes and not know each other (e.g. Storch & Aldosari, 2012; Watanabe & Swain, 2007).

Classroom observation of LREs and implications/relevance for pedagogy

As we noted at the outset, one of the key advantages to observing behaviour of students and teachers in intact classes is the ecological validity of the findings. In this study, three dimensions of that validity merit comment. The first is that the study examined LREs in a variety of common tasks, many of which have not appeared in previous research-designed tasks for the study of LREs (e.g. consensus discussions, interviews about personal experiences, event planning, preparing skits). In addition, two of the most commonly reported tasks in previous research – dictogloss and jigsaw tasks – were not observed in any of the 11 visits to these classes. This in turn resulted in the observation of "normal" as opposed to "imposed" interaction among the students. A second point is that the tasks were all contextualized. We were present for the set up to the pair/group tasks, and, where appropriate, the post-task whole-class debriefing or consolidation. This allowed us to see the influence of the different teachers' pedagogical approaches and of the classroom culture on students' attention to and resolution of language issues. A third point is the advantage of having replicated tasks within the same study. On every one of our visits, there were multiple pairs/groups doing the same task, at the same time, under similar conditions. There were sufficient numbers, therefore, to observe trends within and across tasks, and to observe LRE resolution not only within pairs/groups, but also across them, when students encountered similar issues and shared solutions.

There are caveats, however. Although the context for the activities we observed was well documented, the study was still a snapshot of the dynamics of each of the classrooms, as we were not present on a daily basis over an extended period of time. We did not document teacher/student behaviour with respect to language issues during other activities. For example, we did not observe how feedback on language issues is given at other points in the school day or how grammar (isolated or integrated) and vocabulary are presented and/or reviewed. Nor did we conduct interviews with students to obtain their perspectives on their decisions to focus on language, or to better understand the relationships they had with each other, as has been done in some previous research with adults (eg. Philp et al., 2010).

In addition, although the teachers and students were comfortable with us, there was nevertheless evidence of teachers changing their behaviour to accommodate us. Teacher 1, for example, concentrated more of the pair/group work for the day into the hour or so we were in the class than she normally would have, to allow us to collect as much data as possible during our visit. Teacher 2 realized she did not do much pair/group work and started having students do individualized worksheets on language in pairs and groups, something the students commented favourably on and that the teacher continued to do. As noted above, these activities were not analyzed for this study as they were too language-focused for our purposes, but we offer them as examples of how the researcher presence can affect teacher and student behaviour. In addition, although our initial visits to familiarize students with the operation of the recorders (which they were responsible for) seemed to put them at ease, they were nonetheless conscious of being recorded, as illustrated in this excerpt from a pair of students searching for the word "headband".

> (6) S1: Uhh **bandeau bandeau** *(flipping through workbook pages to try to locate the image and vocabulary item in English)*
> S2: Recorder, how do you say *bandeau*?
> S1: What? Oh **hairband**.
> *a few seconds later, as they finished the task*:
> S2 *(addressing the recorder)*: Thank you for listening to us.

Thus although the ecological validity of descriptive research in actual classrooms clearly generates findings that are relevant to other contexts, assessing the implications for other classroom situations involves the consideration of factors that the chosen research design may not have adequately captured.

Conclusion

Table 12 summarizes the advantages and challenges discussed above of the classroom observation approach we have taken to understanding the characteristics of LREs among francophone children in an intensive ESL program. As noted, most of the challenges were methodological, and many of the advantages were related to the insights gained from working with students and teachers engaged in language learning activities and interactions typically experienced in the three classrooms we observed. This revealed some contextual factors of the classrooms that were associated with the children's attention to language during their oral interactions. The findings also point to other aspects of the classroom context that may merit attention in future research on LREs, using both experimental and observational approaches.

Table 12. Classroom observation of LREs: Summary of advantages and challenges

	Challenges	Advantages
Cost	time-consuming and labour intensive to record, transcribe and analyze	corpus for other projects
Ethics	parental approval for video-recordings; uneven quality of simultaneous audio-recordings of multiple pairs/groups	approval facilitated by focus on existing curriculum
Participant Availability	recruiting teachers; need to develop relationships with teachers and schools	large *N* with intact classes; multiple pairs/groups
Tasks/Instruments	no control over tasks: need to find appropriate metric to compare across tasks of different lengths and types	variety of under-researched task types; expands knowledge base
Teacher Collaboration	teacher behaviour influenced by researcher presence	teacher appreciation of researcher interest in existing practices
Student Motivation	need to normalize presence of researcher and audio recorders; need for preparatory visits	participation enhanced by: peer and task familiarity; student control over audio recorders
Implications for Pedagogy	*generalizability* limited by non-experimental design	*face/ecological validity* of classroom context identification of classroom context factors influencing LREs

Given the finding that young children do focus on language issues during communicative interaction, and that they can also address many of the issues they raise, one avenue that merits further investigation is whether they can be encouraged to expand that focus to include greater attention to grammar and pronunciation issues. Teacher One's practice of sometimes highlighting task-useful forms as part of task instructions appeared to be one way to promote noticing of issues related to language forms that peers could assist each other with. Another is the impact of teachers drawing students' attention to problematic grammar or pronunciation issues such that particular features become the focus for a certain time, allowing students to direct their attention to the use of these forms in their own language and that of their peers. Doughty and Varela, (1998), for example, observed that a teacher's sustained attention to past tense and conditional forms during ESL children's reporting of their science experiments resulted in spontaneous peer corrections of the forms during students' interaction with each other. Horst et al. (2010) report on a series of age-appropriate pedagogical activities for child EFL learners that target grammar and pronunciation challenges that can be traced to L1 influence. In our future work, we would like to employ a more experimental design to examine whether this type of guidance would encourage these children to notice and comment on these features of language during their oral interactions with each other, and to measure the potential impact on their learning of targeted language.

Although not reported on here, the data we have on the students' self-corrections during interaction raises an additional direction for future research. When the students in the current study spontaneously corrected their own speech during oral interaction (that is, when they did not ask for or provide assistance to others), they were much more focused on features of grammar. Indeed, over half of their self-corrections (54%) involved grammar (39% involved vocabulary, 7% pronunciation). This suggests that students may be more focused on grammar than the interactive LREs would suggest; it will be important to examine the nature of these self-corrections to determine the factors that may account for the focus on grammar. Previous research has examined the potential impact of task factors on self-repair (e.g. Nuevo, Adams, & Ross-Feldman, 2011); however learner-initiated self-corrections may also reflect a heightened awareness of language form due to a prior interactive exchange involving the same form, or to the teacher's efforts to highlight these features of language in previous lessons and/or as part of the task set up.

An additional contextual factor that merits further investigation is the impact of both teacher behaviour and students' prior experiences with each other on the roles and relationships that are assumed during pair/group work, and how this in turn may influence not only the students' attention to language issues, but also to their willingness to work together to try to resolve them, as Philp et al.'s (2010) study of adult French L2 students demonstrated.

In a seminal article highlighting the insights SLA research might offer classroom teachers, Lightbown (1985) noted that very little work being done at the time was designed to address pedagogical questions. Consequently, she was cautious about making any recommendations for L2 pedagogy, restricting her synthesis to potential implications and guidance that SLA research might offer teachers. Revisiting the generalizations made in the original article fifteen years later, Lightbown (2000) was able to draw on a number of experimental and observational SLA studies that focused on the teaching and learning relationship. However, she reminded readers of the myriad dimensions that differentiate one classroom context from another, pointing out that that teachers still need to interpret the relevance of classroom findings for their individual teaching situations. The results from the current study support this point: even though there were many shared features among the three classes (age and proficiency of students, length and type of program, L1, L2, student familiarity with each other) there were differences in teaching approaches and classroom culture that were associated with differences in the frequency and characteristics of LREs. The rich description of teacher and student behaviour that results from classroom observations can reveal situational factors related to the phenomenon under investigation; ultimately it is up to individual teachers to identify the relative importance of these factors for their own contexts.

Acknowledgments

An earlier version of this paper was presented at the 2016 American Association for Applied Linguistics in Orlando, Florida. Funding for the research was provided by the FRQSC (Fonds de recherche du Québec – Societé et culture). We would to acknowledge the enthusiastic collaboration of both the teachers and the students, and we thank them for welcoming us into their classrooms. We are also grateful to the team of Concordia University students for their invaluable contribution to the research, including data collection, transcriptions, analyses, and manuscript editing: Katherine Ashmore, Jessica Bate, Phillipa Bell, Bonnie Crawford, Dustin Crowther, Victoria Dwight, Alexandra Imperiale, Juliane Martini, Jessica Prioletta, June Ruivivar, and Tayebeh Shalmani.

References

Bouffard, L. A., & Sarkar, M. (2008). Training 8-year-old French immersion students in meta-linguistic analysis: An innovation in form-focused pedagogy. *Language Awareness*, 17(1), 3–24. https://doi.org/10.2167/la424.0

Bueno-Alastuey, M. C. (2013). Interactional feedback in synchronous voice-based computer-mediated communication: Effect of dyad. *System*, 41(3), 543–559. https://doi.org/10.1016/j.system.2013.05.005

Collins, L. & Muñoz, C. (2016). The foreign language classroom: Current perspectives and future considerations. *The Modern Language Journal*, 100 (1), 133–147. https://doi.org/10.1111/modl.12305

Collins, L., & White, J. (2011). An intensive look at intensity and language learning. *TESOL Quarterly*, 45(1), 106–133. https://doi.org/10.5054/tq.2011.240858

Collins, L., & White, J. (2012). Closing the gap: Intensity and proficiency. In C. Muñoz (Ed.). *Intensive exposure in second language learning* (pp. 45–65). Bristol: Multilingual Matters. https://doi.org/10.21832/9781847698063-006

Collins, L., & White, J. (2014). The quantity and quality of language practice in typical interactive pair/group tasks. *TESL Canada Journal*, 31 (Special Issue 8), 37–67.

Dao, P., Iwashita, N., & Gatbonton, E. (2016). Learner attention to form in task-based ACCESS interaction. *Language Teaching Research*, 21(4), 454–479. https://0-journals-sagepub-com.mercury.concordia.ca/doi/full/10.1177/1362168816651462

Dobao, A. (2012). Collaborative writing tasks in the L2 classroom: Comparing group, pair, and individual work. *Journal of Second Language Writing*, 21, 40–58. https://doi.org/10.1016/j.jslw.2011.12.002

Doughty, C., & Varela, E. (1998). Communicative focus on form. In C. Doughty & J. Williams (Eds.), *Focus on form in classroom second language acquisition* (pp. 114–138). Cambridge: Cambridge University Press.

Ellis, R., Basturkmen, H., & Loewen, S. (2001). Learner uptake in communicative ESL lessons. *Language Learning*, 51(2), 281–318. https://doi.org/10.1111/1467-9922.00156

Fernandez Dobao, A. M. (2012). Collaborative writing tasks in the L2 classroom: Comparing group, pair, and individual work. *Journal of Second Language Writing*, 21(1), 40–58. https://doi.org/10.1016/j.jslw.2011.12.002

Gagné, N., & Parks, S. (2013). Cooperative learning tasks in a Grade 6 intensive ESL class: Role of scaffolding. *Language Teaching Research*, 17(2), 188–209. https://doi.org/10.1177/1362168812460818

Galaczi, E. (2008). Peer-peer interaction in a speaking test: The case of the *First Certificate in English* examination. *Language Assessment Quarterly*, 5(2), 89–119. https://doi.org/10.1080/15434300801934702

Gass, S., Mackey, A., & Ross-Feldman, L. (2005). Task-based interactions in classroom and laboratory settings. *Language Learning*, 55(4), 575–611. https://doi.org/10.1111/j.0023-8333.2005.00318.x

Gass, S., & Mackey, A. (2015). Input, interaction, and output in second language acquisition. In B. VanPatten & J. Williams (Eds.), *Theories in second language acquisition*. New York, NY: Routledge.

Gilabert, R., Baron, J., & Llanes, A. (2009). Manipulating cognitive complexity across task types and its impact on learners' interaction during oral performance. *International Review of Applied Linguistics*, 47, 367–395.

Gass, S., & Mackey, A. (2015). Input, interaction, and output in second language acquisition. In B. VanPatten & J. Williams (Eds.), *Theories in second language acquisition* (pp 180–206). New York, NY: Routledge.

Gilabert, R., Baron, J., & Llanes, A. (2009). Manipulating cognitive complexity across task types and its impact on learners' interaction during oral performance. *International Review of Applied Linguistics*, 47, 367–395. https://0-search-proquest-com.mercury.concordia.ca/docview/347292475/DD031B55F11644FEPQ/9?accountid=10246

Harley, B. (1998). The role of focus-on-form tasks in promoting child L2 acquisition. In C. Doughty & J. Williams (Eds.), *Focus on form in classroom second language acquisition* (pp. 156–173). Cambridge: Cambridge University Press.

Horst, M., White, J., & Bell, P. (2010). First and second language knowledge in the language classroom. *International Journal of Bilingualism*, 14(3), 331–349. https://doi.org/10.1177/1367006910367848

Kagan, S. (1994). *Kagan cooperative learning* (2nd ed). San Clemente, CA: Kagan Publishing.

Kim, Y., & McDonough, K. (2008). The effect of interlocutor proficiency on the collaborative dialogue between Korean as a second language learners. *Language Teaching Research*, 12(2), 211–234. https://doi.org/10.1177/1362168807086288

Kim, Y., & McDonough, K. (2011). Using pretask modelling to encourage collaborative learning opportunities. *Language Teaching Research*, 15(2), 183–199. https://doi.org/10.1177/1362168810388711

Lantolf, J. P., & Appel, G. (1994). Theoretical framework: An introduction to Vygotskian perspectives on second language research. In J. P. Lantolf & G. Appel (Eds.), *Vygotskian approaches to second language research* (pp. 1–32). Westport, CT: Ablex.

Lesser, M. (2004). Learner proficiency and focus on form during collaborative dialogue. *Language Teaching Research*, 8, 55–81. https://doi.org/10.1191/1362168804lr1340a

Lightbown, P. (1985). Great expectations: Second language acquisition research and classroom teaching. *Applied Linguistics*, 6, 173–189. https://doi.org/10.1093/applin/6.2.173

Lightbown, P. (2000). Classroom SLA research and second language teaching. *Applied Linguistics*, 21(4), 431–462. https://doi.org/10.1093/applin/21.4.431

Nuevo, A., Adams, R., & Ross-Feldman, L. (2011). *Task complexity, modified output, and L2 development in learner-learner interaction*. In P. Robinson (Ed.), *Second language task complexity: Researching the cognition hypothesis of learning and performance* (pp. 175–202). Amsterdam: John Benjamins.

Ortega, L. (2009). What do learners plan? Learner-driven attention to form during pre-task planning. In K. Van den Branden, M. Bygate, & J. M. Norris (Eds.), *Task-based language teaching: A reader* (pp. 301–332). Amsterdam: John Benjamins.

Philp, J., Walter, S., & Basturkmen, H. (2010). Peer interaction in the foreign language classroom: What factors foster a focus on form? *Langauge Awareness*, 19(4), 261–279. https://doi.org/10.1080/09658416.2010.516831

Pica, T., Lincoln-Porter, F., Paninos, D., & Linnell, J. (1996). Language learners' interaction: How does it address the input, output, and feedback needs of L2 learners? *TESOL Quarterly*, 30(1), 59–84. https://doi.org/10.2307/3587607

Schmidt, R. (1990). The role of consciousness in second language learning. *Applied Linguistics*, 11, 129–158. https://doi.org/10.1093/applin/11.2.129

Schmidt, R. (1993). Awareness and second language acquisition. *Annual Review of Applied Linguistics*, 13, 206–226. https://doi.org/10.1017/S0267190500002476

Springer, S., & Collins, L. (2008). Interacting inside and outside of the language classroom. *Language Teaching Research*, 12(1), 39–60. https://doi.org/10.1177/1362168807084493

Storch, N. (2002). Patterns of interaction in ESL pair work. *Language Learning*, 52(1), 119–158. https://doi.org/10.1111/1467-9922.00179

Storch, N., & Aldosari, A. (2012). Pairing learners in pair work activity. *Language Teaching Research*, 17(1), 31–48. https://0-journals-sagepub-com.mercury.concordia.ca/doi/full/10.1177/1362168812457530

Swain, M. (1995). Three functions of output in second language learning. In G. Cook & B. Seidlhofer (Eds.), *Principle and practice in applied linguistics: Studies in honour of H. G. Widdowson* (pp. 125–144). Oxford: Oxford University Press.

Swain, M. (1998). Focus on form through conscious reflection. In C. Doughty & J. Williams (Eds.), *Focus on form in classroom second language acquisition* (pp. 64–81). Cambridge: Cambridge University Press.

Swain, M. (2000). The output hypothesis and beyond: Mediating acquisition through collaborative dialogue. In J. P. Lantolf (Ed.) *Sociolinguistic theory and second language learning* (pp. 97–114). Oxford: Oxford University Press.

Swain, M., & Lapkin, S. (1995). Problems in output and the cognitive processes they generate: A step towards second language learning. *Applied Linguistics*, 16, 371–391. https://doi.org/10.1093/applin/16.3.371

Swain, M., & Lapkin, S. (1998). Interaction and second language learning: Two adolescent French immersion students working together. *Modern Language Journal*, 83, 320–337. https://doi.org/10.1111/j.1540-4781.1998.tb01209.x

Swain, M., & Lapkin, S. (2001). Focus on form through collaborative dialogue: Exploring task effects. In M. Bygate, P. Skehan, & M. Swain (Eds.), *Researching pedagogic tasks: Second language learning, teaching, and testing.* (pp. 99–118). New York, NY: Longman.

Tognini, R., Philp, J., & Oliver, R. (2010). Rehearsing, conversing, working it out: Second language use in peer interaction. *Australian Review of Applied Linguistics*, 33(3), 1–28. https://doi.org/10.2104/aral1028

Watanabe, Y., & Swain, M. (2007). Effects of proficiency differences and patterns of pair interaction on second language learning: Collaborative dialogue between adult ESL learners. *Language Teaching Research*, 11(2), 121–142. https://doi.org/10.1177/1362168806607074599

Williams, J. (1999). Learner-generated attention to form. *Language Learning*, 49(4), 583–625. https://doi.org/10.1111/0023-8333.00103

Yilmaz, Y. (2011). Task effects on focus on form in synchronous computer-mediated communication. *The Modern Language Journal*, 95(1), 115–132. https://doi.org/10.1111/j.1540-4781.2010.01143.x

CHAPTER 3

Methodological strengths, challenges, and joys of classroom-based quasi-experimental research
Metacognitive instruction and corrective feedback

Masatoshi Sato and Shawn Loewen
Universidad Andres Bello / Michigan State University

This chapter reports on a classroom-based quasi-experimental study by focusing on its methodological aspects. The study's objectives were twofold: (1) to examine the effect of metacognitive instruction (MI) in which learners were instructed about the benefits of receiving corrective feedback (CF), and (2) to compare the effects of two CF types – input-providing vs. output-prompting CF. Eighty-three EFL learners from four intact classes at a private university in Chile were assigned to one of four conditions: MI plus input-providing CF, input-providing CF only, MI plus output-prompting CF, and output-prompting CF only. The results showed that MI helped learners benefit from CF. Focusing on the ecological validity, we argue that providing learners with interventions that were seamlessly deployed in genuine classroom contexts permitted the examination of authentic classroom instruction with minimal disturbance, thereby allowing the observation of the effects of MI and CF without the potentially confounding variables of researcher intrusion and unfamiliar data collection context.

Keywords: classroom research, ecological validity, metacognitive instruction, corrective feedback, self-regulation

Introduction

The proliferation of corrective feedback (CF) research is evident from a number of meta-analyses and reviews in which a number of CF studies have been examined (D. Brown, 2016; Hattie & Timperley, 2007; Li, 2010; Loewen, 2012; Lyster, Saito, & Sato, 2013; Mackey, 2012; Nassaji & Kartchava, 2017; Plonsky & Brown, 2015; Russell & Spada, 2006). Perhaps, the interest in the topic lies not only in

https://doi.org/10.1075/lllt.52.03sat
© 2019 John Benjamins Publishing Company

its theoretical but also pedagogical relevance. On the one hand, second language acquisition (SLA) researchers, who are interested in how interaction affects L2 learning (see Loewen & Sato, 2017; 2018), investigate moderating variables of CF effectiveness such as type, timing, mode, linguistic targets, learner age, individual differences, and instructor characteristics. On the other hand, CF is a teaching technique that many second language (L2) teachers use (Ellis, Basturkmen, & Loewen, 2001; Lyster & Ranta, 1997) and consider integral to the classroom. Overall, research suggests that CF drives L2 development forward most when learners notice its corrective intent and subsequently produce the correct version of the error (Nassaji, 2016).

Meanwhile, learners' noticing of CF may be facilitated by other types of instruction designed to manipulate L2 processing and learner cognition. One example is metacognitive instruction (MI) that aims to increase the knowledge and control of metacognition (Flavell, 1979; Wenden, 1987). Heightened metacognition helps learners plan, self-monitor, and self-evaluate their learning processes (Veenman, 2011). While scarce in L2 research, some studies have shown that MI leads to an increase in metacognitive knowledge as well as L2 skills (e.g., Vandergrift & Baker, 2015). It is reasonable to assume that if informed about the advantages of CF and prepared to receive it, learners will more likely notice and benefit from CF. The current study, therefore, incorporated MI into CF and examined the two types of instruction.

Corrective feedback

Ever since Lyster and Ranta's (1997) CF classroom observation study, researchers have categorized the ways in which L2 teachers react to L2 errors in the classroom. Recent classifications suggest that CF is comprised of two dimensions (Lyster et al., 2013; Sheen & Ellis, 2011). The first relates to whether CF provides or withholds the corrected version of an error. Input-providing CF supplies learners with reformulations in response to their errors, thereby providing positive evidence, that is, linguistic information about what is allowed in the target language. In contrast, output-prompting CF withholds the correct version of the error, allowing learners the opportunity to self-correct and produce the correct linguistic form on their own. The second dimension concerns the explicitness of CF, comparing more explicit and more implicit feedback. Explicit CF has been argued to promote noticing of CF more than implicit CF through overt negative evidence (e.g., indication of the error and/or metalinguistic comments) (Ellis, Loewen, & Erlam, 2006).

The comparison of different types of CF, however, is grounded in different theoretical frameworks. While some researchers may be interested in the psycholinguistic processes triggered by negative evidence, others may be interested in the practice opportunities created by CF. As Lyster et al. (2013) noted, a skill-learning perspective is "less focused on the extent to which CF is either explicit or implicit, because its concern is less with instances of noticing CF and more with the opportunities afforded by CF for consolidating oral skills through contextualized practice" (p. 5). In addition, the distinction between explicit and implicit CF requires caution, because whether or not a learner notices CF may not be relative to the discoursal form of the given CF. Indeed, D. Brown's (2016) meta-analysis of CF excludes the implicit/explicit distinction on these grounds. For example, it is possible that a learner may not notice an explicit type of CF, such as an explicit correction, even when the teacher's intention is to overtly correct the error. It is also possible that a learner notices a conversational recast and subsequently practices the correct form even when the teacher provides a recast implicitly without any corrective intent (see Nicholas, Lightbown, & Spada, 2001; Sato, 2011). Hence, on the one hand, the discoursal explicitness of CF should not be equated with the explicitness of learners' L2 processing. On the other hand, it is theoretically and pedagogically important to investigate how CF can be processed explicitly (i.e., noticed) regardless of its discoursal forms.

Meanwhile, a variable found to affect the effectiveness of CF is the linguistic structure targeted by the correction. Yilmaz (2012) compared explicit corrections and recasts on two structures in Turkish – plural and locative – and found that the more salient structure (i.e., plural) benefitted more from CF. However, Li (2014), who compared recasts and metalinguistic correction on Chinese classifiers and perfective aspect, reported that only recasts had differential effects on the two target structures. Li's study showed that recasts had a longer lasting effect on the less salient structure. Given such mixed findings, further investigation into how linguistic structures mediate CF effectiveness is warranted. The current study controlled the discoursal implicitness of CF and examined another type of instruction – metacognitive instruction (MI) – hypothesized to affect the impact of CF, on two linguistic targets that differed in their perceptual saliency and communicative value.

Metacognitive instruction

If increasing CF's noticeability positively affects its effectiveness (Mackey, 2006), by either invoking negative evidence or by pushing the learner to practice partially-developed knowledge, a *pedagogical* question is how teachers can enhance learners' noticing of CF. One way of achieving this may be to help learners develop metacognitive knowledge that can be accessed during communicative interaction. MI is a type of instruction that enhances metacognition and metacognitive knowledge. The construct of metacognition, which has widely been examined in cognitive psychology since the 1970s, was defined by Flavell (1976) as "one's knowledge concerning one's own cognitive processes and products. ... Metacognition refers, among other things, to active monitoring and consequent regulation and orchestration of these processes" (p. 232). Simply put, metacognition is composed of different types of metacognitive knowledge that enhances the learners' awareness of their own learning processes and allows them to regulate those processes.

In a seminal paper, Flavell (1979) categorized metacognitive knowledge into three components: (1) person knowledge (the knowledge a person has about him/herself and others as cognitive processors); (2) task knowledge (the knowledge a person has about the information and resources in order to undertake a task); and (3) strategy knowledge (knowledge regarding the strategies that are likely to be effective in achieving goals and undertaking tasks). To put the construct in the L2 context, learners may come to realize that they (*person knowledge*) frequently make grammatical errors during communicative activities (*task knowledge*). Consequently, they may think that they should pay more attention to the teachers' (also *person knowledge*) responses to their utterances (*strategy knowledge*). MI aims to influence the different types of knowledge concurrently. Successful MI, therefore, results in self-regulated (or autonomous) learning whereby learners "set goals for their learning and then attempt to monitor, regulate and control their cognition" (Pintrich, 2000, p. 453). The relationships between metacognition and learning success have been found in different areas such as mathematical problem-solving and scientific reasoning (see Veenman, Van Hout-Wolters, & Afflerbach, 2006).

In the field of L2 teaching/learning, Wenden (1987) was the first to point out the potential of metacognition in relation to the development of self-regulated learning as well as L2 knowledge. By defining self-regulation as skills through which "learners manage, direct, regulate, guide their learning, i.e., planning, monitoring, and evaluation" (p. 519), Wenden (1998) suggested that L2 instructors should not only teach the language itself but also provide learners with guidance in "improving and expanding their knowledge about learning" (p. 531). Since Wenden's proposal, such pedagogical efforts have been applied primarily to the teaching of listening. In Vandergrift and Tafaghodtari's (2010) experiment, university-level learners of French were taught a set of metacognitive strategies. For example, participants were instructed to predict types of information they would hear before actual listening. Then, they were told to verify their prediction during listening (self-monitoring). The results showed that the experimental learners outperformed the control group in listening comprehension and those learners exhibited heightened awareness of their learning processes after the intervention (see also Goh & Taib, 2006).

Although MI in the field of L2 teaching/learning has been examined in relation to improvement of listening comprehension (see Vandergrift & Baker, 2015), reading comprehension (see Karimi, 2015), and writing proficiency (see Teng & Zhang, 2016), its effect on grammatical development has not been investigated. The current study, therefore, explores how MI about the benefits of CF impacts L2 development observed in spontaneous production. Accordingly, two research questions were formed:

RQ1: How do implicit input-providing and implicit output-prompting corrective feedback differentially affect the L2 development of two grammatical features?

RQ1: Does metacognitive instruction moderate the effects of the two types of corrective feedback?

Empirical study

Participants

The study was conducted in four intact English-as-a-foreign-language (EFL) classes at a large private university in Chile, with 83 L1 Spanish students and four teachers. The classes were different sections of the same course, using the same textbook and syllabus. There were 22 females and 61 males; their ages ranged from 20 to 25 with an average of 22.3 ($SD = 0.9$). The English classes were mandatory for second-year commerce major students and were held twice a week for 1.5 hours each time. All students in the current study were below B1 proficiency (the Common European Framework of References for Languages), even though they had previously studied English for an average of 6.8 years ($SD = 0.8$).

The four teachers (three females and one male) were all experienced teachers with more than 10 years of teaching. They were L1 Spanish speakers with near-native levels of English proficiency. The curriculum at the university advocated communicative approaches and the language of instruction was primarily English; the curriculum states that the program is "committed to using teaching/learning strategies that utilize the best practices of the communicative approach and task-based learning approach."

Overall design

The four intact classes were assigned to one of four conditions: (1) MI plus input-providing CF (henceforth, MI+IP[1]: Class A: $n = 22$); (2) input-providing CF only (IP-only: Class B: $n = 22$); (3) MI plus output-prompting CF (MI+OP: Class C: $n = 20$); and (4) output-prompting CF only (OP-only: Class D: $n = 19$). At the onset of the intervention, while it was assumed that (1) the targeted morpho-syntactic structures were easy to understand conceptually, and (2) the learners had received grammar lessons on the structures prior to the current study, we provided all groups with explicit rule explanations of the target structures, in order to ensure that the learners possessed explicit knowledge of them. The intervention was implemented during teacher-fronted activities for three weeks, totaling approximately 240 minutes of communicative interaction between the teachers and their students (60 minutes of researcher-developed activities plus 180 minutes of textbook-based activities). Participants in the MI conditions were exposed to additional 60 minutes of MI. Figure 1 depicts the overall design of the study.

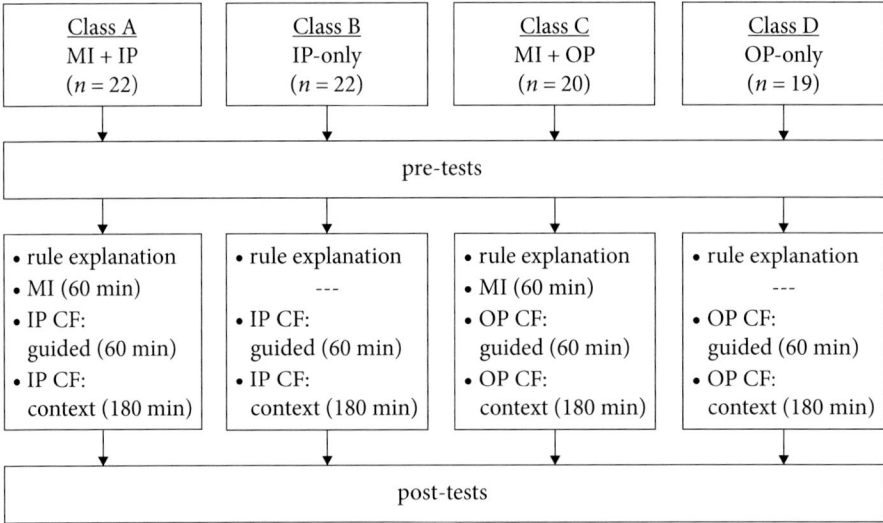

Figure 1. Overall design

---

1.   We chose to label CF types according to their characteristics of IP and OP rather than their discourse functions such as conversational recasts and clarification requests. This was because (1) the discourse moves may not accurately depict how implicitly/explicitly a learner processes given CF, and (2) IP/OP labels do not imply explicitness/implicitness.

Intervention

Target structures
The intervention targeted two English linguistic forms: third-person-singular *-s* (henceforth, 3sg-*s*) and possessive determiners (PDs), both of which have been found to pose difficulties for L2 English learners (Dulay & Burt, 1974; Zobl, 1985). The structures were chosen based on their different degrees of saliency and communicative value. First, the perceptual saliency of the two target structures was operationalized according to Goldschneider and DeKeyser (2005), that is, "how easy it is to hear or perceive a given structure" (p. 47). Based on morphosyntax, we hypothesized that the perceptual saliency of the free morpheme PDs would be higher than that of bound morpheme 3sg-*s* (see Loewen, Erlam, & Ellis, 2009). In addition, the communicative value of PDs is arguably higher than 3sg-*s* (see Carpenter, Jeon, MacGregor, & Mackey, 2006). While omission of 3sg-*s* during interaction may not cause a communication breakdown, errors related to PDs (omission or wrong PDs) may.

Activities
Two separate sets of activities were used to elicit the target structures. The first set was designed by the researchers and aimed to ensure that the learners in all groups received a baseline amount of CF on the target structures. The activities were picture description tasks delivered via PowerPoint slides. In each picture, there were females and males engaged in an action involving different objects with different grammatical genders in Spanish. For each slide, the teacher pointed to a person, and asked a learner to describe the person's routine. For example, in one of the pictures, "Every 18th (the Chilean national holiday in September)" was shown and the picture included three females and a male having a drink together. When the teacher pointed to one of the females, a learner was supposed to say, for example, "Every September the 18th, she gets together with her friends." Hence, the activity elicited 3sg-*s* and PDs by juxtaposing the possessor and the possessed entity. The activities were implemented in each group and took approximately 10 minutes per class, totalling 60 minutes of the researcher-developed activities.

The second set of activities derived from the theme-based textbook (e.g., celebrations, health, etc.) called *Touchstone Level 2* (McCarthy, McCarten, & Sandiford, 2008). For the period of the intervention, the classes focused on a unit called "appearances." The learners engaged in various communicative activities describing other people's appearances and habits. For instance, in one of the activities, the learners were asked to choose a family member and describe his/her features, as in the following example (the excerpts in this manuscript are from short classroom observations conducted by the researchers):

Teacher: So, what does your grandmother look like?
Student: She has funny hair. *His* hair is always...messy.
Teacher: Oh yeah? *Her* hair is messy, huh? Like how?

The combined number of teacher-fronted activities in this unit varied from 25–35 minutes depending on classes. However, all groups engaged in the textbook-based activities approximately 180 minutes in total over six lessons.

Corrective feedback

During the above activities, teachers were asked to provide CF as implicitly as possible. Teachers participated in training sessions (described subsequently) to ensure appropriate CF delivery. The current study followed Lyster et al.'s (2013) taxonomy where conversational recasts and clarification requests were placed at the implicit end of the continuum of IP and OP dimensions, respectively. Conversational recasts were operationalized following Lyster and Ranta's (1997) definition: "the teacher's reformulation of all or part of a student's utterance, minus the error" (p. 46). Unlike Sheen and Ellis' (2011) definition of conversational recasts stating they often take the form of "confirmation checks where the reformulation is followed by a question tag" (p. 594), conversational recasts in the current study included any teacher's response that included the correct linguistic form without any emphasis. Clarification requests were operationalized as the teacher's attempt to elicit more information about the meaning of the learner's erroneous utterance where "no direct indication of the presence of an error" was made (Loewen & Nabei, 2007, p. 367). The teachers were simply asked to pretend that they did not understand what the learner said. Some forms of clarification requests presented during the teacher training sessions were: "Sorry. I didn't understand"; "Can you repeat what you said?"; and "Huh?".

For either CF type, the teachers were asked to provide feedback whenever they noticed an error. Importantly, the teachers were trained not to add any emphasis to the feedback, not to interrupt the communicative flow, and, most importantly, not to overtly direct the student's attention to the error. In addition, teachers were asked not to provide CF more than once even when a learner repeated the same error in response to CF; however, they were encouraged to provide the assigned type of CF to other types of errors than those involving the target structures. These decisions were made in order to tease apart the impact of MI by keeping the discoursal forms of CF as implicit as possible. For instance, we suspected that if a teacher provided conversational recasts multiple times on the same error during the same episode, the recasts might become explicit to the learner regardless of the existence of MI.

Metacognitive instruction

In terms of MI, the current study followed two frameworks from psychology and L2 research. First, we adapted Veenman et al.'s (2006, p. 9) three principles for successful MI: (1) embedding MI in the content matter to ensure connectivity; (2) informing learners about the usefulness of metacognitive activities, to make them exert the initial extra effort; and (3) prolonged training to guarantee the smooth and sustained application of metacognitive activity. Second, the current study applied Wenden's (1998, p. 531) step-wise procedure of MI: (1) elicitation of learners' metacognitive knowledge; (2) articulation of what has come to awareness; (3) confrontation with alternative views; and (4) reflection on the appropriateness of revising, expanding one's knowledge.

We adjusted Veenman et al.'s and Wenden's MI frameworks for CF as the target of MI delivered in intact classrooms, which resulted in a five-stage MI: (1) introduction to CF; (2) explanation of CF's effectiveness; (3) class discussion of CF; (4) getting ready to receive CF; and (5) reminder of CF. With PowerPoint slides, the learners in the MI groups were first provided with the definition of CF and told that the objective of CF is to correct students' errors when they are communicating with the teacher. Second, the teachers explained how CF helps students improve their speaking skills. The teachers were aware of the relevant theories (e.g., noticing hypothesis, output hypothesis, and skill acquisition theory) from the teacher training sessions. Also, the slides included several examples of CF. The explanation stage was followed by class discussion where the teacher answered questions from the students. The slides ended with a remark "*Be on the lookout for them [CF], so that you can improve your speaking!!!*" Those four stages were delivered for three out of six class meetings for the MI groups (approximately 15 minutes each class). For the three remaining classes, the teachers spent a few minutes at the beginning of class and before teacher-fronted activities to remind the students of CF, which was operationalized as the final stage of MI (see Figure 1). The only difference between the MI+IP and MI+OP groups was the CF examples. For the MI+IP group, recasts were shown and for the MI+OP group clarification requests.

Developmental tests

Picture description tasks were developed and administered before and after the intervention, to examine the learners' development of their spontaneous oral production skills. In this task, learners were asked to describe a set of seven pictures each depicting routines of a group of people. First, the learners were instructed to describe each character's weekly routine, which elicited 3SG-*s*. There were three females and two males in each picture, and they interacted with each other over a certain object that juxtaposed the possessor and possessed entity to elicit PDs. Two sets of seven pictures were prepared for the pre- and post-tests, the only difference being the actions taking place in the pictures.

Scoring was done using target-like use of the target structures (Ellis & Barkhuizen, 2005). First, accurate use in obligatory contexts was identified. Any non- or mis-suppliances of the structures were coded as incorrect. In order to examine differential effects of the intervention on L2 development among the four classes, a two-step statistical analysis was conducted. The tests of normality indicated that the post-test scores of the MI+IP group were not normally distributed (Kolmogorov-Smirnov: $p = .04$); however, we proceeded with the analysis because the other groups at both testing times met the assumption (see Blanca, Arnau, López-Montiel, Bono, & Bendayan, 2013). The first step involved repeated-measures (RM) ANOVAs on PDs and 3SG-s separately. The RM ANOVAs and the following post-hoc pairwise comparisons indicated that, for both structures, (1) there were significant time effects and (b) the between comparisons were affected by the differences at the time of the pre-test. Subsequently, the second analysis was done in which the pre-test scores were factored in as the covariates (i.e., ANCOVAs: see justification in Keselman et al., 1998). Hence, we use the results from the RM ANOVAs in order to interpret the effect of the intervention over time (within-group) while we rely on the results from the ANCOVAs to discuss the differential effects of the intervention among the groups (between-group). For post-hoc single comparisons, Bonferroni tests were used and the alpha level for all tests of significance was set at .05. The effect sizes using Cohen's *d* were calculated based on the adjusted means. We used Plonsky and Oswald's (2014) criteria to interpret the magnitude of the effect sizes.

Results and discussion[2]

Tables 1 and 2 display the means and standard deviations of 3SG-s and PDs at the pre- and post-tests. The RM ANOVA of the 3SG-s scores yielded a significant main effect of time ($F(1, 79) = 39.32$, partial $\eta^2 = .332$, $p < .001$) as well as a main

---

2. An effect size, such as partial η_2 and *d*, indicates the magnitude of a statistical result. For instance, one can compare the magnitudes of two different comparisons based on the effect sizes (Class A vs. Class B and Class A vs. Class C). Covariates (e.g., in ANCOVAs) are characteristics that participants possess prior to an experiment. In the current study, the learners possessed different degrees of L2 knowledge prior to the experiment and their knowledge was factored in in the analysis.

interaction effect ($F(3, 79) = 4.27$, partial $\eta^2 = .140, p = .008$). The pairwise comparisons showed that the three groups that significantly increased their scores over time were MI+IP ($p < .001; d = .97$), MI+OP ($p < .001; d = .86$), and OP-only ($p = .011; d = .70$). The IP-only group's difference between the pre- and post-test was not significantly different ($p = .651; d = .09$). The RM ANOVA of PDs also showed a significant main effect for time ($F(1, 79) = 21.26$, partial $\eta^2 = .212, p < .001$); however, the interaction effect was not significant: $F(3, 79) = 2.49$, partial $\eta^2 = .086$, $p = .066$. The pairwise comparisons showed that the MI+IP ($p = .003; d = .54$), MI+OP ($p = .002; d = .51$), and OP-only ($p = .006; d = .51$) groups significantly improved the scores over time while the IP-only group did not ($p = .999; d < .00$). The effect sizes for 3sg-*s* were all medium and those for PDs were rather small.

The ANCOVA of the 3sg-*s* scores yielded a statistically significant group effect, $F(3, 78) = 3.89$, partial $\eta^2 = .130, p = .012$, suggesting significant differences among the four groups at the time of post-test after factoring in the pre-test scores. The post-hoc pairwise comparisons revealed that the MI+IP group outperformed the IP-only group ($p = .004; d = 4.15$). However, the MI+IP group did not outperform MI+OP ($p = .948; d = 0.09$) or OP-only group ($p = .195; d = 1.84$). In addition, the MI+OP group outperformed the IP-only group ($p = .005; d = 4.14$) but not OP-only group ($p = .184; d = 1.89$). There was no significant difference between IP-only and OP-only groups ($p = .132; d = 2.15$). The ANCOVA on the PD scores also detected a statistically significant main effect, $F(3, 78) = 2.77$, partial $\eta^2 = .096, p = .047$. Similar to the results of 3sg-*s*, both the MI+IP group ($p = .022; d = 3.31$) and MI+OP group ($p = .017; d = 3.45$) outperformed the IP-only group, while neither of them showed a superior effect to the OP-only group (*MI+IP, $p = .930; d = 0.12$: *MI+OP, $p = .815; d = 0.33$). There was no significant difference between the MI+IP and MI+OP groups ($p = .878; d = 0.21$). However, for PDs, the OP-only group showed a higher developmental pattern than the IP-only group at the time of the post-test ($p = .033; d = 3.07$). The effect sizes from the ANCOVAs were all large.

Table 1. Accuracy scores (%) for third person singular -s

Groups	pre-test		post-test	
	M	SD	M	SD
MI+IP ($n = 22$)	10.99	16.12	30.77	24.03
IP-only ($n = 22$)	15.27	22.86	17.16	17.71
MI+OP ($n = 20$)	10.39	19.81	30.74	26.85
OP-only ($n = 19$)	12.75	12.90	24.34	19.70

Table 2. Accuracy scores (%) for possessive determiners

Groups	pre-test		post-test	
	M	SD	M	SD
MI+IP ($n = 22$)	54.88	25.16	68.91	26.57
IP-only ($n = 22$)	52.11	31.21	52.12	36.86
MI+OP ($n = 20$)	51.02	30.19	66.91	31.59
OP-only ($n = 19$)	52.72	29.77	66.66	24.98

The findings are threefold. First, OP-CF and MI facilitated the development of 3SG-s and PDs as shown by the significant improvement of the three groups over time. However, IP-CF did not affect L2 development of either structure positively. Second, MI facilitated the effectiveness of CF especially for IP-CF. This was the case for both 3SG-s and PDs. There was no clear evidence suggesting a positive effect of MI on OP-CF. Given that both the MI-OP and OP-only groups showed significant improvement over time, however, we argue that MI did not have an *additional* benefit for OP-CF. In other words, it seems that MI helped learners process conversational recasts explicitly that may not be otherwise noticed due to their implicit nature of the discoursal form (see discussion of depth of processing in Leow, 2015). Furthermore, we suspect that (1) clarification requests alone were sufficiently effective thereby masking the effect of MI, and/or (2) MI was not enough to assist learners to process clarification requests explicitly due to their discourse nature, that is, clarification of meaning. Third, the two types of CF affected the two linguistic structures differently when MI was considered in the between-groups analysis; as stated above, the structures arguably entail different degrees of perceptual saliency and communicative value. While the IP-CF and OP-CF had a comparable effect on the development of 3SG-s (see Loewen & Nabei, 2007; McDonough, 2007), the development of PDs was affected by CF types whereby the OP type was more effective than IP type (see Ammar & Spada, 2006; Lyster, 2004). Overall, the effectiveness of MI and CF was mediated by linguistic targets (see Sato & Loewen, 2018 for a fuller discussion).

Pedagogical implications

Although not all SLA research needs to have direct pedagogical implications (Sato & Loewen, 2019-a; Spada, 2015), we personally feel the need for our own research to be directly relevant to the classroom. To that end, the current study was an attempt to further our understanding of CF, along with an additional element, namely MI that (1) might have the ability to impact the effectiveness of CF, and

(2) is relatively easy to implement in the classroom. Based primarily on the results of the current study, as well as our observations, we offer the following pedagogical implications.

Corrective feedback

The results from our study support previous studies showing that CF can be effectively provided during communicative L2 lessons. However, our study also showed that IP-CF assisted L2 development only when it was accompanied with MI. Based on our methodological choices of aligning intervention with teachers' preferred CF behaviors (which will be further explained), we can make suggestions concerning (1) the amount and types of CF and (2) teacher training of CF.

Amount and types of feedback

From a classroom point of view, we acknowledge that the amount of CF the learners in the current study received was most likely beyond regular teaching practice, especially when CF targets specific grammatical structures. Hence, teachers should not expect the extent of L2 development in a few weeks that was observed in the current study. At the same time, the results suggest that providing CF on a few specific morphosyntactic structures is effective on the development of those structures. Hence, teachers might want to consider pre-determining linguistic structures to target intensively with CF, in accordance with the lesson plans (see Ellis, 2001).

With regards to types of CF, teachers should be aware of the potential of other types of CF with which they might be less comfortable or less familiar. We suggest that teachers flexibly employ different types of CF based on (1) learners' knowledge of a particular linguistic structure, (2) communicative appropriateness, (3) task objectives, (4) learner psychology, and (5) instructional contexts. For example, in our study, although IP-CF contributed to L2 development to a small extent, it is unreasonable to expect learners to benefit from OP-CF when they possess no knowledge of the targeted structure (see Goo & Mackey, 2013 vs. Lyster & Ranta, 2013). As Lyster et al. (2013) emphasized, "[t]he most effective teachers are likely to be those who are willing and able to orchestrate, in accordance with their students' language abilities and content familiarity, a wide range of CF types that fit the instructional context" (p. 30). Nonetheless, providing the right type of CF to the right learner at the right moment is no easy job. This point leads us to the following suggestion concerning teacher education.

Training in corrective feedback

Teachers have different teaching styles, including the way in which they correct (or do not correct) students' errors. Some teachers may believe that recasts are better because they do not embarrass the student, while some teachers believe prompts are better because the student is pushed to practice. Additionally, some teachers avoid correcting L2 errors at all cost based on the principle of pure communicative language teaching (see A. Brown, 2009).

Because of this variability, we considered it imperative to ensure that participating teachers were comfortable providing the types of CF required for this study. Therefore, prior to the selection of the participating teachers, we conducted classroom observations of six teachers. Two teaching patterns were focused on. First, we chose teachers who advocated communicative teaching (see Spada & Fröhlich, 1995), wherein the primary attention of the students was drawn to meaning rather than form; we thought that the manipulation of perceptual saliency via CF and MI could otherwise be compromised. Second, we observed CF provision patterns of the selected four teachers so that we could assign them to a group that approximated their regular teaching styles. This was because if a teacher changes her teaching style suddenly, her students may notice the change which may affect the degree of CF noticeability (see Lyster & Mori, 2006).

To further ensure that teachers provided the type of feedback required for the study, the first author provided extensive CF training sessions. The teachers were paired according to their preferred CF type and invited to the researcher's office separately. The sessions involved not only the explanation of the nature of the study but also discussion and practice of CF. First, the teachers were asked to read Lyster et al. (2013) prior to the first session. Second, during the sessions, the researcher gave a short lecture about CF. Third, the paired teachers practiced CF in front of the researcher and the researcher commented on how they could improve the provision of the assigned CF while maintaining their regular teaching patterns. Finally, the teachers were asked to practice the assigned CF in a different class that was not part of the current study. The researcher visited those classes and gave comments on their CF patterns. Only after the training did the actual data collection start.

Given the successful training sessions, we recommend CF training for pre- and in-service teachers. While it is not easy to change teachers' beliefs or teaching styles (see Underwood, 2012), we believe that it is important to raise teachers' awareness of CF. For example, even though Kamiya and Loewen (2013) found that an ESL teacher who read several research articles on CF focused on the parts that supported his beliefs and discounted those parts with which he did not agree, their study found that giving teachers the opportunity to reflect on their beliefs was helpful. Consequently, we argue that it is important to inform teachers that correcting L2 errors is a good thing to do. Theoretical information may help them understand the effects of CF. Observations of other teachers' classes or teachers video-taping their own lessons are effective ways of raising CF awareness as well (see Vásquez & Harvey, 2010). Such training can be incorporated in a pedagogy class for pre-service teachers. Additionally, a language program can set up a workshop designed to train in-service teachers.

Metacognitive instruction

In addition to an investigation of the well-known phenomenon of CF, the current study explored an instructional technique that has been rarely used in interactionist research, namely MI. This instruction might have resulted in developing the three types of metacognitive knowledge (i.e., person, task, and strategy), all of which are important for teaching and learning. First, *person knowledge* pertaining to learners' beliefs about themselves and others may have been influenced by the intervention. For example, the whole class discussion of and practice with CF might have eliminated possible embarrassment and reduced learners' anxiety (see Zhang & Rahimi, 2014). Second, regarding *task knowledge*, the learners in the MI groups may have come to realize that the goal of the communicative activities can include the development of grammatical knowledge. Without the benefit of such MI, L2 learners may believe that the goal of communicative activities is simply task completion (e.g., answering the teacher's questions).

Third, and most importantly, the MI groups' *strategic knowledge*, which entails "what strategies are, why they are useful, and specific knowledge about when and how to use them" (Wenden, 1998, p. 519), may have been improved. Due to the MI, the learners presumably became more aware of provision and function of CF, and were thus able to benefit from it more than students in the comparison groups, who did not receive MI. However, we remain cautious in discussing the learners' metacognition because we did not implement an independent measure of metacognitive knowledge. Overall, MI arguably heightened the noticeability of implicit CF on less perceptually salient linguistic features. Hence, teachers can use MI to help learners (1) process CF explicitly regardless of its discoursal form, and (2) notice morphosyntactic structures that are not perceptually salient or communicatively redundant, such as 3SG-*s*.

In terms of implementation of MI, unlike CF, the participating teachers were not provided with training that focused on how to deliver the instruction. Rather, after the researchers briefed them on the gist of MI, the teachers simply followed PowerPoint slides that the researchers created. Also, the instruction was short (60 minutes over six classes). Therefore, we argue that (1) a teacher does not require extensive knowledge or training for using MI in the classroom; (2) the instruction does not necessarily involve much preparation time; (3) the instruction does not use up teaching time; and (4) the instruction is effective. Thus, we recommend that teachers adopt MI for boosting the effectiveness of CF. It is easy to prepare and implement. However, it is important that teachers are aware of the fact that MI is *instruction about instruction*; otherwise, learners may perceive MI as traditional grammar instruction.

Methodological take-away points

Ecological validity

One of the greatest methodological strengths of classroom-based research is its ecological validity, which is "the degree of similarity between a research study and the authentic context that the study is purportedly investigating" (Loewen & Plonsky, 2016, p. 56). In the current study, the only element manipulated by the researchers was part of the instruction. Everything else – the teachers, students, classroom, materials, schedule, etc. – was part of the participants' regular activities, thereby minimizing the chances of the researcher introducing some element into the classroom that would have a substantial impact, either negative or positive, on the results of the research. The MI intervention was delivered by the classroom teachers. We used the instructional materials from the intact classes to elicit communicative interaction. This interaction, where CF was provided, was carried out between classroom teachers and their own students. This interaction was not manipulated by the researchers (apart from CF and its types). This interaction was not videotaped, and the researchers refrained from being present in the classroom (except for short observations). Below is a list of methodological decisions, we believe, that increase the ecological validity of a study while maintaining the internal and external validity:

a. the intervention materials incorporate the existing lesson plans;
b. the intervention is delivered in the classroom setting during regular class time;
c. the intervention is given by the classroom teacher;
d. the intervention is understood and supported by the teacher;
e. the researcher is not present during the intervention; and
f. the rigor of data collection procedure, testing tools, and data analysis, etc. is ensured.

With regards to Decision (a), researchers, including ourselves, tend to go to the classroom and administer a "one-off research activity" (McDonough, 2015, p. 227), hoping that we capture learning behaviors in a real world setting. However, learner behaviors may be altered when an unfamiliar element is introduced to their regular learning environment, thereby the researcher may fail to observe an accurate picture of what is going on in the classroom. To minimize such experimental intrusion, the researcher may want to adjust the intervention material according the existing curriculum. The same argument applies to Decisions (b) and (e); if learners are pulled out of the classroom and asked to interact with an unfamiliar research assistant in a laboratory, their behaviors, including their attention to language, would most likely be altered (Foster, 1998; but see Gass, Mackey, & Ross-Feldman, 2005). As for Decisions (c) and (d), we recruited four teachers who were assigned to two CF conditions. As explained, the assignment considered their regular teaching styles and they went through intensive training. Those decisions, we believe, increased the intervention's validity as to the four teachers provided their assigned types of CF.

At the same time, classroom-based research also presents threats to internal and external validity, which is related to Decision (f). The goal of any experimental study is, by definition, to discover a causal relationship (e.g., the relationship between a specific type of L2 instruction and the change in a specific aspect of L2 knowledge), and it is the use of precise procedures and researcher control that allows for confidence in the generalizability of a study (Shadish, Cook, & Campbell, 2002). In classroom-based research, however, the researcher has very little control over confounding variables, such as differences in participants or treatment, that might impact the results of the study. In our case, for example, the proficiency levels of the learners within and across the classes varied more than we hoped for based on the institutional class assignments. Gender proportions within and across the classes also varied. It is most likely the case that there was also a wide range of individual differences (e.g., phonological and working memories) among the participants.

Perhaps, given the paucity of comparative studies between classroom and laboratory settings as well as the dynamics and the messiness (from a research standpoint) of classroom L2 learning, it is safe to resort to the idea of ecological validity in understanding the effect of MI and CF in the current study. We agree, therefore, that "high ecological validity comes with a trade-off in the form of reduced experimental control over other variables" (McDonough, Crawford, & De Vleeschauwer, 2016, p. 189), but in the end, we endeavored to increase ecological validity while maintaining internal and external validity as much as possible (see also Sato & Loewen, 2019-b).

Challenges and joys of classroom research

In spite of a researcher's best efforts to minimize validity threats, there are numerous challenges to (quasi-experimental) classroom-based research. One often hears or reads about problems or incidents like the ones below, and we will illustrate here how some of the issues listed may have played a role in the current study:

a. There is no school or teacher who fits the purpose of the study;
b. There is no school or teacher who is willing to participate in the study;
c. There is insufficient time to implement the intervention due to the school schedule;
d. There is no space and/or time for administering individualized tests;
e. One or more students do not agree to participate in the study, even though whole class observation is a crucial part of the research;
f. The classroom is not conducive to audio-visual recording. Oddly configured rooms can result in students being left out of the video, and classroom noise can negatively impact audio recordings;
g. During the researcher's purposeful absence from the classroom, the recording equipment is tampered with by a student playing with the recorder;
h. A class is cancelled without advanced notice;
i. One or more students stop coming to the class;
j. Students are not engaged with the class and not paying attention to the intervention;
k. Students behave differently from regular classes; and
l. One or more students are reluctant to engage with the developmental tests.

Some of these challenges are avoidable. For instance, for Challenges (a), (b), (c), (d), (e), (f), and (g), the researcher can make creative adjustments to the design or timing of the intervention prior to the data collection. Indeed, our study was originally planned to be implemented in the first semester of the academic year. However, due to a student strike, we had to reschedule the data collection to the second semester (we were truly lucky that this did not happen in the midst of data collection).

Probably, one of the most frustrating challenges is sudden class cancellations (Challenge h) during the treatment, because a researcher cannot predict them. Reasons for cancellation vary from the teacher getting sick to the school cancelling instructional activities. In our case, one week prior to the scheduled intervention, a new university chancellor was elected. Subsequently, the university cancelled all classes on the intervention date for celebration. Fortunately, we were able to adjust data collection dates. Unscheduled interruptions can end an entire study depending on research objectives, however. For example, if a researcher is interested in examining spacing effects (the effect of intervals between practice), one cancelled class is sufficient to send the entire project to the grave.

Another challenge is that classroom-based research typically suffers from participant attrition (Challenge i). Students may withdraw from the course. Some of them simply do not come to class. Even when all students come to class, some of them may skip the post-test. In those cases, a researcher may have to eliminate those students from the data set. In our study, the four classes originally had 123 students in total, yet the sample size was reduced to 83 at the end. Student engagement with research is a double-edged sword (Challenges j, k, and l). While it is fundamental that students are paying attention to the intervention (otherwise, how can we talk about the effect of the intervention?), we do not want them to act differently for the sake of research (the Hawthorne effect). Such behavior diminishes ecological validity. In addition, different degrees of student engagement, combined with uncontrollable individual differences in intact classes, may lead to undesirably large standard deviations (which was unfortunately the case in our dataset). Large standard deviations are problematic because the interpretation of the mean differences (i.e., the effect of the intervention) could be unreliable. Finally, classroom researchers need to deal with ethical issues specific to classroom-based research. For instance, knowing CF brings about positive learning effects regardless of its type, is it ethical to set up a control group that does not receive any CF (see Gass & Sterling, 2017 for a comprehensive review of ethical issues)?

Probably, classroom-based researchers were unenthusiastically nodding while reading the challenges list, but laboratory-based researchers were thinking about the negative impacts of the challenges on validity. Again, it is ultimately the researcher's personal choice as to whether the data should be collected in the classroom. Should you choose to conduct a classroom-based quasi-experimental study, however, you need to act quickly and creatively when, for instance, you discover that half of the class is absent because it is the Thursday before a long weekend.

Despite the challenges that come with unforeseeable data collection challenges, classroom-based research gives us the joy of working with teachers in a real learning setting. In reflecting on her career in classroom-based research, Lightbown (2016: 199–200) wrote:

> [o]ur research group saw teachers who amazed us by their energy, their knowledge, and their genuine joy when students succeeded – or at least showed that they were trying. Regardless of teaching method, the materials, or the external sociocultural circumstances, we saw teachers who made good use of the precious time available for learning, got students excited about learning, and helped them develop the tools to keep learning outside the classroom. … What was clear in every classroom, however, was that the nature of the interaction between teacher and students would be the most important determinant in learning outcomes.

Despite the challenges outlined above, we enjoyed working with the teachers and learned much from them. During the teacher training sessions, for example, we learned about their beliefs regarding CF and MI. Observing how the teachers implemented the MI gave us several ideas for research as we recognized that metacognitive knowledge concerns classroom-specific behaviors (person knowledge). Sitting in a classroom is always a refreshing reminder of what it means to be language learners and language teachers, and observing classroom interaction gives us a reality-check opportunity about what our research is intended to contribute to. We believe that the methodological challenges are intimately linked with those benefits.

Conclusion

The current study opens up a new research avenue for MI while providing some confirming evidence about CF. In this chapter, we focused on the methodological aspects of the study. We argued that such a classroom-based quasi-experimental design, on the one hand, runs a risk of diminishing internal and external validity (generalizability) due to the difficulty of controlling classroom procedures. On the other hand, this design increases ecological validity that helps link research and practice (see the introduction to this volume). While we supported ecological validity that comes with classroom research in this chapter, we both conduct laboratory-based research as well. In conclusion, we concur with Spada (2015), who argued that misapplication of SLA research to L2 pedagogy happens when "there is a failure to take into consideration the context in which the research has been carried out" (p. 70). It is not a matter of which data collection methods are better than others. Rather, it is the research objective (theoretical and pedagogical) and the researcher's personal belief (generalizability or ecological validity) that should drive the central methodological decisions.

Acknowledgment

This work was partially supported by the Fondo Nacional de Desarrollo Científico y Tecnológico from the Ministry of Education of Chile (FONDECYT: 1181533) as well as PIA (CIE160009) from the Chilean National Commission of Science and Technology (CONICYT), awarded to the first author.

References

Ammar, A., & Spada, N. (2006). One size fits all? Recasts, prompts and L2 learning. *Studies in Second Language Acquisition*, 28(4), 543–574. https://doi.org/10.1017/S0272263106060268

Blanca, M. J., Arnau, J., López-Montiel, D., Bono, R., & Bendayan, R. (2013). Skewness and kurtosis in real data samples. *Methodology*, 9, 78–84. https://doi.org/10.1027/1614-2241/a000057

Brown, A. (2009). Students' and teachers' perceptions of effective foreign language teaching: A comparison of ideals. *The Modern Language Journal*, 93(1), 46–60. https://doi.org/10.1111/j.1540-4781.2009.00827.x

Brown, D. (2016). The type and linguistic foci of oral corrective feedback in the L2 classroom: A meta-analysis. *Language Teaching Research*, 20(4), 436–458. https://doi.org/10.1177/1362168814563200

Carpenter, H., Jeon, S., MacGregor, D., & Mackey, A. (2006). Recasts as repetitions: Learners' interpretations of native speaker responses. *Studies in Second Language Acquisition*, 28(2), 209–236. https://doi.org/10.1017/S0272263106060104

Dulay, H. C., & Burt, M. K. (1974). Natural sequences in child second language acquisition. *Language Learning*, 24(1), 37–53. https://doi.org/10.1111/j.1467-1770.1974.tb00234.x

Ellis, R. (2001). Introduction: Investigating form-focused instruction. *Language Learning*, 51(s1), 1–46. https://doi.org/10.1111/j.1467-1770.2001.tb00013.x

Ellis, R., & Barkhuizen, G. (2005). *Analysing learner language*. Oxford: Oxford University Press.

Ellis, R., Basturkmen, H., & Loewen, S. (2001). Learner uptake in communicative ESL lessons. *Language Learning*, 51(2), 281–318. https://doi.org/10.1111/1467-9922.00156

Ellis, R., Loewen, S., & Erlam, R. (2006). Implicit and explicit corrective feedback and the acquisition of L2 grammar. *Studies in Second Language Acquisition*, 28(2), 339–368. https://doi.org/10.1017/S0272263106060141

Flavell, J. H. (1976). Metacognitive aspects of problem solving. In L. B. Resnick (Ed.), *The nature of intelligence* (pp. 231–235). Hillsdale, NJ: Lawrence Erlbaum Associates.

Flavell, J. H. (1979). Metacognition and cognitive monitoring: A new area of cognitive–developmental inquiry. *American Psychologist*, 34(10), 906–911. https://doi.org/10.1037/0003-066X.34.10.906

Foster, P. (1998). A classroom perspective on the negotiation of meaning. *Applied Linguistics*, 14(1), 1–23. https://doi.org/10.1093/applin/19.1.1

Gass, S., Mackey, A., & Ross-Feldman, L. (2005). Task-based interactions in classroom and laboratory settings. *Language Learning*, 55(4), 575–611. https://doi.org/10.1111/j.0023-8333.2005.00318.x

Gass, S., & Sterling, S. (2017). Ethics in ISLA. In S. Loewen & M. Sato (Eds.), *The Routledge handbook of instructed second language acquisition* (pp. 577–596). New York, NY: Routledge.

Goh, C., & Taib, Y. (2006). Metacognitive instruction in listening for young learners. *ELT Journal*, 60(3), 222–232. https://doi.org/10.1093/elt/ccl002

Goldschneider, J., & DeKeyser, R. (2005). Explaining the "natural order of L2 morpheme acquisition" in English: A meta-analysis of multiple determinants. *Language Learning*, 55(1), 27–77. https://doi.org/10.1111/j.0023-8333.2005.00295.x

Goo, J., & Mackey, A. (2013). The case against the case against recasts. *Studies in Second Language Acquisition*, 35(1), 127–165. https://doi.org/10.1017/S0272263112000708

Hattie, J., & Timperley, H. (2007). The power of feedback. *Review of Educational Research*, 77(1), 81–112. https://doi.org/10.3102/003465430298487

Kamiya, N., & Loewen, S. (2013). The influence of academic articles on an ESL teacher's stated beliefs. *Innovation in Language Learning and Teaching*, 8, 205–218. https://doi.org/10.1080/17501229.2013.800077

Karimi, M. N. (2015). L2 multiple-documents comprehension: Exploring the contributions of L1 reading ability and strategic processing. *System*, 52, 14–25. https://doi.org/10.1016/j.system.2015.04.019

Keselman, H., Huberty, C., Lix, L., Olejnik, S., Cribbie, R., Donahue, B., Levine, J. (1998). Statistical practices of educational researchers: An analysis of their ANOVA, MANOVA, and ANCOVA analyses. *Review of Educational Research*, 68(3), 350–386. https://doi.org/10.3102/00346543068003350

Leow, R. (2015). *Explicit learning in the L2 classroom*. New York, NY: Routledge.

Li, S. (2010). The effectiveness of corrective feedback in SLA: A meta-analysis. *Language Learning*, 60(2), 309–365. https://doi.org/10.1111/j.1467-9922.2010.00561.x

Li, S. (2014). The interface between feedback type, L2 proficiency, and the nature of the linguistic target. *Language Teaching Research*, 18(3), 373–396. https://doi.org/10.1177/1362168813510384

Lightbown, P. (2016). From language learner to language learning researcher. In R. Ellis (Ed.), *Becoming and being an applied linguist* (pp. 175–211). Amsterdam: John Benjamins. https://doi.org/10.1075/z.203.08lig

Loewen, S. (2012). The role of feedback. In S. Gass & A. Mackey (Eds.), *The Routledge handbook of second language acquisition* (pp. 24–40). New York, NY: Routledge.

Loewen, S., Erlam, R., & Ellis, R. (2009). The incidental acquisition of third person-s as implicit and explicit knowledge. In R. Ellis, S. Loewen, C. Elder, R. Erlam, J. Philp, & H. Reinders (Eds.), *Implicit and explicit knowledge in second language learning, testing and teaching* (pp. 262–280). Clevedon: Multilingual Matters. https://doi.org/10.21832/9781847691767-013

Loewen, S., & Nabei, T. (2007). Measuring the effects of oral corrective feedback on L2 knowledge. In A. Mackey (Ed.), *Conversational interaction in second language acquisition: A collection of empirical studies* (pp. 361–377). Oxford: Oxford University Press.

Loewen, S., & Plonsky, L. (2016). *An A-Z of applied linguistics research methods*. New York, NY: Palgrave Macmillan. https://doi.org/10.1007/978-1-137-40322-3

Loewen, S., & Sato, M. (2017). Instructed second language acquisition (ISLA): An overview. In S. Loewen & M. Sato (Eds.), *The handbook of instructed second language scquisition* (pp. 1–12). New York, NY: Routledge. https://doi.org/10.4324/9781315676968

Loewen, S., & Sato, M. (2018). State-of-the-art article: Interaction and instructed second language acquisition. *Language Teaching*, 51(3), 285–329. https://doi.org/10.1017/S0261444818000125

Lyster, R. (2004). Differential effects of prompts and recasts in form-focused instruction. *Studies in Second Language Acquisition*, 26(3), 399–432. https://doi.org/10.1017/S0272263104263021

Lyster, R., & Mori, H. (2006). Interactional feedback and instructional counterbalance. *Studies in Second Language Acquisition*, 28(2), 269–300. https://doi.org/10.1017/S0272263106060128

Lyster, R., & Ranta, L. (1997). Corrective feedback and learner uptake: Negotiation of form in communicative classrooms. *Studies in Second Language Acquisition*, 19(1), 37–66. https://doi.org/10.1017/S0272263197001034

Lyster, R., & Ranta, L. (2013). Counterpoint piece: The case for variety in corrective feedback research. *Studies in Second Language Acquisition*, 35(1), 1–18. https://doi.org/10.1017/S027226311200071X

Lyster, R., Saito, K., & Sato, M. (2013). State-of-the-art article: Oral corrective feedback in second language classrooms. *Language Teaching*, 46(1), 1–40. https://doi.org/10.1017/S0261444812000365

Mackey, A. (2006). Feedback, noticing and instructed second language learning. *Applied Linguistics*, 27(3), 405–430. https://doi.org/10.1093/applin/ami051

Mackey, A. (2012). *Input, interaction, and corrective feedback in L2 learning*. Oxford: Oxford University Press.

McCarthy, M., McCarten, J., & Sandiford, H. (2008). *Touchstone* 2. Cambridge: Cambridge University Press.

McDonough, K. (2007). Interactional feedback and the emergence of simple past activity verbs in L2 English. In A. Mackey (Ed.), *Conversational interaction in second language acquisition: A collection of empirical studies* (pp. 323–338). Oxford: Oxford University Press.

McDonough, K. (2015). Perceived benefits and challenges with the use of collaborative tasks in EFL contexts. In M. Bygate (Ed.), *Domains and directions in the development of TBLT: A decade of plenaries from the international conference* (pp. 225–245). Amsterdam: John Benjamins. https://doi.org/10.1075/tblt.8.08mcd

McDonough, K., Crawford, W. J., & De Vleeschauwer, J. (2016). Thai EFL learners' interaction during collaborative writing tasks and its relationship to text quality. In M. Sato & S. Ballinger (Eds.), *Peer interaction and second language learning: Pedagogical potential and research agenda* (pp. 185–208). Amsterdam: John Benjamins. https://doi.org/10.1075/lllt.45.08mcd

Nassaji, H. (2016). Anniversary article Interactional feedback in second language teaching and learning: A synthesis and analysis of current research. *Language Teaching Research*, 20(4), 535–562. https://doi.org/10.1177/1362168816644940

Nassaji, H., & Kartchava, E. (Eds.) (2017). *Corrective feedback in second language teaching and learning: Research, theory, applications, implications*. New York, NY: Routledge.

Nicholas, H., Lightbown, P., & Spada, N. (2001). Recasts as feedback to language learners. *Language Learning*, 51(4), 719–758. https://doi.org/10.1111/0023-8333.00172

Pintrich, P. (2000). The role of goal orientation in self-regulated learning. In M. Boekaerts, P. Pintrich, & M. Zeidner (Eds.), *Handbook of self-regulation* (pp. 451–502). Cambridge, MA: Academic Press. https://doi.org/10.1016/B978-012109890-2/50043-3

Plonsky, L., & Brown, D. (2015). Domain definition and search techniques in meta-analyses of L2 research (Or why 18 meta-analyses of feedback have different results). *Second Language Research*, 31(2), 267–278. https://doi.org/10.1177/0267658314536436

Plonsky, L., & Oswald, F. L. (2014). How big is 'big'? Interpreting effect sizes in L2 research. *Language Learning*, 64, 878–912. https://doi.org/10.1111/lang.12079

Russell, J., & Spada, N. (2006). The effectiveness of corrective feedback for the acquisition of L2 grammar. In J. Norris & L. Ortega (Eds.), *Synthesizing research on language learning and teaching* (pp. 133–162). Amsterdam: John Benjamins.

Sato, M. (2011). Constitution of form-orientation: Contributions of context and explicit knowledge to learning from recasts. *Canadian Journal of Applied Linguistics*, 14(1), 1–28.

Sato, M. (2013). Beliefs about peer interaction and peer corrective feedback: Efficacy of classroom intervention. *The Modern Language Journal*, 97(3), 611–633. https://doi.org/10.1111/j.1540-4781.2013.12035.x

Sato, M., & Loewen, S. (2018). Metacognitive instruction enhances the effectiveness of corrective feedback: Variable effects of feedback types and linguistic targets. *Language Learning*, 68(2), 507–545. https://doi.org/10.1111/lang.12283

Sato, M., & Loewen, S. (2019-a). Do teachers care about research? The research-pedagogy dialogue. *ELT Journal*, 73. https://doi.org/10.1093/elt/ccy048

Sato, M., & Loewen, S. (2019-b). Towards evidence-based second language pedagogy. In M. Sato & S. Loewen (Eds.), *Evidence-based second language pedagogy: A collection of instructed second language acquisition studies*. New York, NY: Routledge.

Shadish, W. R., Cook, T. D., & Campbell, D. T. (2002). *Experimental and quasi-experimental designs for generalized causal inference.* Boston, MA: Houghton Mifflin.

Sheen, Y., & Ellis, R. (2011). Corrective feedback in language teaching. In E. Hinkel (Ed.), *Handbook of research in second language teaching and learning* (Vol. 2, pp. 593–610). New York, NY: Routledge.

Spada, N. (2015). SLA research and L2 pedagogy: Misapplications and questions of relevance. *Language Teaching*, 48(1), 69–81. https://doi.org/10.1017/S026144481200050X

Spada, N., & Fröhlich, M. (1995). *COLT. Communicative orientation of language teaching observation scheme: Coding conventions and applications.* Sydney: National Center for English Language Teaching and Research.

Teng, L. S., & Zhang, L. J. (2016). A questionnaire-based validation of multidimensional models of self-regulated learning strategies. *The Modern Language Journal*, 100(3), 674–701. https://doi.org/10.1111/modl.12339

Underwood, P. R. (2012). Teacher beliefs and intentions regarding the instruction of English grammar under national curriculum reforms: A Theory of Planned Behaviour perspective. *Teaching and Teacher Education*, 28(6), 911–925. https://doi.org/10.1016/j.tate.2012.04.004

Vandergrift, L., & Baker, S. (2015). Learner variables in second language listening comprehension: An exploratory path analysis. *Language Learning*, 65(2), 390–416. https://doi.org/10.1111/lang.12105

Vandergrift, L., & Tafaghodtari, M. H. (2010). Teaching L2 learners how to listen does make a difference: An empirical study. *Language Learning*, 60(2), 470–497. https://doi.org/10.1111/j.1467-9922.2009.00559.x

Vásquez, C., & Harvey, J. (2010). Raising teachers' awareness about corrective feedback through research replication. *Language Teaching Research*, 14(4), 421–443. https://doi.org/10.1177/1362168810375365

Veenman, M. V. (2011). Learning to self-monitor and self-regulate. In R. Mayer & P. Alexander (Eds.), *Handbook of research on learning and instruction* (pp. 197–218). New York, NY: Routledge.

Veenman, M. V., Van Hout-Wolters, B. H., & Afflerbach, P. (2006). Metacognition and learning: Conceptual and methodological considerations. *Metacognition and Learning*, 1(1), 3–14. https://doi.org/10.1007/s11409-006-6893-0

Wenden, A. L. (1987). Metacognition: An expanded view on the cognitive abilities of L2 learners. *Language Learning*, 37(4), 573–597. https://doi.org/10.1111/j.1467-1770.1987.tb00585.x

Wenden, A. L. (1998). Metacognitive knowledge and language learning. *Applied Linguistics*, 19(4), 515–537. https://doi.org/10.1093/applin/19.4.515

Yilmaz, Y. (2012). The relative effects of explicit correction and recasts on two target structures via two communication modes. *Language Learning*, 62(4), 1134–1169. https://doi.org/10.1111/j.1467-9922.2012.00726.x

Zhang, L. J., & Rahimi, M. (2014). EFL learners' anxiety level and their beliefs about corrective feedback in oral communication classes. *System*, 42, 429–439. https://doi.org/10.1016/j.system.2014.01.012

Zobl, H. (1985). Grammars in search of input and intake. In S. Gass & C. Madden (Eds.), *Input in second language acquisition* (pp. 329–344). Rowley, MA: Newbury House.

CHAPTER 4

Integrating instructed second language research, pragmatics, and corpus-based instruction

Kathleen Bardovi-Harlig, Sabrina Mossman and Yunwen Su
Indiana University / University of Texas at El Paso / The University of Utah

This paper discusses the issues raised by implementing instruction in language classrooms for the purpose of researching the effects of instruction on second language acquisition. We examine the process of developing and implementing novel corpus-based instruction for the teaching of pragmatic routines in a study that compared the use of teacher-developed corpus-based materials to guided, hands-on corpus searches by learners (Bardovi-Harlig, Mossman, & Su, 2017). We use this study as the impetus for reflection on the experimenters' role in materials and activities development and the difference between experimental instruction and classroom teaching. We further discuss the role of learner proficiency levels and grammatical and lexical development in response to instruction, teacher collaboration, and generalizability to other contexts.

Keywords: pragmatics, pragmatic formulas, corpus-based instruction, corpus-based materials, corpus searches, instructional effects, materials development, instructional design

Introduction

Designing, implementing, and interpreting instructional effects studies present many challenges not encountered when conducting other types of acquisition research. While the design considerations are quite similar, the addition of one or more instructional components adds not only a measure of complexity, but also all the variables related to teaching including, but not limited to, teachers, development of materials and activities, and instructional delivery. In order to examine the role played by the various factors in instructional effect studies, we discuss a study in which we implemented corpus-based instruction in two different ways for the teaching of pragmatic routines (Bardovi-Harlig, Mossman, & Su, 2017). First,

https://doi.org/10.1075/lllt.52.04bar

we developed lessons that were teacher-directed by extracting authentic conversations from an academic corpus to serve as input and creating noticing activities to accompany them. Next, we developed pragmatics lessons in which the students engaged in hands-on searches of the same academic corpus. This approach was new to pragmatics instruction, new to us, and new to the learners, so it provided us an opportunity to reflect anew on the interface of pragmatics, teaching, research, and the institutions in which we work.

In the following sections, we discuss the importance of authentic materials for the teaching of pragmatics, review the research that led to our study, and then briefly present our most recent work comparing supported corpus searches to corpus-based materials in the teaching of pragmatics. We draw on this study to reflect on the instructional and methodological issues that arise in planning and delivering language instruction for research purposes, and the subsequent integration of such instruction into regular language classes.

Background

Authentic materials in pragmatics

Readers are likely to be less familiar with the issues related to teaching pragmatics than other linguistic domains because it is a relative newcomer compared to the more established areas of grammar, pronunciation, and vocabulary. Informally, pragmatics is the knowledge of how to say what to whom when and in what context (Bardovi-Harlig, 2013). Levinson (1983) defines pragmatics as encompassing at least five main areas: deixis, conversational implicature, presupposition, speech acts, and conversational structure. This chapter is concerned with speech acts and the pragmatic routines used to realize them. Pragmatic routines are tied to a specific speech act. Speech act research is often concerned with illocutionary force – the intended impact of an utterance – and perlocutionary force – how listeners perceive the impact of the utterance. Pragmatic routines, such as *I agree, You're right*, and *That's true*, help convey the illocutionary force of agreement and should encourage the listener to perceive the utterance as an agreement as well.

Because pragmatics deals with language use, pragmatics researchers interested in instruction have argued that the teaching of pragmatics should draw primarily on authentic language materials (Cohen & Ishihara, 2013). Nevertheless, like the early surveys (Bardovi-Harlig, et al, 1991; Boxer & Pickering, 1995; Williams, 1988; Vellenga, 2004), even recent surveys of textbooks show that the pragmatics depicted in conversations is often contrived and does not illustrate how speakers interact (Bardovi-Harlig, Mossman, & Vellenga, 2015a; Cheng & Cheng, 2010; Cohen &

Ishihara, 2013; Ren & Han, 2016). For teachers to supplement textbooks by collecting their own authentic language samples requires such an investment of time that it may not be practical beyond special projects. The advent of free online corpora has dramatically changed that. Corpus searches are ideal for searching words and phrases. Thus, searching for multiple-word expressions related to pragmatics, like pragmatic routines, is very straightforward.[1]

Research – teaching trajectory

Our interest in the teaching and learning of pragmatic routines comes from two sources: work on teaching pragmatics that argues for the use of authentic materials (discussed briefly above) and research on the L2 acquisition of pragmatic routines and conventional expressions. Whereas pragmatic routines are tied to speech acts, conventional expressions are tied to speech acts, realized in specific contexts, and are moreover the preferred expression used in that context (Bardovi-Harlig, 2009; Erman & Warren, 2000). Prior to 2005, research reports often concluded by hypothesizing that learners would be more successful pragmatically if they could use the same conventional expressions that expert speakers use (Bardovi-Harlig, 2006). That led to a series of acquisition studies (Bardovi-Harlig 2009, 2010; Bardovi-Harlig & Bastos, 2011; Bardovi-Harlig, Bastos, Burghardt, Chappetto, Nickels, & Rose, 2010) that showed that learners recognized some expressions, but not others; of the expressions they recognized, they could use some, but not others. As a result, Bardovi-Harlig and Vellenga (2012) undertook an instructional effect study to teach conventional expressions. They used focused noticing activities with written transcripts of authentic-scripted language from *Friends* as input. Learners were assessed orally via a computer-delivered oral discourse completion task (DCT). Results showed a significant increase in recognition and production of target expressions.

The increase was encouraging in that the improvement was statistically significant but not dramatic (as shown by small to medium effect sizes), and we wanted to investigate whether adding oral practice to the noticing activities would enhance the instructional effects. As we were planning a follow-up study to include oral production, we met with teachers from the intensive English program with which we work, hoping that they could help us fine-tune the instruction. However, the teachers also had a problem that they wanted to solve. They wanted help with the teaching of pragmatics related to academic group work, and most

---

1.   In contrast, pragmatic tagging of a corpus is still experimental. See Taguchi, Kaufer, Gómez-Laich, & Zhao (2016).

particularly agreements and disagreements, following the program curricular goals for low-advanced university-bound students.[2] We undertook the project, and added clarifications to agreements and disagreements because they are frequently found to precede potential disagreements, and a well-placed clarification can eliminate the need for a disagreement (Bardovi-Harlig & Salsbury, 2004; Pomerantz, 1984).

We designed a study around authentic uses of pragmatic routines for agreement, disagreement, and self- and other-clarifications that were identified via a search of English for academic purposes (EAP) textbooks and verified for frequency of occurrence in an academic corpus, Michigan Corpus of Academic Spoken English (MICASE; Simpson, Briggs, Ovens, & Swales, 2002). MICASE was selected for its relevance to academic preparation; moreover, the University of Michigan, where the recordings took place, has regional proximity to our campus, and is a peer institution in the Big Ten Academic Alliance. Using MICASE as our source for authentic input ensured that it would be compatible with our pedagogical goals. Moreover, the corpus is user friendly and reliable, thus we could promote its use to teachers with confidence.

We created corpus-based written materials and re-recorded input, and devised a number of focused noticing activities and production opportunities that gave all students equal opportunities for oral practice (Bardovi-Harlig, Mossman, & Vellenga, 2015b). We found that learners performed significantly better after instruction as measured by a computer-delivered oral group-work simulation. That could have been the end of the story; however, renewed interest in the role of awareness and noticing in the acquisition of pragmatics (Bardovi-Harlig, 2018; Clennell, 1999; Tomlinson, 1994) in light of compatible claims for the role of noticing and autonomy in data driven-learning which also uses corpus searches (Boulton, 2010; Vyatkina, 2016), led us to investigate whether learners would show an advantage if they were to search the corpus themselves, and whether this might lead learners to use the corpus as a resource independently after instruction (see also the concept of "involvement load" Hulstijn & Laufer, 2001).

In the next study we returned to our previously published work using teacher-developed corpus-based materials (from Bardovi-Harlig, Mossman, & Vellenga, 2015b) and we compared it to essentially the same pragmatics instruction, substituting corpus searches for the original corpus-based excerpts presented by teachers. The details of this study are presented in Bardovi-Harlig, Mossman, and Su (2017). We present an abbreviated sketch of the study in the next section.

---

2.   At the time we designed the study, the relevant student-learning outcome for Level 5 read: (By the end of the session you will be able to....) Participate successfully in small group discussions with the ability to express opinions, agree, disagree, take turns, and negotiate for meaning.

The study: Comparing corpus materials and corpus searches

The study we consider here compared the efficacy of teaching pragmatic routines in two corpus-based conditions and a control condition in which the test was administered twice without pragmatics instruction. Our research questions for that study were:

1. Is there a difference between the performance of a group that receives teacher-developed corpus-based materials and the performance of a group that performs teacher-guided corpus searches, as measured by the production of speech acts and pragmatic routines in an oral group-work simulation task?
2. Does the corpus search group engage in corpus searches independently, beyond instructional activities?

Instruction

Sixteen pragmatic routines were selected on the basis of frequency of occurrence, distributed across the targeted speech acts (agreements, 6; disagreements, 3; self-clarifications, 2; other-clarifications, (5). Nine expressions met or exceeded the threshold of 10 occurrences per million words established by Biber, Johansson, Leech, Conrad, & Finegan, 1999), with four between 10 and 18 occurrences/million and five between 30 and 35 occurrences /million (Table 1). An additional seven expressions occurred between 65 and 120 times per million words (exceeding the count for frequent multiword units of 40 occurrences per million words proposed by Biber, Conrad, & Cortes, 2004).

The first condition used corpus materials (CM) designed by teacher-researchers based on searches using MICASE. The teacher-designed materials had accompanying noticing activities designed to help learners increase their pragmatic awareness of patterns, asymmetries, occurrence, and placement of the routines in academic conversations. The second condition implemented student-conducted hands-on corpus searches (CS) using MICASE. The student-conducted searches contained detailed instructions for carrying out the search and directed student attention to specific characteristics of the transcript in order to mirror the information available from the corpus materials; corpus searches had additional information about frequency. The CM and CS conditions offered three opportunities for the noticing of each of the 16 pragmatic routines. The CM and CS conditions were balanced for content, number of noticing opportunities, and overall length of instruction. For CS, a frequency search replaced one distributional search in CM. There was one frequency search per speech act (agreement, disagreement, and clarification), which replaced noticing activities of the more general type employed in CM. Every other aspect of the instruction was the same (Table 2).

Table 1. Lesson outline

	Lesson one	Lesson two	Lesson three	Lesson four
Speech Acts	Agreement	Agreement Disagreement	Self-Clarification Other-Clarification	Other-Clarification
Routines (frequency in words per million)	*That's right* (90+)	*I agree* (35+)	*What I mean* (100+)	*You're saying* (90+)
	You're right (75+)	*I agree with* (10+)	*In other words* (10+)	*What you're saying* (35)
	That's true (65+)			
	Good point (18+)	*Yeah but* (120+) *Okay but* (90+)	*Do you mean* (36+) *What do you mean* (27+)	
		I agree but (10)	*I have a question* (35+)	

Table 2. Distribution of activities

Activities	Corpus materials	Corpus search
Warmup: Interpreting ambiguous pictures (pair work)		13–22 minutes
Input w/noticing activities	Conversation excerpts from MICASE 93–100 minutes	Concordance lines from MICASE search 100–105 minutes
Aural Input: Recorded excerpts from MICASE		16–18 minutes
Production: Games progressively adding speech acts (Group work)		51–64 minutes

Four 50 minute lessons were developed. Each lesson began with warm-up activities, moving to focused noticing, aural input, and production; the distribution of the pragmatic routines is listed in Table 1 and shared activities are listed in Table 2. The lesson plans, Power-Points, handouts, practice activities and games were given to the teachers. Teachers and researchers met before the pedagogical unit began and before each of the four lessons. Teachers were provided with scripts to assure comparability of metapragmatic information across classes and instructors. Examples (1) and (2) show examples of conversational excerpts used in the CM group. Example (1) shows an agreement example and (2) shows a self-clarification example. The target routines are underlined in the examples, but were not underlined in the materials given to the students. In the example below, students are guided to recognize that *That's a good point* is an impersonal expression. This is later contrasted with *That's right* which is also impersonal and *You're right* which is a personal expression.

(1) Agreement activity CM

> ***Teacher Script***: Some agreements are personal like "You're right," but some are impersonal, like "that's true." "You're right" is an agreement expression that comments on the speaker's view. It's more personal because it says "you." Look at the following examples using the phrase "good point". Which ones are personal and which ones are impersonal? Mark them with an I or a P. [depending on time, this pair activity (involving reading aloud) can be shortened into a whole class activity]
>
> ---
>
> **Dialogue 2   I   P**
>
> ---
>
> A: … you could go back to that sorta argument you know? But, that's not really the argument. All it's saying is that, the number three's like, wherever you're thinking you are, that's where you are.
> B: Um, right I think that's I think <u>that's a good point</u>. I think actually both of these are really good points because, um, <LAUGH> yeah you could, could be giving us a new way of trying to figure out where your real point of view is.
> **Transcript ID:** SEM475JU084

Self-clarifications were part of the third lesson. In Example (2) students are asked to notice which self-clarification expressions occur in three different dialogues and to circle the appropriate expression for the dialogue in the table.

(2) **Self-clarification Noticing CM**

> Dialogue A
> A: It has to be exposed, right? In order to develop a significant erosion or surface, our sediments have to be exposed to the elements. <u>In other words</u>, we need rain, we need rivers, we need, uh wind, all of those, uh factors that are going to, uh help weather down or erode the surface, uh so that uh we develop what is known as an unconformity.
>
> ---
>
>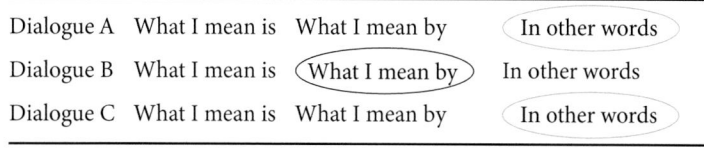
>
> | | | | |
> |---|---|---|---|
> | Dialogue A | What I mean is | What I mean by | (In other words) |
> | Dialogue B | What I mean is | (What I mean by) | In other words |
> | Dialogue C | What I mean is | What I mean by | (In other words) |

Example (3) presents a disagreement example in the CS condition in which the learner is directed to do a search of the disagreement routines. This is an example of the frequency searches students conducted in the CS condition; frequency information was unique to the CS condition.

(3)   **Disagreement search: CS (Frequency)**

> Do people really use "Yeah but" frequently to show disagreement? Let's find out, and while we are at it, let's look at some other possible combinations of agreement expression plus "but" in MICASE. Search for each of the expressions in the table below in MICASE and write down how many times each of them appears.
>
> | Expression | Frequency |
> |---|---|
> | Yeah, but | (233) |
> | Okay, but | (170) |
> | That's true, but | (8) |
> | That's a good point, but | (1) |
> | You're right, but | (3) |
> | That's right, but | (1) |

In Example (4) learners are asked to focus on words or punctuation that follows the other-clarification expression *What do you mean*? Sometimes the expression stands alone as a question (?), and sometimes it takes a noun or a sentence introduced by "by" and sometimes by Ø.

(4)   Other-Clarification CS

> Search for "what do you mean" in MICASE. Look at the first 12 results in the list (from Transcript LAB575JU095 to Transcript OFC300JU149). Write down the word or punctuation that immediately follows "what do you mean" for each of the examples.
>
> what do you mean + 1 word/punctuation
>
> | | |
> |---|---|
> | 1. ? | 7. that |
> | 2. ? | 8. you |
> | 3. he | 9. by |
> | 4. , | 10. by |
> | 5. ? | 11. by |
> | 6. strength | 12. by |

Pretest-posttest

The assessment task was a computer-delivered oral group work simulation task. The task consisted of 30 items, 10 agreement, 10 disagreement, and 10 clarification scenarios, with two training items and two practice items for a total of 34 items. Students were given 10 seconds to respond to a scenario that included the topic of the conversation, their position on the topic, and an aural student turn. The agreement and disagreement scenarios included 5 items that explicitly stated what the students thought "you think that small cars save gas," and 5 items that stated the students' positions relative to the speaker's turn "you think {the same thing/ something different} from your classmate". Clarification scenarios were divided into self- and other-clarifications. Other clarifications were prompted by a range of directions including "Ask about the word 'X' or take a guess" and "{Check/Verify} your understanding." Self-clarifications were prompted by "People look confused. You say:" All other responses were prompted with "You say:". The full task with audio files and transcripts may be retrieved from IRIS <http://www.iris-database. org/iris/app/home/index>. Examples (4) and (5) present an agreement and a self-clarification item, respectively.

(5) Agreement item
     Your group is discussing transportation and cars. You have the same opinion as your classmate.
     Classmate [audio only]: People who take the bus are more responsible environmentally than people who drive cars.
     You say:

(6) Self-Clarification item
     Your classmate has asked you to finish the project for the group.
     You say: I am not saying that I won't do it, just that other people should contribute.
     People look confused. You say: _____

Questionnaire

All learners were given a questionnaire with three background questions. The CS questionnaire additionally included three questions related to conducting the searches: (1) Did you do all of the MICASE searches in the lessons yourself? (yes/ no; if no explain); (2) Did you do additional MICASE searches on your own (not part of the assignments)? (yes/no); (3) If you circled YES, what did you search for? (6 lines provided for sample words or phrases).

Participants

Eight intact classes participated, seven were Level 5 communication classes in a seven-level intensive English program and one was a comparable credit-bearing class for matriculated university students. All six instructors were regularly appointed ESL instructors in the same programs. Only students who completed both the pretest and the posttest and three of the four instructional class periods were included, resulting in 54 participants. All classes reported six to eight native languages. Twenty-six students were in the five CM classes; 17 were in the two CS classes and, 11 were in the two control classes. Students in the control group only had to attend the pretest and posttest.

Analysis

All responses were scored by two raters, once for speech act clarity and once for use of a pragmatic routine for that speech act. An agreement in an agreement context received 1 point. All others received no points. Disagreements in disagreement contexts received 1 point, all others zero, and so on. Accurate production of pragmatic routines for agreements received 1 point in agreement scenarios, disagreement routines in disagreement contexts received 1 point, and clarification routines in clarifications received 1 point. All others received no points.

Results

Production data

A one-way ANOVA performed on the pretest scores showed that the groups performed comparably before instruction. Mixed-model ANOVAs with pretest-posttest as the within-subjects variable and treatment condition as the between-subject variable (corpus-materials/corpus-search/control) were conducted to examine the effect of instruction.

An overview of the results shows that all groups performed better on speech acts than pragmatic routines; students were able to clearly express the appropriate speech acts even without the target expressions (Table 3, Figure 1). All groups improved from pretest to posttest for both speech acts and pragmatic routines, but the gains of the control group were minimal compared to the gains of the experimental groups (Table 3, Figure 1). Results of mixed-model ANOVAs showed significant interactions between pretest-posttest and condition on both speech act scores (F (2, 51) = 4.777, p = .013, partial $\eta2$ = .158) and scores for pragmatic routines (F (2, 51) = 6.147, p = .004, partial $\eta2$ = .194).

Table 3. Production of speech acts and pragmatic routines, by treatment condition, pretest and posttest

	Corpus-materials (N = 26)				Corpus-search (N = 17)				Control (N = 11)			
	Pretest		Posttest		Pretest		Posttest		Pretest		Posttest	
	M	SD	M	SD	M	SD	M	SD	M	SD	M	SD
Speech Acts (k = 30)	.582	.166	.809	.118	.519	.164	.629	.197	.541	.302	.597	.238
Pragmatic Routines	.137	.106	.404	.224	.126	.111	.401	.268	.183	.125	.196	.110

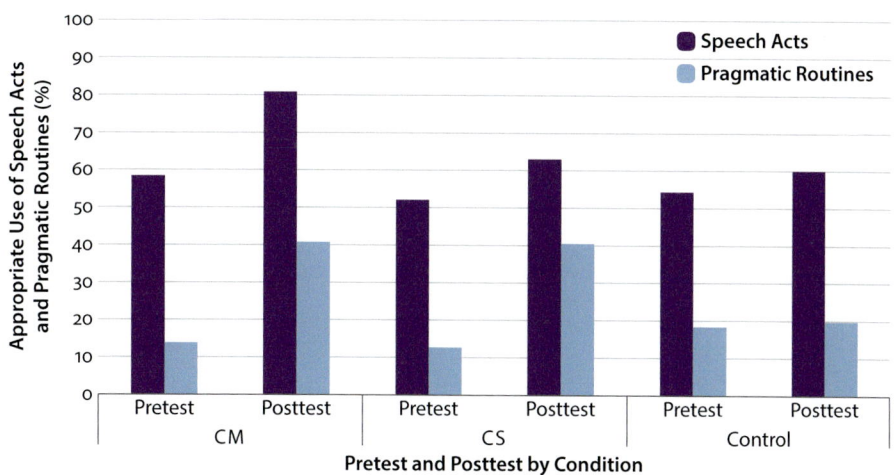

Figure 1. Speech Acts and Pragmatic Routines, by instructional condition, pretest and posttest

Considering agreements (Figure 2), disagreements (Figure 3), and clarifications (Figures 4 and 5) separately shows that they behaved differently. All three groups improved from the pretest to posttest on their speech act scores for agreements and disagreements with similar gains. The results of mixed-model ANOVAs showed no significant effects of interaction between condition and pretest-posttest, but did show significant main effects for pretest-posttest (agreement: $F(1, 51) = 18.821, p < .001$, partial $\eta^2 = .270$; disagreement: $F(1, 51) = 5.642, p = .021$, partial $\eta^2 = .100$).

CM showed greater improvement than CS on production of agreement routines (Figure 2), but less improvement on production of disagreement routines (Figure 3); the control group showed minimal improvement on agreement routines

(Figure 2) and a decrease on disagreement routines (Figure 3). Effects of interaction between condition and pretest-posttest were significant on use of pragmatic routines for both agreement (F (2, 51) = 4.916, p = .011, partial η^2 = .162) and disagreement (F (2, 51) = 3.695, p = .032, partial η^2 = .127).

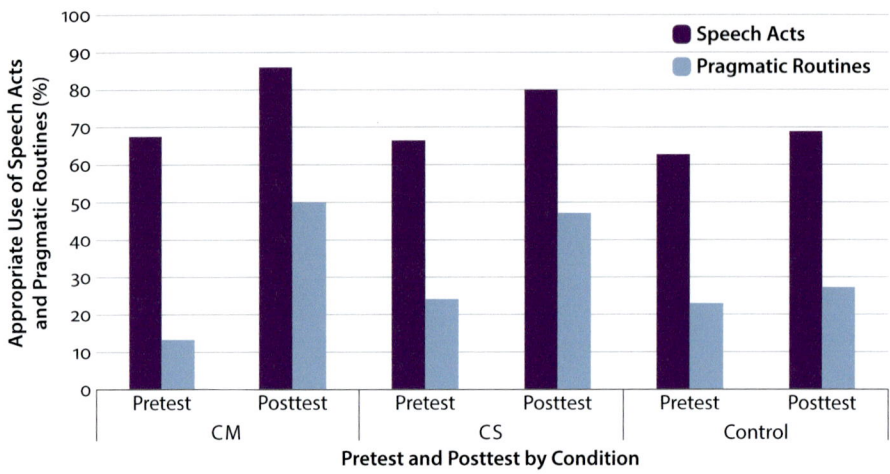

Figure 2. Agreements and agreement routines, by instructional condition, pretest and posttest

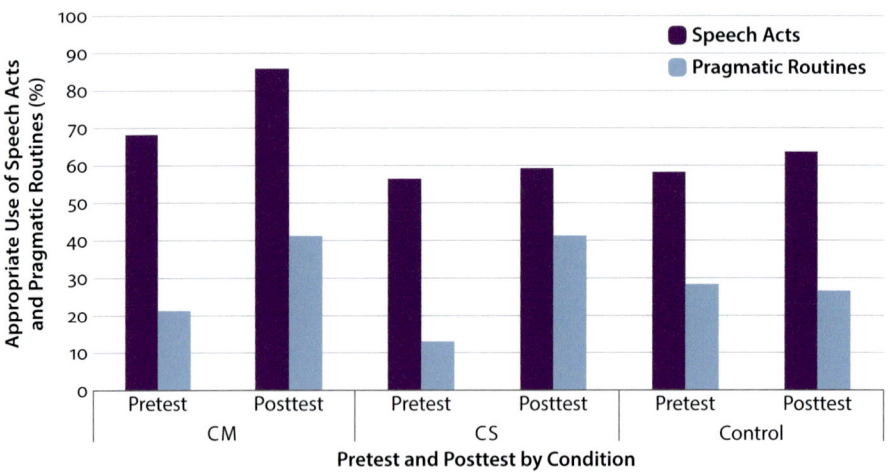

Figure 3. Disagreements and disagreement routines, by instructional condition, pretest and posttest

Clarifications showed lower pretest scores than agreements and disagreements, for all groups; other-clarifications scored higher than self-clarifications (Figures 4 and 5). CM showed greater improvement on expressing the speech act of other-clarification than CS and the control group (Figure 4). The effect of interaction between condition and pretest-posttest was significant on realization of speech acts (F (2, 51) = 8.798, p = .001, partial η^2 = .257). CS, however, showed greater improvement on using pragmatic routines for other-clarifications than CM did; the control showed no improvement. The effect of interaction between condition and pretest-posttest was significant on the use of pragmatic routines (F (2, 51) = 5.282, p = .008, partial η^2 = .172).

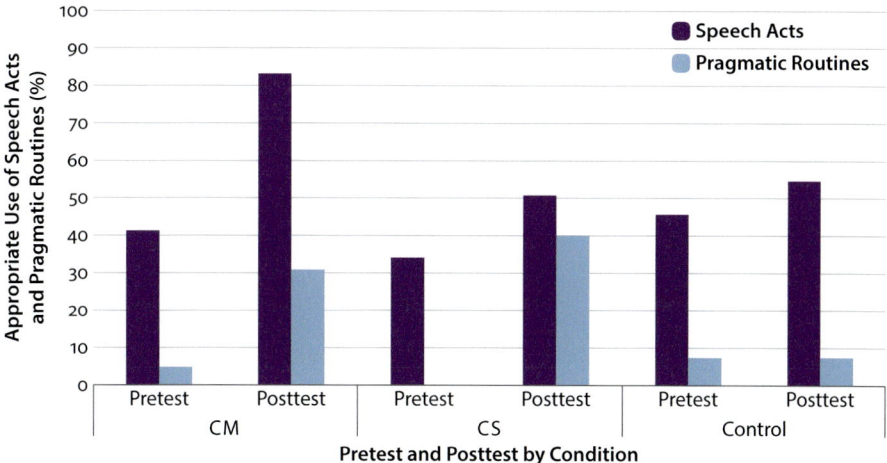

Figure 4. Other-Clarifications and pragmatic routines, by instructional condition, pretest and posttest

CM and CS performed similarly on improvement for self-clarifications on both speech act clarity and appropriate use of pragmatic routines (Figure 5). The effect of interaction between condition and pretest-posttest was not significant but the main effect of pretest-posttest was significant (speech act: F (1, 51) = 9.150, p = .004, partial η^2 = .152; pragmatic routine: F (1, 51) = 11.612, p = .001, partial η^2 = .185). This means that all groups improved their scores for self-clarification from the pretest to posttest, but the gains between the groups show no significant differences.

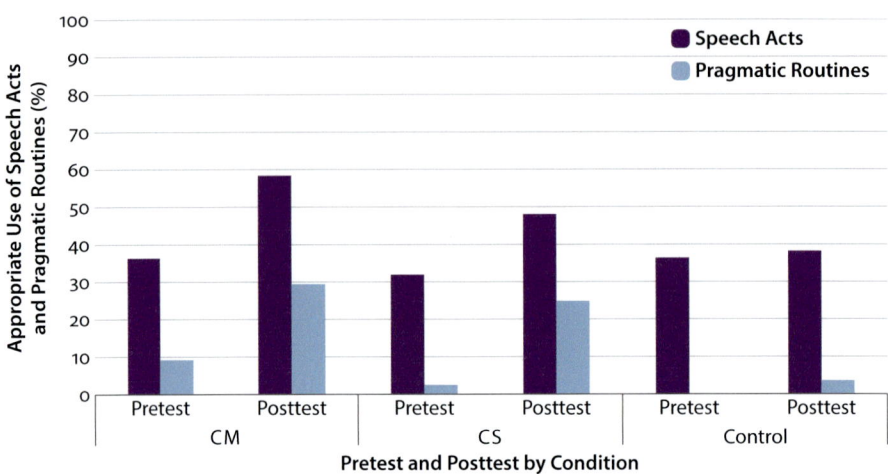

Figure 5. Self-Clarifications and pragmatic routines, by instructional condition, pretest and posttest

Independent searches

In response to the questionnaire, seven students of the seventeen in CS reported that they searched for words and phrases independently. They reported searching for single words such as *yeah*, *okay*, *gosh*, *yup* and *nope* and phrases such as *OMG! got it!*, *got you!*, *that's wassup*, *you're welcome* and *are you sure*? An additional three students who participated in the instruction, but were not included in the study due to having missed the pretest, also reported conducting searches independently (bringing the number of students who did so to 10 of the twenty students who received instruction). The teacher who helped us pilot the CS materials reported that pilot students began searching for words independently as soon as they were introduced to MICASE.

Discussion

This section discusses issues specifically related to the interpretation of the results of this study. The following sections reflect on the relationship of research to pedagogy more broadly. Here, we discuss three main issues: the comparison of CM and CS conditions, the learning, teaching, and testing of clarifications, and finally, the relation of syntax and lexicon to pragmatic development, as related to this study.

CS and CM comparisons revisited

Whereas our original conception of the study was a simple comparison of hands-on searches by the students with corpus-based materials from the teacher, the results caused us to think about the role that format plays in presentation of conversation and its potential benefits. CM excerpts presented an entire speech act in conversational format with speakers and turns clearly labeled. CS searches resulted in lists of concordance lines (input enrichment) on which the pragmatic routine was centered and bolded (input enhancement, Vyatkina, 2016), but the text that preceded and followed the routine is presented in a single line in which neither speakers nor turns are indicated. Both presentations enhance the input, but in different ways. The benefits of CM seem to be both increased speech act clarity and increased use of pragmatic routines. The benefits of CS seem to be increased use of pragmatic routines and the potential for self-initiated corpus searches, which may impact future learning. Pedagogically, in nonexperimental conditions, these approaches could be combined for maximum benefit to the learners.

Regarding the second point of comparison, because the corpus-search condition was designed after we had run our first study testing the use of corpus-based materials, only the CS students received the questionnaire asking whether they had conducted corpus searches on their own. This precludes comparison of the groups on this point. However, no other group was introduced to MICASE or shown how to conduct searches. We did in fact hope that by labeling all excerpts in the CM handouts with the MICASE transcript number and listing the website on the worksheets that the students would explore on their own, but we have no evidence of that.

Learning, teaching, and testing clarifications

Clarifications are much less frequently studied than agreements and disagreements in the experimental pragmatics literature, and thus we review issues of item construction and learner performance here.

Self-clarification

Every group showed its lowest production scores for self-clarification in both pretest and posttest. There were no models in the pragmatics literature for eliciting self-clarifications in a controlled production task, so we created a prompt and piloted it (and all the questions) in written format before recording. "People look confused" oriented the students to the need for self-clarifications, and "you say:" cued them to speak, as in Example (6), repeated here.

(7)   Your classmate has asked you to finish the project for the group.
      You say: I am not saying that I won't do it, just that other people should
      contribute.
      Screen only: People look confused. You say: _____

These items might have been inherently more difficult than the other speech acts
because respondents had to accept the premise that they had said something confusing in an earlier turn.

   The results also showed that students could accomplish a self-clarification
without using the targeted routines. Students either attempted to repeat the original sentence as in (7a) or paraphrased it without a preceding self-clarification
expression as in (7b). Other self-clarification responses show the same pattern.

(8)   Responses to Scenario (6)
      a.   I'm not saying I won't do it, but let other people of the group contribute.
      b.   I think the people the adult people have to do that because I do that before.

Given that self-clarifications can be successful without clarification routines, it may
be necessary to constrain what can be said by providing a preceding statement as
in Example (8).

(9)   Your classmate has asked you to finish the project for the group.
      You say: I am not saying that I won't do it, just that other people should
      contribute.
      Your classmate says: You don't like the project?
      You say: _____

Turns including target expressions such as "Are you saying that," and "Do you
mean" both run the risk of priming the corresponding expression. A "bare" request
for clarification such as "You don't like the project?" or "Don't you like the project?"
may suffice, but more testing needs to be done to develop additional contexts.

Other-clarification

In an attempt to make the other-clarification items credible, we used expressions that
were difficult enough for learners to realistically ask about. In Example (9), we asked
students to "check your understanding of the saying," but may have overestimated
their familiarity with the saying "You can lead a horse to water, but you cannot make
it drink." One student in the CM group responded, "What is horse water?"

(10)   Your group is talking about motivating other people. Your classmate uses a
       proverb. Check your understanding of the saying.
       Your classmate says: You can lead a horse to water, but you cannot make it drink.
       You say:_____

Learner responses to (9) in (10a-b) showed that they did not know the proverb. The response in (10d) showed that the student knew the proverb, but like the response in (10c) was an agreement, rather than a clarification. In contrast, the learner who produced (10e) was successful on all counts, satisfying the production of the speech act, using the targeted pragmatic routine, and avoiding repeating the expression.

(11) a. I think the hot water is not is the bad for our body
      b. Actually, I don't understand the question...sorry,
      c. Yes, that's true.
      d. Yeah that's true because not always you can convince people to do what you want.
      e. What do you mean by that?

A possible account of item difficulty is that the lexical items that we used in three of the five other-clarification items (*leap year*, *current events*, and *lead a horse to water*) may have been too hard for the students. They may have been so focused on understanding the meaning that they did not have the extra resources to attend to the prompt. The fact that more than half of the students produced the target expressions in both of the other-clarification items (*banned*, and an item linking *children* and *money*) in the posttest suggests the potential for improvement after the instruction. Other-clarifications may have been further influenced by the lack of a single repeated prompt format.

Syntax and lexicon as variables in pragmatic development

The relative low use of *What I mean (is/by)*, and the nonuse of *You're saying* and *What you're saying* in the student production suggests that syntactic complexity could further influence the production rates of clarifications. Learners used stand-alone routines, such as *in other words* and *I have a question* more robustly than the expressions that require complements, e.g. *what I mean is/by, you're saying*, and *what you're saying*. This is consistent with similar findings in Vercellotti and Packer (2016) in which learners produced fewer embedded clauses than was expected based on research on written production. They found that in free spoken production tasks, complement-taking predicates were produced later than other clause types, such as adverbial and relative clauses as well as non-finite clauses which were expected to be the most difficult to produce. The authors discuss the possibility that in addition to the syntactic complexity of embedded clauses, the students may consider embedding not especially useful for communication, which could contribute to their reluctance to use it.

In this study, teachers reported that students expressed difficulty in distinguishing the different types of complements that follow *do you mean* and *what do you mean.* The observation by teachers is echoed by the low use of *What I mean (is/by)*, and the nonuse of *You're saying* and *What you're saying* on the posttest. This suggests that when pragmatic routines that require syntactically complex complements are taught, carefully designed scaffolding is needed to facilitate the learning process, especially for the corpus-search condition. In such cases, the noticing of syntactic contexts, analogous to noticing use, is unlikely to be enough. Learners may need explicit discussion of complement types followed by communicative use. One model for teaching the communicative function of grammar is found in Felix-Brasdefer and Cohen (2012), which provides a guide for designing lessons for pragmatic in-struction in a Spanish FL classroom. By explicitly demonstrating the pragmatic im-portance of the grammatical structures, the perceived usefulness of the grammatical structure may increase, leading to a greater willingness to use them.

Returning to the lexicon, recall that unfamiliar words and phrases may have made the other-clarification items difficult for reasons unrelated to pragmatics. Other responses suggest that unfamiliar vocabulary may have also affected indi-vidual learners. For example, when directed to disagree with the statement "Global warming is a myth," some learners elaborated their disagreements in ways that suggested that they understood aural delivery of "global warming" but not "myth." The learner response in (11a) reflects an understanding of "myth" whereas the response in (11b) does not.

(12) a.   Yeah, but I think it is not myth because oh sea level is increase. (CS5)
      b.   That's right and the temperature is rising in the world and if has temper-ature is increasing we'll lose a lot of thing (CS17)

To address issues of lexical knowledge in a revised task, we would need to either control the familiarity of words or phrases, or have enough items to level out the effect of familiarity.

The final area in which we observed the interface of linguistic development and instruction is knowledge of contractions. The CS pilot teacher reported that learners typed in search phrases – the pragmatic routines – often eliminating con-tractions, using for example, *you are right* for *you're right.* We had not anticipated problems with noticing the components of the pragmatic routines at the level of contractions or the ability of students to faithfully type them into the searches, but this is consistent with reports by learners that they hear uncontracted forms of common expressions as often as contracted forms (e.g., *You are welcome* and *You're welcome*) whereas native speakers report hearing the contracted forms more often (Bardovi-Harlig, 2010). In this case, it prevents the learners from returning useful search results.

The connection of syntactic complexity and the apparent need for teaching complements with the clarification routines and the students' substitution of full forms for contracted forms when typing the pragmatic routines in the searches reminds us that pragmatics instruction should not be conceived of as independent units as we do for experimental teaching, but integrated with instruction in syntax and morphosyntax, and very likely, with pronunciation and lexis, for optimal effect.

Integrating research and teaching

In this section we discuss how instruction for research differs from classroom instruction and issues of materials development. We then move on to discuss issues of participant availability, experimental control, and teacher collaboration, as well as generalizability to other educational contexts, languages, and linguistic constructs.

Experimentalizing instruction

Many of the issues that we encountered are actually a direct result of the limitations imposed by adhering to a strict research design, and therefore can be resolved when the instruction is implemented in a regular classroom. For example, having greater flexibility in deciding how much time is spent on each lesson may help resolve some of the challenges of teaching self-clarifications. Teachers may combine corpus-materials and corpus-search exercises in ways they feel maximize the benefits of each type of instruction.[3] With additional time, teachers can also allow the students to go "off script" if they have questions about other types of expressions, other speech acts, and other ways to use the corpus. In the case of production activities, game play, which is both beneficial and entertaining for the students, can be extended. The need to balance the number of CM noticing activities with the number of CS noticing activities and the number of noticing events for each speech act was another constraint on the research that could be eliminated in classroom instruction. This would allow teachers to mix and match CM and CS exercises in ways that they find most effective, at points where they are most needed.

These potential adaptations of the lessons in a real classroom (i.e. a non-experimental classroom) are not simply hypothetical; one of the authors had the opportunity to implement them in an authentic class when she taught a section of the course for which the materials were designed after the experiment had concluded. She combined both corpus materials and corpus searches without dramatically increasing class time spent on the lessons by assigning the CS exercises for homework. As an added component of the homework, students were required to

---

3. For an example of how corpus-searches and corpus-based materials can be combined, and a a study of the relative efficacy of doing so, see Bardovi-Harlig, Mossman, Rothgerber, Su, & Swanson (in press).

carry out searches for additional expressions they were curious about. Students did so quite enthusiastically, particularly at the beginning, searching for expressions such as *same here, I'd say that, me too, okey-doke,* and *I don't go along with you on that.* Students also looked up individual words such as *personally, frankly, definitely,* and *surely.* Assigning independent searches as homework not only capitalized on learners' interest in searching the corpus on their own, but also ensured it was not left up to individual motivation. Other ways to do this might be to establish a class wiki or bulletin board where students can post their discoveries, among other things. In the experiment, however, we did not give teachers suggestions for possible assignments, nor did we ask the teachers to encourage independent searches outside the class to assure the comparability between the two instructional conditions being examined.

Materials and activities development

There were a number of issues with designing the corpus searches. The searches had to be directed for three reasons: (a) empirical evidence from pragmatics shows that learners do not notice pragmatics on their own; (b) noticing had to be comparable to that provided by the corpus-based teacher-designed materials; and, (c) the amount of time spent in the two conditions had to be comparable. The two conditions were comparable in the study, but they are not necessarily equal in terms of the development of materials and activities or implementation. CM materials have a clear target of instruction that appears in conversation excerpts supplied by the instructor, along with a variety of companion activities. In contrast, CS materials require that the developer try to anticipate what a student will think and do, and then based on those assumptions, create a pathway to the target through student searches. However, there is no guarantee that the student will do what is expected. Therefore, in addition to creating the pathway, the developer has to integrate opportunities for the teacher to redirect the students toward the target if they go in another direction.

Finally, carrying out the searches in class can take longer than simply presenting the teacher-prepared results from the searches, and as a result, they could potentially take up a greater portion of the allotted class time. We had to tightly control this for the study. We considered balancing time alone, but realized that doing so might sacrifice the number of routines that could be covered. Instead we settled on teaching students how to search the corpus prior to the pretest by using unrelated course materials. We balanced the number of noticing events and we balanced the total instructional time for each lesson and the complete unit. The importance of how much time searches can take should not be ignored because time is always limited and ideally class time should be used in a way that leads to the most effective outcome for the students.

An additional concern for activity development is variety. The variety of CS activities is more limited than that of CM. With teacher-input students are given the search results, and the presentation of those results can vary greatly. A creative materials developer can provide some variety in student-search exercises as well, and we did so in our study, but there are limitations. Regardless of what type of additional activity the students engage in, the exercises always begin with a search of the corpus – this is unchanging. Thus, there is the potential for CS lessons to become tedious, and this could possibly decrease students' willingness to do them or reduce attention, thereby reducing the effectiveness of the exercises.

Participant availability

Participant availability is always an issue. We had no trouble getting access to classes since our work addresses program curricular goals, but we have no control over program enrollment. When we ran the first part of the study (the CM condition), enrollment in intensive English programs across the U.S. was robust. That meant that we could run multiple sections in the same session. We ran two classes as control group in the following session. In contrast, by the time we ran the CS condition, enrollments around the country had dropped significantly, and we had to run the same condition in two consecutive sessions. With the pilot, it took us three sessions to complete the CS condition.[4] The intensive English program limits its class size to 15 students, enrolling about 8–15 students per class. While small classes are advantageous for language teaching and learning, they present a challenge for research and necessitate using multiple sections of the same course either in the same term (enrollment permitting) or in subsequent terms.

For a treatment study, attendance is a second issue. It is not enough for students to be assigned to a treatment condition; they must actually attend the class to receive the instruction. We set the bar at three of four instructional periods and completion of both the pretest and the posttest, which is a total of five of six days. Fortunately, the students in the two corpus-search classes had very good attendance; no students missed class and only two students arrived 15 minutes late for a single class session.

In the corpus-materials condition we had many more students who had much poorer attendance. Only 31 students completed both the pretest and posttest, and only 26 of those attended at least three classes. The CM instruction ran during the second spring session bordered by spring break and summer vacation, and it could be that that session is not ideal for data collection over multiple days.

---

4. Because we ran only a single condition for any one term, all students enrolled in Level 5 in the same term received the same instruction as all other students in Level 5.

Experimental control

There are three important components of experimental control in our study: equivalence of treatment conditions, fidelity in instruction, and the use of computer-delivered simulated group work for assessment. The two conditions were identical except for the teacher-prepared corpus excerpts and the supported corpus searches. We had already completed and published the study on the corpus-based materials condition when we conceived of testing the corpus-search condition to enhance noticing. We therefore designed the corpus-search conditions to match the corpus-materials, even when some revision would have been preferable. This is a research induced problem, which we would not have encountered in teaching. This could be resolved by developing materials for two or more conditions in tandem.

To assure fidelity of instruction, we provided the lesson plans, the Power Points, game boards with pieces and play money, and a checklist for teachers to fill out and to use to report any noteworthy events. The lesson plans suggested teacher scripts in order to provide teachers with the necessary metapragmatic information, and to assure that both conditions got the same information. All teachers met with us five times: once for an overview of the instruction and once for each of four lessons. We do not know how closely the teachers followed the scripts, although their completed checklists show that they covered all the elements of the lessons.

Finally, the computer-delivered group work simulation gives everyone a turn unlike real group work where if one person speaks, it may eliminate the need for a turn by another speaker (cf. LoCastro's 1997 work on disagreement). The board games used for oral practice also ensured turns for all learners and introduced unpredictability through advancing along the board and drawing cards with instructions. Authentic group work can be used to supplement the practice activities that allot equal turns to all students.

A final note on experimental control comes from the case of a student in CS who was excluded from the study for replaying items on the test, which we could hear on his digital recording. Taguchi (2007) has identified listening comprehension as a potential constraint on pragmatic performance, and we saw evidence of that in the case of this student. Replaying and slowing the task may have simplified the listening component for him. This case demonstrates the importance of working with oral input, oral production, and oral assessment tasks in the teaching of pragmatics for conversations. The corpus search mode is visual (as is the main input for CM), and that is why we provided aural input and multiple production activities in advance of asking the students to complete the conversation simulation posttest.

Teacher collaboration

Since we were invited by teachers to help them meet the instructional goals of an English for Academic Purposes (EAP) program, our content was immediately relevant to teachers who were on the whole happy to teach the units. We enlisted teachers who were assigned to the communication classes in our targeted instructional level to teach the units. This assures that the lessons are perceived by the students as part of the ongoing instruction in the class, and eliminates the chance of researcher bias when the researcher teaches the experimental units. This means that we had to familiarize the teachers with the content (pragmatics and pragmatic routines) and with our approach (focused noticing with metapragmatic summaries by the teachers).

Most teachers were very enthusiastic about the units, but they did differ according to when they wanted the materials delivered. One teacher wanted them the same day so the lesson would be fresh, and all materials at hand. Another teacher requested advanced delivery so that she could review the materials. She objected to the games (which were designed to simulate the unpredictability of turn-taking in a multi-party conversation such as group work) and wanted to get to the "real" work of the semester. Nonetheless, she delivered the lessons professionally and her students did as well as others in the same condition. She also gave very detailed accounts of the use of the materials that helped with spacing the lessons and made the procedures smoother. Collaboration with teachers is essential to instructional effects studies regardless of teachers' enthusiasm for or faith in the project. Our experience shows that despite their varying approaches, all the teachers delivered the lessons professionally and gave us very helpful comments.

One teacher additionally worked with us during the pilot of the corpus search materials. He provided valuable information about the searches, the level of involvement, and the length of the lessons. In addition, he made important observations that enriched our understanding of the effect of instruction. He let us know that students were searching the corpus independently; he also noticed that some students had very low frequency numbers compared to others, and a little detective work revealed that, as noted earlier, some students were searching for full forms rather than for contracted forms. We subsequently attempted to circumvent this in modified search directions.

Teachers who delivered the lessons undoubtedly contributed to the success of the instruction. Because teachers are a potential "confound" in instructional effects studies, researchers' support for teachers is essential, which includes meeting with them before each lesson to go through the teaching materials and to answer questions, and afterwards to collect feedback in order to revise subsequent lessons.

Generalizability to other contexts

This study was an outgrowth of teaching conventional expressions for social interactions using the *Friends* corpus of online fan transcriptions (Bardovi-Harlig & Vellenga, 2012). We also explored the use of three different corpora for teaching pragmatic routines for different purposes, including speech among friends (Bardovi-Harlig & Mossman, 2016). We thus feel reasonably confident in suggesting that corpus-based teaching for pragmatic routines and conventional expressions can be extended to other contexts, providing the corpus is relevant to the target speech register. This approach to instruction could be used to teach a variety of speech acts that utilize pragmatic routines. (See, for example, Furniss, 2016, for use of the Russian National Corpus in teaching pragmatic routines.) With time, a teacher could use a corpus to develop conversational excerpts in a number of ways, but for searches by classes, we suggest working with lexical units (words, phrases, and expressions) because they are searched so easily. At present, corpora are generally not tagged for speech acts, and thus working with the lexicon is most promising at this time.

Expanding the use of corpus-based instruction to other settings should not be a problem as long as the goals are consistent with the corpus selected. However, expanding to languages other than English can be limited by the availability of corpora or the availability of free online corpora. Even some of the free online English corpora limit the number of searches without registration.

Concluding reflections

What started out as an investigation into the second language acquisition of conventional expressions as a pragmatic resource (Bardovi-Harlig, 2009) led to explorations into the teaching of formulaic sequences for pragmatics. At the same time, a request for assistance in teaching pragmatics for academic group work from teachers in our intensive English program directed our attention to pragmatic routines used in agreements, disagreements, and clarifications. Our working relationship with the teachers in our intensive English program became one of our most valuable assets in our study.

Our pedagogical approach to the use of authentic language in pragmatics instruction (see also Ishihara & Cohen, 2010; Cohen & Ishihara, 2013) further led us to the use of free online corpora in the selection and development of input. Our work confirmed that corpus-based instruction is especially helpful for the teaching of pragmatics, which by its nature requires authentic language use. In our work, we varied the primary user of the corpus – from teachers to students – and concluded that nonexperimental instruction can combine the two approaches to capitalize on their strengths.

Whereas other areas of instruction may fit into established curricula more easily, for instruction in pragmatics in particular, researchers have to look for ways to work pragmatics into existing curricular categories (such as "communication" or "conversation") because most language programs teach little or no pragmatics. The present study has illustrated the positive effects of corpus-based instruction on learning pragmatics in class. Future research may lead to the development of approaches with out-of-class corpus-based activities and support, complemented by in-class communicative activities. Integrating relevant pedagogical advances to language instruction into established curricula remains the final collaborative step in research on instructional effects.

Acknowledgments

We thank the instructors, John Rothgerber and Kyle Swanson, who administered the lessons, Michael Frisby of the Indiana Statistical Consulting Center, Indiana University, and the Center for Language Technology (CeLT), Indiana University, and their staff for providing technical expertise in recording and formatting the computer tasks and assistance during the elicitation sessions. Audio-editing was done by Natasha Branch.

References

Bardovi-Harlig, K. (2006). On the role of formulas in the acquisition of L2 pragmatics. In K. Bardovi-Harlig, C. Félix-Brasdefer, A. S. Omar (Eds.), *Pragmatics and language learning*, (Vol. 11, pp. 1–28). Honolulu, HI: University of Hawai'i, National Foreign Language Resource Center.

Bardovi-Harlig, K. (2009). Conventional expressions as a pragmalinguistic resource: Recognition and production of conventional expressions in L2 pragmatics. *Language Learning*, 59, 755–795. https://doi.org/10.1111/j.1467-9922.2009.00525.x

Bardovi-Harlig, K. (2010). Recognition of conventional expressions in L2 pragmatics. In G. Kasper, H. t. Nguyen, D. R. Yoshimi, & J. K. Yoshioka (Eds.), *Pragmatics and language learning* (Vol. 12, pp. 141–162). Honolulu, HI: University of Hawai'i, National Foreign Language Resource Center.

Bardovi-Harlig, K. (2013). Developing L2 pragmatics. *Language Learning*, 63(Suppl.1), 68–86. https://doi.org/10.1111/j.1467-9922.2012.00738.x

Bardovi-Harlig, K. (2018). Pragmatic awareness in second language acquisition. In P. Garret & J. Maria Cots (Eds.), *Routledge handbook of language awareness.* (pp. 323–338). UK: Taylor & Francis.

Bardovi-Harlig, K., & Bastos, M.-T. (2011). Proficiency, length of stay, and intensity of interaction and the acquisition of conventional expressions in L2 pragmatics. *Intercultural Pragmatics* 8, 347–384. https://doi.org/10.1515/iprg.2011.017

Bardovi-Harlig, K., Bastos, M.-T., Burghardt, B., Chappetto, E., Nickels, E., & Rose, M. (2010). The use of conventional expressions and utterance length in L2 pragmatics. In G. Kasper, H. t. Nguyen, D. R. Yoshimi, & J. K. Yoshioka (Eds.), *Pragmatics and language learning* (Vol. 12, pp. 163–186). Honolulu, HI: University of Hawai'i, National Foreign Language Resource Center.

Bardovi-Harlig, K., Hartford, B. A. S., Mahan-Taylor, R., Morgan, M. J., & Reynolds, D. W. (1991). Developing pragmatic awareness: Closing the conversation. *ELT Journal*, 45, 4–15. https://doi.org/10.1093/elt/45.1.4

Bardovi-Harlig, K., & Mossman, S. (2016). Corpus-based materials development for teaching and learning pragmatic routines. In B. Tomlinson (Ed.) *SLA research and materials development for language learning* (pp. 250–267). New York, NY: Taylor and Francis.

Bardovi-Harlig, K., Mossman, S., Rothgerber, J., & Su, Y., & Swanson, K. (in press). Revisiting clarifications: Self- and other-clarifications in corpus-based pragmatics instruction. In M. Sato & S. Loewen (Eds.), *Evidence-based second language pedagogy: A collection of instructed second language acquisition studies*. New York: Routledge.

Bardovi-Harlig, K., Mossman, S., & Su, Y. (2017). The effect of corpus-based instruction on pragmatic routines. *Language Learning & Technology*, 21, 76–103.

Bardovi-Harlig, K., Mossman, S., & Vellenga, H. E. (2015a). Developing corpus-based materials to teach pragmatic routines. *TESOL Journal*, 6, 499–526. https://doi.org/10.1002/tesj.177

Bardovi-Harlig, K., Mossman, S., & Vellenga, H. E. (2015b). The effect of instruction on pragmatic routines in academic discussion. *Language Teaching Research*, 19, 324–350. https://doi.org/10.1177/1362168814541739

Bardovi-Harlig, K., & Salsbury, T. (2004). The organization of turns in the disagreements of L2 learners: A longitudinal perspective. In D. Boxer & A. D. Cohen (Eds.), *Studying speaking to inform second language learning* (pp. 199–227). Clevedon: Multilingual Matters.

Bardovi-Harlig, K., & Vellenga, H. E. (2012). The effect of instruction on conventional expressions in L2 pragmatics. *System*, 40, 77–89. https://doi.org/10.1016/j.system.2012.01.004

Biber, D., Conrad, S., & Cortes, V. (2004). If you look at ...: Lexical bundles in university teaching and textbooks. *Applied Linguistics*, 25, 371–405. https://doi.org/10.1093/applin/25.3.371

Biber, D., Johansson, S., Leech, G., Conrad, S., & Finegan, E. (1999). *Longman grammar of spoken and written English*. London: Longman.

Boulton, A. (2010). Data-driven learning: Taking the computer out of the equation. *Language Learning*, 60, 534–572. https://doi.org/10.1111/j.1467-9922.2010.00566.x

Boxer, D., & Pickering, L. (1995). Problems in the presentation of speech acts in ELT materials: The case of complaints. *ELT Journal*, 49, 44–58. https://doi.org/10.1093/elt/49.1.44

Cheng, W., & Cheng, P. (2010). Correcting others and self-correcting in business and professional discourse and textbooks. In A. Trosborg (Ed.), *Pragmatics across languages and cultures* (Vol. 7 of *Handbooks of pragmatics*, pp. 443–466). Berlin: Mouton de Gruyter.

Clennell, C. (1999). Promoting pragmatic awareness and spoken discourse skills with EAP classes. *ELT Journal*, 53, 83–91. https://doi.org/10.1093/elt/53.2.83

Cohen, A. D., & Ishihara, N. (2013). Pragmatics. In B. Tomlinson (Ed.), *Applied linguistics and materials development* (pp. 113–126). London: Bloomsbury Academic.

Erman, B., & Warren, B. (2000). The idiom principle and the open choice principle. *Text*, 20, 29–62. https://doi.org/10.1515/text.1.2000.20.1.29

Félix-Brasdefer, J. C., & Cohen, A. D. (2012). Teaching pragmatics in the foreign language classroom: Grammar as a communicative resource. *Hispania, 95*, 650–669. https://doi.org/10.1353/hpn.2012.0124

Furniss, E. A. (2016). Teaching the pragmatics of Russian conversation using a corpus-referred website. *Language Learning & Technology, 20*(2), 38–60.

Hulstijn, J., & Laufer, B. (2001). Some empirical evidence for the involvement load hypothesis in vocabulary acquisition. *Language Learning, 51*, 539–558. https://doi.org/10.1111/0023-8333.00164

Ishihara, N., & Cohen, A. D. (2010). *Teaching and learning pragmatics: Where language and culture meet.* London: Longman.

Levinson, S. C. (1983). *Pragmatics.* Cambridge: Cambridge University Press.

LoCastro, V. (1997). Pedagogical intervention and pragmatic competence development. *Applied Language Learning, 8*, 75–109.

Pomerantz, A. (1984). Agreeing and disagreeing with assessments: Some features of preferred/dispreferred turn shapes. In J. M. Atkinson & J. Heritage (Eds.), *Structures of social action: Studies in conversation analysis* (pp. 57–101). Cambridge: Cambridge University Press.

Ren, W., & Han, Z. (2016). The representation of pragmatic knowledge in recent ELT textbooks. *ELT J, 70*, 424–434. https://doi.org/10.1093/elt/ccw010

Simpson, R. C., Briggs, S. L., Ovens, J., & Swales, J. M. (2002). *The Michigan Corpus of Academic Spoken English.* Ann Arbor, MI: The Regents of the University of Michigan. <https://quod.lib.umich.edu/m/micase/>

Taguchi, N. (2007). Development of speed and accuracy in pragmatic comprehension in English as a foreign language. *TESOL Quarterly, 41*, 313–338. https://doi.org/10.1002/j.1545-7249.2007.tb00061.x

Taguchi, N., Kaufer, D., Gómez-Laich, M. P., & Zhao, H. (2016). A corpus linguistics analysis of on-line peer commentary. In K. Bardovi-Harlig, & J. C. Félix-Brasdefer (Eds.), *Pragmatics and Language Learning* (Vol. 14, pp. 357–370). Honolulu, HI: University of Hawai'i, National Foreign Language Resource Center.

Tomlinson, B. (1994). Pragmatic awareness activities. *Language Awareness, 3*, 119–129. https://doi.org/10.1080/09658416.1994.9959850

Vellenga, H. E. (2004). Learning pragmatics from ESL and EFL Textbooks: How likely? *TESL-EJ, 8* (2).

Vercellotti, M. L., & Packer, J. (2016). Shifting structural complexity: The production of clause types in speeches given by English for academic purposes students. *Journal of English for Academic Purposes, 22*, 179–190. https://doi.org/10.1016/j.jeap.2016.04.004

Vyatkina, N. (2016). Data-driven learning for beginners: The case of German verb-preposition collocations. *ReCALL, 28*, 207–226. https://doi.org/10.1017/S0958344015000269

Williams, M. (1988). Language taught for meetings and language used for meetings: Is there anything in common? *Applied Linguistics, 9*, 45–58. https://doi.org/10.1093/applin/9.1.45

The roles of explicit instruction and guided practice in the proceduralization of a complex grammatical structure

Natsuko Shintani
Kobe Gakuin University

This chapter reports a classroom-based experimental study focusing on the effects of providing metalinguistic explanation (ME) before asking learners to perform a practice activity involving story reconstruction on their acquisition of a grammatical structure. The task required learners to comprehend the oral narrative with the help of a written script and illustrations describing the story and then to reconstruct the story while referring to the illustrations and a list of keywords. Three instructional conditions were compared: the ME+Task where the learners received ME and then completed a story reconstruction task, the Task Only, where learners just completed the task, and the ME Only where they just received the ME. This chapter also considers the relevance of the study to classroom practice. It will provide suggestions for teaching limited-proficiency learners a complex grammatical structure. The chapter concludes with a consideration of the ecological validity and pedagogical implications of this study.

Keywords: explicit instruction, skill-learning theory, presentation-practice-production (PPP), grammar acquisition, text reconstruction

Introduction

Skill-learning theory claims that proceduralisation occurs when learners draw on declarative knowledge of a grammatical structure as they practise it receptively or productively. Automatization occurs later when learners have extensive opportunities to practise the structure under real operating conditions (DeKeyser, 2015). This theory supports a commonly used second language (L2) teaching approach called 'presentation, practice, and production (PPP)', where metalinguistic information is provided (presentation), learners produce the target language feature in controlled exercises (practice), and then they have opportunity to produce the

https://doi.org/10.1075/lllt.52.05shi

target form in meaningful activities (production). However, little research has investigated the effects of providing practice opportunities after establishing explicit language knowledge. The main purpose of this chapter is to investigate whether metalinguistic explanation by itself develops explicit knowledge and whether opportunity for practice the target structure immediately following metalinguistic explanation develops procedural knowledge.

Empirical study

Skill-acquisition theory claims that L2 learning, particularly for adult learners, is effective if the learners are first equipped with explicit knowledge of the language that they use in subsequent practice activities to help proceduralise their knowledge. The proceduralised knowledge then becomes automatized when there are extensive opportunities for using the structure in communicative tasks (DeKeyser, 2015). This theory supports presentation-practice-production (PPP), where *a priori* explicit instruction involving metalinguistic explanation is followed by controlled exercises and then by communicative activities that require the learners to use the target feature. The explicit instruction aims at equipping learners with explicit grammar knowledge to utilise it. In traditional forms of language pedagogy, explicit instruction is typically followed by decontextualised controlled exercises. DeKeyser (2015) explains that producing a linguistic form, which learners have declarative knowledge of, initially takes place in a conscious and controlled manner, as it requires referring to declarative language knowledge during production. He argues that only cumulative experiences of spontaneous production will help learners to acquire the fully automatised knowledge necessary to use the feature easily in communication. The claim is also supported by transfer-appropriate processing (TAP) theory, which argues that the learning environment that best promotes rapid, accurate retrieval later on of what was learned is that in which the psychological demands placed on the learner resemble those that will be encountered later in natural settings (Lightbown, 2007).

In language pedagogy, a 'controlled' teaching activity is one that is highly structured with a closed, 'correct' answer while a 'free' activity is one that involves real-world language use and leads to negotiated and/or unpredicted responses (Brown, 2007). However, it is not easy to distinguish 'controlled' and 'free' production activities. The two categories constitute a continuum, on which another type of activity – often referred to as 'guided' – can be placed. Guided activities can be structured but open-ended, and although learners' production is still controlled, they allow for unpredictable responses (Brown, 2007). Guided activities have been widely used by teachers when learners need support to produce specific linguistic targets in a context that emphasizes meaning. The current study employed one such activity, a story reconstruction (SR) task. The SR task required learners to re-produce a story-length text with some support (i.e., using keywords and pictorial cues). Although this task controls learners' production, it allows for unpredicted responses and aims to direct learners' attention to the meaning of the story, which might facilitate proceduralisation of the features of L2 included in the story.

Focusing on the above theoretical claims, the current study investigated whether isolated explicit instruction by itself develops explicit knowledge (Krashen, 1982; Ellis, 1994), and that opportunity for guided production after establishing explicit knowledge assists the development of proceduralised knowledge (DeKeyser, 2015). Although there are a number of studies that have investigated the effects of a priori explicit instruction followed by controlled exercises (e.g., Doughty, 1991; Li, Ellis, & Zhu, 2016; Robinson, 1997; Sanz & Morgan-Short, 2004; VanPatten, 2009; VanPatten & Oikkenon, 1996), few studies have investigated the combination of a priori ME and a guided production activity.

In one such study, Li, Ellis, and Zhu (2016) investigated the effects of a priori explicit instruction combined with oral tasks for Chinese middle school learners of English as a foreign language (EFL). The learners were divided into four experimental groups and one control group. The experimental groups attended a two-hour treatment session in which they performed two dictogloss tasks in groups, followed by an oral reporting session. Each group received a different type of instruction: (1) simply performing the two oral tasks, (2) receiving explicit instruction before performing the tasks, (3) receiving within-task feedback but no explicit instruction, and (4) receiving both explicit instruction and within-task feedback. Relevant to my study is the comparison between the conditions (1) and (2) as this addresses the effect of explicit instruction prior to performing a task. Acquisition was measured by a grammaticality judgment test (GJT) and an elicited imitation test (EIT) as a pretest, immediate posttest and delayed posttest. The group that received explicit instruction showed greater gains than the group that just performed the task on the GJT. On the EIT, no effect was observable for either the explicit instruction plus task group or the task only group. Li et al. interpreted the results as showing that explicit instruction was helpful in enhancing the learners' explicit knowledge but did not their implicit knowledge. However they noted that the limited effects may have been because the low-proficiency learners were not developmentally ready to acquire the target feature.

Li et al.'s study warrants extension. It did not include a condition in which learners just received explicit instruction (i.e. without completing the oral task). Including an ME only condition would help confirm the role of ME by itself. Also, pedagogical validity would be enhanced by including multiple instructional sessions rather than just the one session as in Li et al. Experiencing multiple sessions increases the opportunity for using the explicit knowledge obtained from the ME. Repetition of tasks, particularly when they are conducted over time, might enhance learning opportunities and better facilitate automatisation. Furthermore, Li et al. measured learners' implicit knowledge using an EIT but it is also important to measure learning using a meaningful production test.

Investigating the role of *a priori* ME before the opportunity for meaningful production is pedagogically important. Providing metalinguistic explanation before requiring the learners to practise the target grammatical feature has been a widely used teaching practice in the second language (L2) classroom. The typical three-stage approach, presentation – practice – production (PPP), corresponds with the development of the three elements involved in language learning, i.e. declarative, procedural, and automatized language knowledge. However, studies have reported that in many foreign language classrooms, teachers tend to devote most of the class time to the first two stages of PPP (i.e. presentation and controlled practice) and provide little or no opportunity for communicative practice due to the limited class time and the need to implement the entire structural syllabus (Adams & Newton, 2009). However, as pointed out earlier, highly controlled practice may have little effect on learners' ability to use the language in communication (Lightbown, 2000). It is thus important to investigate the effect of the opportunity for extensive production in a freer activity after providing explicit instruction. Guided production practices might cater to learners with limited ability for spontaneous oral production. The current study undertook to investigate this.

With these points in mind, the study reported in this chapter addressed the following research questions:

1. Does ME alone promote learners' (a) explicit knowledge of the target grammatical structure and (b) accurate production of the target grammatical structure in a guided oral production task?
2. Does performing story reconstruction tasks promote learners' (a) explicit knowledge of the target grammatical structure and (b) accurate production of the target grammatical structure in a guided oral production task?
3. Does ME followed by performing story reconstruction tasks promote learners' (a) explicit knowledge of the target grammatical structure and (b) accurate production of the target grammatical structure in a guided oral production task?
4. Is there any difference in the effect that these different treatments have on learners' (a) explicit knowledge of the target grammatical structure and (b) accurate production of the target grammatical structure in a guided oral production task?

These questions were investigated by comparing a group that received both ME and oral tasks with two other groups that received either treatment: one that only received ME and one that only completed the oral tasks. The effects were measured in terms of the learners' ability to correct errors in the target structure and their accuracy in an oral production task. The former is considered to measure analytical, declarative type of knowledge, which is in favour of the ME instruction. The latter aimed to measure the accuracy in an oral production, which should be in favour of the oral task treatment. Learners in the study received four treatment sessions over four weeks in university-level English classes.

Method

Participants

The participants in the study were 121 university economics majors in five English oral communication classes in Japan. The students were low to intermediate English learners (TOEIC scores ranging from 350 to 700, equivalent to TOEFL paper-based scores of 400 to 550). Any student who had lived in an English-speaking country for more than six months was removed from the analysis on the assumption that he or she might have achieved automatized linguistic knowledge in a different learning context from that found in Japan. The rest of the participants ($n = 111$) were randomly divided into four groups as follows: (a) metalinguistic explanation (ME) + a story reconstruction task (Task), (b) Task only, (c) ME only, and (d) a control group. The experimental groups participated in seven sessions over nine weeks. A total of 92 participants attended all seven sessions (23 in the ME+Task group, 23 in the ME Only group, 24 in the Task Only group, and 22 in the control group). Data from these participants were included in this study.

Design

The research project lasted nine weeks (see Figure 1). After the pretest (Week 1), the three experimental groups received four instructional sessions (ME+Task, Task Only, or ME Only) over weeks 2 – 5. All four groups completed an error correction test and a story retelling task similar to the treatment tasks. The EC test was completed as a pretest (Week 1) and delayed posttest (Week 9) while the story-retelling task was completed as a pretest (Week1), an immediate posttest (Week 6) and a delayed posttest (Week 9).

Groups	ME+Task	ME only	Task only	Control
Week 1		Error correction test		
(Pretest)		SR tests 1, 2 and 3 (counterbalanced)		
Weeks 2–5		ME (10 min)		––
(4 treatment sessions)	SR task	––	SR task	––
	(20 min)		(20 min)	
Week 6		SR tests 1, 2 and 3 (counterbalanced)		
(Immediate posttest)				
Week 9		SR tests 1, 2 and 3 (counterbalanced)		
(Delayed posttest)		Error correction test		

Note: *ME* = metalinguistic explanation, *SR task/test* = Story reconstruction task/ test

Figure 1. Research design

Target structure

The target structure was the English past counterfactual conditional (e.g. *If it had been fine yesterday, we would have had a barbecue.*). Studies have shown that English conditional is difficult to acquire for L2 learners because of its syntactically and semantically complex structure (Celce-Murcia & Larsen-Freeman, 1999). Japanese learners of English tend to have particular difficulty in encoding two functions involved in this structure: hypotheticality and past time reference (Izumi, Bigelow, Fujiwara, & Fearnow, 1999). University students in Japan, regardless of their major, do not usually have solid control over this structure despite possessing some explicit knowledge of the construction (Izumi et al., 1999; Shintani, Ellis, & Suzuki, 2014).

Treatment materials

Metalinguistic explanation (ME) sheets
Four ME sheets were created (see Appendix A for an example). Each of them consisted of a written explanation of the past counterfactual conditional structure and a short confirmation exercise that required the students to apply and consolidate their metalinguistic knowledge by referring to the explanation. The explanation and the instructions were provided in Japanese (the L1) to assist the learners' understanding.

Story reconstruction tasks
Seven stories, ranging from 358 to 399 words in length, were created for the treatment and testing materials. Each story included four sentences using the past counterfactual conditional structure. Five descriptive pictures were created for each of

the seven stories. A professional narrator recorded the stories. Four of the seven stories were used in the treatment sessions, and the other three were used for the pre-, post-, and delayed posttests.

A story reconstruction (SR) video file was created for each story (see Appendix B). The video clip contained three sections. In the first section, the learners saw Japanese instructions for the task procedures. The second section provided an audio narration of the story (the first listening) whilst the screen showed the story's script. The third section played the audio text again (the second listening) whilst the screen showed the five pictures representing the story.

In addition to the video clip, a story reconstruction sheet was created as a PDF file (Appendix C). It consisted of one page of instructions and five pages with one page for each of the five pictures shown during the listening stage and keywords next to each picture. Verbs were shown in their base form (e.g., *play* for the form *played* in the actual sentence). For the past counterfactual conditional sentences, the sheet provided keywords based on the following criteria: (a) 'if', (b) the base form of the verb used in the *if*-clause and the main clause, and (c) key nouns used in the sentence. For example, keywords for the sentence 'If he had married her, he would have had delicious meals every day' included 'if', 'marry', 'have' and 'delicious meals'. The participants were expected to produce the original sentence using the key words.

Treatment procedures

The treatment sessions took place in a classroom at the university where all participants were allocated an individual computer screen and a headset. The learners first downloaded a folder that included the ME sheet (in Microsoft Word format), the SR video file (in WAV format), and the SR sheet (in PDF format) onto their desktops from the central folder.

The ME+Task and ME only groups first read through the ME sheet on the individual computer screen for 10 minutes. After 10 minutes, the researcher asked them to save the ME sheet on their individual computers and to open the SR task WAV file to start the task. The Task only group immediately started the SR task without accessing the ME sheet. Immediately after the WAV video was finished, the researcher asked the learners to open the SR sheet, which instructed them to re-tell and audio-record the story using the individual headsets and audio-recording software, Sound Recorder. Ten minutes were given for the recording. There was no preparation time given for reconstruction of the story. The researcher then asked the learners to submit their audio files to an online folder shared with the researcher. The ME+Task and ME only groups were also asked to submit their completed ME sheet.

Testing materials

Two tests, an error correction (EC) test and three story reconstruction (SR) tests, were used to measure the treatment effects.

Error correction (EC) test
The EC test was designed to measure the learners' explicit knowledge of the past counterfactual conditional. The test consisted of 16 decontextualized sentences, each containing a single error. Four sentences included errors in the use of the past counterfactual conditional, the use of the auxiliary 'have' and the past participle in the *if*-clauses, and the use of the auxiliary 'have' and the past participle in the main clauses. The other 12 included other grammatical errors (e.g., the definite article, the verb tense and 3rd person '-s') as distracters. The test asked the learners to first identify the errors in the sentences and then write the correct forms. One point was awarded if the participant provided the correct form for each item. No point was awarded for identifying the error but failing to provide the correct form. The test was conducted as a pretest and as a delayed posttest with the item order randomised on each occasion.

Story reconstruction (SR) tests
Three of the seven stories written for this study were used as the story reconstruction tests. The tests were counterbalanced by dividing each group into three sub-groups, each of which completed the three tests with a different order as pretest, posttest, and delayed posttest.

Coding and scoring

The participants' audio-recorded story reconstruction speech were transcribed and first analysed in terms of the number of past counterfactual conditional sentences attempted by each learner. When a student produced a sentence corresponding to one of the past counterfactual conditional sentences, it was coded as one target sentence. When the produced sentence included only the *if*-clause or the main clause of the original sentence, it was counted as 0.5 of a target sentence. When a learner produced a full sentence including an *if*-clause corresponding to one of the past counterfactual conditional sentences, it was coded as one target sentence. Next, the scoring system used by Shintani et al. (2014) (summarised in Table 1) was used to code for accuracy in the three SR tests.

Table 1. Criteria for scoring the past-counterfactual conditional

Clause	Criteria	Features	Components	Point
if-clause	1	the perfect aspect	*have* (aux) + verb	1.0
(maximum 2	2	the past tense	*had*	0.5
points)	3	the past participle (PP) form	correct form of PP	0.5
main clause	4	the modal in the past tense	past modal	1.0
(maximum 3	5	the perfect aspect	*have* (aux) + verb	1.0
points)	6	the auxiliary form	correct form of *have* (aux)	0.5
	7	the PP form	correct form of PP	0.5
			Total possible	5

The total score for each student was calculated by averaging the accuracy scores of produced sentences as follows:

$$\frac{\text{Total points scored}}{\text{Number of attempted conditional sentences}}$$

Statistical analyses

Statistical analyses were conducted using SPSS version 23. Cronbach's alpha was used to estimate the reliability of the EC test and the three SR tests. Alpha was .82 for the four target items. Those for the 7 categorical items used to score the three SR tests (pretest) were .89, .88, and .85, respectively. A graduate research assistant coded the data and the researcher coded 15% of the data, of which inter-rater reliability was assessed. Cohen's kappa was calculated as ranging from $k = .91$ to $k = .94$, showing that, overall, the raters achieved a high level of agreement. The comparative analyses employed repeated-measures ANOVAs followed by planned multiple comparisons using Bonferroni adjustments. Partial eta-squared ($\eta p2$) and Cohen's d were used to estimate effect sizes. Effect sizes were interpreted as small ($d = .40$), medium (.70), and large (1.00), following Plonsky and Oswald's (2014) recommendations.

Results

Comparative results for the error correction (EC) tests

Table 2 shows the descriptive statistics for the EC tests (pretest and delayed posttest). The maximum possible score was 4.

Table 2. Descriptive statistics for the error correction (EC) test

Groups	N	Pretest		Delayed posttest	
		Mean	SD	Mean	SD
ME+Task	23	1.00	.74	2.52	1.24
Task only	23	1.04	.77	1.78	1.17
ME only	24	.83	.87	2.12	1.33
Control	22	1.09	.75	1.32	.89

A repeated measures ANOVA showed that there were significant main effects for time (F (1, 88) = 107.95, $p < .01$, $\eta^2 = .55$) and for time × group (F (3, 88) = 11.91, $p < .01$, $\eta^2 = .29$) but not for group (F (3, 88) = 1.73, $p = .17$, $\eta^2 = .06$). Bonferroni pairwise comparisons showed that the three experimental groups improved their mean scores at statistically significant levels from pretest to delayed posttest (ME+Task: $p < .01$, $d = 1.52$; Task only: $p < .01$, $d = .76$; ME only: $p < .01$, $d = 1.17$), whilst the control group did not ($p = .45$, $d = .29$).

As for differences among the groups, there were no statistically significant differences on the pretest. On the posttest, the ME+Task group outperformed the control group ($p < .01$, $d = 1.13$) while the other two experimental groups did not (Task Only: $p = 1.00$, $d = .45$; ME Only: $p = .06$, $d = .72$). Table 3 provides the within-effect sizes (pretest-posttest) and between-effect sizes (compared with the control group) for each group. The overall results indicate that all of the treatments, including simply completing the task, improved the learners' ability to correct errors in the test. The effect sizes indicate that the effect of the treatment on the test scores was the largest for the ME+Task group followed by the ME Only, and the Task Only groups. The effect for the control group was marginal.

Table 3. Summary of the EC test results

Groups	Within-group *d*	Between-group *d*	
		Pretest	Posttest
ME+Task	1.52*	−.12	1.13*
Task Only	.76*	−.07	.45
ME Only	1.17*	−.33	.72
Control	.29	–	–

* = The differences were statistically significant; *ME* = metalinguistic explanation; *Task* = story reconstruction task; *Control* = the control group; *Within-group* = the comparison between the pretest and the posttest; *Between-group* = the comparison between the experimental and the control group

The results for the story reconstruction (SR) tests

Table 4 shows the means and standard deviations for and the accuracy scores for the past counterfactual conditional sentences in the SR tests (pre-, post-, and delayed posttests). The maximum possible score was 5 (i.e. the average scores of attempted sentences).

Table 4. Descriptive statistics for the story reconstruction tests

Group	N	Pretest		Posttest		Delayed posttest	
		Mean	SD	Mean	SD	Mean	SD
ME+Task	23	.38	.89	1.61	1.38	1.50	1.51
Task Only	23	.63	.86	1.25	1.02	1.05	1.01
ME Only	24	.67	1.00	1.21	1.31	.82	.96
Control	22	.53	.85	.52	.62	.61	.65

ME = metalinguistic explanation; *Task* = story reconstruction task; *Control* = the control group

A repeated measures ANOVA showed that there were significant main effects for time (F (2, 176) = 24.01, $p < .01$, $\eta^2 = .21$) and for time × group (F (6, 176) = 4.33, $p < .01$, $\eta^2 = .13$) but no significant effect for group (F (3, 88) = 2.07, $p = .11$, $\eta^2 = .07$). Bonferroni pairwise comparisons showed there were no statistically significant group differences in the pretest. For the two posttests, there were a number of within- and between-group differences with different patterns for the immediate posttest and the delayed posttest.

Within-group comparisons between the pretest and posttest showed that the three experimental groups improved their mean scores at statistically significant levels with small to large effect sizes (ME+Task: $p < .01$, $d = 1.08$; Task Only: $p = .01$, $d = .67$; ME Only: $p = .01$, $d = .47$). On the delayed posttest, only the ME+Task group maintained the statistically significant gain against the pretest with a large effect size ($p < .01$, $d = .92$) while the gains were no longer significant for the Task Only group ($p = .11$, $d = .46$) and the ME Only group ($p = .20$, $d = .16$) with small to marginal effect sizes. The control group did not show any significant improvement with marginal effects over the three tests.

There were no significant differences between any of the four groups on the pretest. The post-treatment measurements showed that only the ME+Task condition performed significantly better than the control group on both of the posttests (posttest: $p = .01$, $d = 1.03$; delayed posttest: $p = .44$, $d = .78$). The other experimental groups failed to differ significantly from the control group both on the posttest (Task Only: $p = .20$, $d = .88$; ME Only: $p = .26$, $d = .68$) and delayed posttest (Task Only: $p = 1.00$, $d = .53$; ME Only: $p = 1.00$, $d = .26$) although the small to medium effect sizes for these groups indicated some positive effects for these treatments. There were no significant differences between any of the experimental groups on either of the two posttests.

Table 5 summarises the SR test results. Overall the three experimental groups performed better than the control group. All experimental groups significantly improved from pretest to posttest, but the gains were all reduced on the delayed posttest. Only the ME+Task group showed a clear advantage over the control group. This group also showed a significant durable gain over the control group on the delayed posttest. Overall, the ME+Task group showed the greatest gain, followed by the Task Only group. The ME Only group showed a small effect on the posttest, which became marginal on the delayed posttest.

Table 5. Summary of the SR test results

Groups	Within-group		Between-group		
	Pre-Post	Pre-Delayed	Pretest	Posttest	Delayed
ME+Task	1.08*	.92*	−.17	1.03*	.78*
Task Only	.67*	.46	.12	.88	.53
ME Only	.47*	.16	.15	.68	.26
Control	.01	.11	–	–	–

* = The differences were statistically significant; *ME* = metalinguistic explanation; *Task* = story reconstruction task; *Control* = the control group; *Within-group* = the comparison between the pretest and the posttest; *Between-group* = the comparison between the experimental and the control group

Discussion

Research question 1 asked whether metalinguistic explanation (ME) alone promotes learners' (a) explicit knowledge of the target grammatical structure and (b) accurate production of the target grammatical structure. Explicit knowledge was measured using the EC test that required the learners to correct the target structure in decontextualized short sentences. Unsurprisingly, the results indicated that the ME alone led to explicit knowledge of the target feature, and the effect was large ($d = 1.17$). The results support the claims that explicit instruction can help to develop explicit knowledge (Krashen, 1982; Ellis, 1994).

The SR test measured the learners' ability to produce the target structure accurately. The ME Only group showed some improvement in accuracy on the posttest ($d = .47$) but not on the delayed posttest ($d = .16$). The ME Only condition did not provide opportunity for using the form meaningfully. Considering the near-zero scores on the SR pretest, the learners presumably had not proceduralized the target structure at the start of the study. Overall, then the results support DeKeyser's (2015) claim that without opportunities to apply metalinguistic knowledge in practice activities, proceduralisation will not occur. It is possible of course that the explicit knowledge resulting from the ME might assist proceduralisation over time if learners subsequently draw on it when trying to communicate, as Ellis (1994) has suggested. However, the fact that the gain in explicit knowledge was not maintained suggests that the ME alone treatment was of limited value even in this respect.

Research question 2 asked about the effectiveness of just performing the SR tasks (without ME). As Table 3 showed, the Task Only group showed significant improvement on the EC test with a medium effect ($d = .71$) even without the metalinguistic rule explanation. The results showed that completing SR tasks four times helped the learners to improve their explicit knowledge, suggesting that the learners analysed the target form in the process of comprehending the input in the SR tasks and then reconstructing the texts orally. The nature of the target structure might have helped this. The past counterfactual conditional is meaning-conveying, which, as Leow et al. (2003) suggested, can promote noticing of the target feature when encountered. If the target feature had been simpler or less salient (e.g. third person singular -s) the Task Only treatment might have not been so effective.

As for the development of procedural knowledge measured by the SR test, the Task Only group initially showed significant improvement ($d = .67$) but the effect was reduced to a non-significant level ($d = .46$) in the delayed post-test. This group failed to show a significant advantage over the control group but the effect sizes were medium for both tests: $d = .88$ and $d = .53$ on the posttest and delayed posttest respectively. The results suggest that text reconstruction alone did help development of procedural knowledge of the past counterfactual conditionals, but only to a limited extent. A possible explanation is that the SR tasks might have burdened the learners' working memory, preventing them from noticing and analysing the form with the result that they found it difficult to use it in subsequent production. Studies have shown that increased cognitive complexity limits the self-repair that learners undertake and that can promote L2 learning (Gilabert, 2007; Révész, Sachs, & Hama, 2014; Robinson, 2001). This might have been particularly true for the participants in this study, who had limited prior knowledge of the target feature as shown by the pretest scores.

Research question 3 addresses the effects of the treatment involving a combination of ME and the SR tasks. The results suggest that this combination promoted learners' explicit knowledge. The large, significant effects for both within-group ($d = 1.52$) and between-group ($d = 1.13$) comparisons for the EC test (Table 3) point to the effectiveness of this treatment in developing the learners' explicit knowledge. This group also demonstrated significant improvement in the SR tests, both immediate and delayed, indicating that the ME+Task led to oral accuracy and the effect was durable. The overall test results for this group, thus, suggest that providing ME followed by a guided production task improves both explicit knowledge and accuracy in oral production.

Research question 4 asked whether there is any difference in the effect that the three different treatments had on learning. As for explicit knowledge measured by the EC test, the ME+Task condition was found to be the most effective, followed by the ME Only, with the Task Only condition proving the least effective (Table 3). The ME+Task condition was clearly more effective than the Task Only condition (the effect size differences are $d = .55$ for within-group comparison and $d = .68$ for between-group comparison), indicating that the *a priori* ME helped the learners analyse the form of the target feature. The ME+Task group, however, also showed a larger between-group effect size than the ME Only group. The results suggest that having opportunities for comprehending and producing the target form by performing the SR tasks consolidated what they had learned from the ME. The results suggest that completing a text reconstruction task after establishing explicit knowledge aids the development of explicit knowledge. It seems that the SR tasks helped the learners to pay attention to the form of the target structure and analyse it.

Regarding gains in accuracy, the ME+Task also showed the largest effect. The second most effective condition was the Task Only with the ME Only the least effective (Table 5). It has to be reminded, however, that the treatment and testing tasks followed the same procedures. The groups that completed SR tasks practiced the tasks while the ME Only group did not, which might have contributed to accuracy in production. Only the ME+Task group demonstrated a clearly durable effect. This group also outperformed the Task Only group ($d = .4$). The results shows that the learners in the ME+Task group were able to utilize the declarative knowledge gained from the ME as a crutch to help them produce the conditional sentences in the SR tasks (DeKeyser, 2007). The findings support skill-acquisition theory, which emphasizes the importance of practice opportunities for the development of proceduralised knowledge (DeKeyser, 2015).

Pedagogical implications

The current study made the case for providing metalinguistic explanation before production practice for at least in the context investigated in this study – teaching a complex structure to learners with low oral productive ability. The fact that the Task Only condition had a limited effect on explicit knowledge and on accurate production suggested that the learners could not effectively internalise the target structure while comprehending and re-producing a relatively long story. *A priori* explicit instruction enhanced their explicit knowledge of the target feature, which might have helped them to make a form-meaning mapping when processing the input and to monitor their production in output. If the ME helped accuracy when performing the tasks, it might have helped proceduralization. The findings, thus, suggest that a priori explicit instruction is not harmful but is helpful for low proficiency learners who can use it as a crutch when producing (DeKeyser, 1998, p. 49) but also requires opportunity for productive practice.

The study also illustrates how *a priori* explicit instruction can be provided in a written handout and that metalinguistic knowledge acquired in this way is available when performing an oral production task. Written handouts are easily prepared and implementation requires minimum time in the classroom (in this study, the learners had 10 minutes to study the handout). Arguably, such an approach is more economical than extensive oral explanation although this remains to be shown.

The study demonstrated that SR tasks afford opportunities for incidental learning. An SR task requires the learners to first listen to or read a story and then reproduce the entire story. Thus, it directs learners' attention to the meaning of the story but also provides exposure to a number of exemplars of the target structure. Learning might take place when learners receive the input (comprehending the story) but also when they are reconstructing the story. The learners might *notice the hole* (i.e., become aware of knowledge gap; Doughty & Williams, 1998) when re-producing the story and become aware of their inability to re-construct some language features accurately. Also, through repeating the same type of task, learners might pay greater attention to linguistic form when they receive the input for the next story.

The SR tasks used in the current study were focused tasks (i.e. they were designed to elicit the production of the target structure). Four sentences containing past counterfactual conditionals were embedded in each story. Such tasks can be used to create a context for the use of a linguistic target while still satisfying the main criterion for a task, namely that the primary focus is on meaning (Ellis, 2003).

Ecological validity of the current study

A key issue in the kind of study I have reported is to what extent it achieves ecological validity. While views differ about whether the results of laboratory-based studies can be generalized to the classroom, it is surely the case that studies that mirror more closely what happens in actual classrooms will carry more weight with teachers.

Ecological validity is, however, not an absolute quality of a study. Rather, a study can achieve ecological validity to a greater or lesser extent depending on the nature of setting (whether the research setting was similar to the real-world language classroom), the instructional treatment (whether the treatment tasks were similar to those commonly used in the classroom), and the measurements obtained (whether the tests tapped the kind of knowledge needed in real-world communication).

Setting

The setting of this study was a real classroom. The entire data was collected in a regular classroom during a single semester. It took place in the same computer rooms that the class took place in. Although the researcher was present in the class, the lecturer for the course conducted all the treatment sessions. The participants were used to computer-mediated instruction and to audio-recording their oral production using headsets. Thus, the study achieved high ecological validity in terms of the research setting.

Instructional treatment

The instruction focused narrowly on a single grammatical structure. This is typical of English classrooms in Japan. The target structure was the past counterfactual conditional. It was chosen because previous studies showed that university students in Japan had limited productive knowledge of this structure. To achieve validity, however, it is important to select a structure that is acquirable by the learners. There is little sense in designing instruction that caters to incidental acquisition for a structure that is clearly beyond the students' current level of development. Arguably, this was a weakness in the Li *et al*.'s study referred to earlier. The results of my study indicated that although the past hypothetical conditional was difficult for these learners it was acquirable. Even those participants with near-zero initial production knowledge of the structure improved their accuracy as a result of the instruction.

The study operationalised the ME+Task condition by providing a metalinguistic explanation and guided production practice activity – an instructional approach that has high validity for the Japanese context. *A priori* ME was used to develop learners' explicit knowledge before performing an oral task which is a common practice in English language classrooms in Japan (Shintani, 2016). Including ME was also justified by the fact that the target structure was clearly a challenging one. To ensure the viability of the SR tasks, they were designed in consultation with the lecturer of the classes used in this study and proved successful in eliciting attempted use of the target structure.

However, the treatment received by other groups did not correspond to any pedagogically valid type of instruction. In particular, the ME Only group just studied the ME sheet without engaging in any follow-up production practice. This can hardly be said to constitute sound pedagogic practice. The fact that the ME took up less time the ME+Task condition – perhaps the reason why it was less effective – also raises doubts about its ecological validity. It is doubtful whether a teacher would be very happy to just let students do nothing after completing an activity. The justification for the ME only condition was entirely theoretical, raising a question not just about its ecological validity but, in retrospect, its ethical acceptability.

Measurement

The EC test served as a measure of declarative knowledge. I do not think I can claim that such a test has ecological validity for these students. Such a test does not tell us anything about the procedural knowledge needed in oral communication – the main purpose of the course they were taking. The teacher of the classes did not use such a test in evaluating the students' performance. The justification for including such a test was entirely theoretical – I wanted to see if the different treatments had any effect on learners' explicit knowledge.

However, the SR tasks can claim to be ecologically valid. They were of the same type as used in the treatment. This is pedagogically sound as ideally tests used to measure students' abilities should match the kinds of activities used for instruction. The SR tests also reduced the potential problem of the skill-specificity of proceduralised knowledge. If learners automatize their language knowledge through a certain learning process (e.g. reconstructing stories), then there is a likelihood that it is transferable when performing in a similar condition. One major advantage of using an SR test is that it allows researchers to ensure that there are occasions for the use of the target structure. A major problem with production tasks in an experimental study is that the use of the target structure is not 'task essential' (Loschky & Bley-Vroman, 1993), particularly because learners with limited proficiency tend to avoid difficult structures when they are focussed on communication (Samuda, 2001). The SR tests, however, successfully elicited the target feature in the oral production task. By using the same task types with the same procedures for the treatment and testing, it was possible to achieve the theoretical aim of investigating whether learning took place in a way that was ecologically valid.

Issues of ecological validity, however, remain. The SR tests did not provide an opportunity for engaging in truly spontaneous communication. Arguably, the tests only measured the ability to reconstruct the L2 sentences but not the ability to use the target structures in a totally free context. Also, as the tasks provided L2 input first, we cannot exclude the possibility that the learners were able to produce the target sentences by simply memorising them rather than through accessing their linguistic system. Another ecological validity issue is the delayed post-tests. The current study conducted delayed posttest three weeks after the immediate posttest. Delayed post-tests are not a feature of normal classroom practice. It might be argued, however, that teachers could usefully include delayed testing in order to establish whether the effect of their instruction is durable and whether they needed to provide further instruction directed at the same target structure.

Comparability of studies

It is customary to compare the results of a study with those of previous studies and where the results differ to seek an explanation. The results of the current study showed that a *priori* metalinguistic explanation followed by a story reconstruction task enhanced the learning of both explicit language knowledge and the accuracy in oral production. The results partially replicate Li et al. (2016) in that a priori explicit instruction also enhanced their learners' explicit knowledge. However, whereas Li et al. reported no effect on oral accuracy, the current study found that learners improved their accuracy in the oral reconstruction tests. How can the difference in the results of these two be explained?

I want to argue that seeking an explanation is problematic given that studies vary in so many different ways that it is impossible to determine what factors can account for the differences. To illustrate this problem I carried out a comparison of the current study and Li et al. Table 6 shows that they differed in numerous ways – the choice of target structure, the participants, medium of the instruction, the instructional tasks, and the types of measurement. Any one of these factors might account for the different results making any explanation entirely speculative.

Table 6. Design differences in Li et al. (2016) and the current study

	Li et al. (2016)	Current study
Target structure	Past passive voice	Past counterfactual conditional
Participants	Junior high schoolers in China	University students in Japan
Prior knowledge of the target structure	Mixed	Low
Medium of instruction	Face-to-face	Computer-mediated
Metalinguistic explanation	Oral	Written
Text reconstruction task		
Number of tasks	2	4
Number of target feature input in one task	45 (15 cases in one story × story told 3 times for each task)	8 (4 cases in one story × story played twice for each task)
Type of reconstruction	dialogic	monologic
Reconstruction aids	list of keywords	pictures with keywords
Learning measurement	Grammaticality judgement test Oral elicited imitation test	Error correction test Story reconstruction test

Yet, comparing the results of different studies is essential if we are to arrive at convincing generalizations. Meta-analyses go some way to achieving this but struggle to take account of the full range of design variables that might impact on instructional effects. An additional way forward might be to conduct careful replications of existing studies, varying their design in very specific ways. One might investigate, for example, whether replicating the current study using the same type of measurements as in Li *et al.* would produce the same or different results. Replications of studies are often encouraged but in fact rarely happen. They can not only help to confirm the results of the original study but to pinpoint factors that will allow for meaningful comparisons with other studies

References

Adams, R., & Newton, J. (2009). TBLT in Asia: Constraints and opportunities. *Asian Journal of English Language Teaching*, 19, 1–17.

Brown, H. D. (2007). *Teaching by principles: An interactive approach to language pedagogy* (3rd ed.). New York, NY: Pearson Education.

Celce-Murcia, M., & Larsen-Freeman, D. (1999). *The grammar book*. New York, NY: Heinle & Heinle.

DeKeyser, R. M. (1998). Beyond focus on form: Cognitive perspective on learning and practicing second language grammar. In C. Doughty & J. Williams (Eds.), *Focus on form in classroom second language acquisition* (pp. 42–63). Cambridge: Cambridge University Press.

DeKeyser, R. M. (2007). *Practice in a second language: Perspectives from applied linguistics and cognitive psychology*. Cambridge: Cambridge University Press
https://doi.org/10.1017/CBO9780511667275

DeKeyser, R. M. (2015). Skill Acquisition Theory. In B. VanPatten & J. Williams (Eds.), *Theories in second language acquisition: An introduction*. New York, NY: Routledge.

Doughty, C. (1991). Second language instruction does make a difference. *Studies in Second Language Acquisition*, 13(04), 431–469. https://doi.org/10.1017/S0272263100010287

Doughty, C., & Varela, E. (1998). Communicative focus on form. In C. Doughty & J. Williams (Eds.), *Focus on form in classroom second language acquisition* (pp. 114–138). Cambridge: Cambridge University Press.

Ellis, N. (1994). Introduction: Implicit and explicit language learning – An overview. In N. Ellis (Ed.), *Implicit and explicit learning of language* (pp. 1–31). London: Academic Press.

Ellis, R. (2003). *Task-based language learning and teaching*. Oxford: Oxford University Press.

Gilabert, R. (2007). Effects of manipulating task complexity on self-repairs during L2 oral production. *IRAL– International Review of Applied Linguistics in Language Teaching*, 45(3), 215–240. https://doi.org/10.1515/iral.2007.010

Izumi, S., Bigelow, M., Fujiwara, M., & Fearnow, S. (1999). Testing the output hypothesis: Effects of output on noticing and second language acquisition. *Studies in Second Language Acquisition*, 21, 421–452. https://doi.org/10.1017/S0272263199003034

Krashen, S. (1982). *Principles and practice in second language acquisition*. Oxford: Pergamon.

Li, S., Ellis, R., & Zhu, Y. (2016). Task-based versus task-supported language instruction: An experimental study. *Annual Review of Applied Linguistics*, 36, 205–229.
https://doi.org/10.1017/S0267190515000069

Lightbown, P. M. (2007). Transfer appropriate processing as a model for classroom second language acquisition. In Z. Han & E. Park (Eds.), *Understanding second language process* (pp. 27–44). Clevedon: Multilingual Matters.

Loschky, L., & Bley-Vroman, R. (1993). Grammar and task-based methodology. In G. Crookes & S. Gass (Eds.), *Tasks and language learning: Integrating theory and practice* (pp. 123–167). Clevedon: Multilingual Matters.

Révész, A., Sachs, R., & Hama, M. (2014). The effects of task complexity and input frequency on the acquisition of the past counterfactual construction through recasts. *Language Learning*, 64(3), 615–650. https://doi.org/10.1111/lang.12061

Robinson, P. (1997). Generalizability and automaticity of second language learning under implicit, incidental, enhanced, and instructed conditions. *Studies in Second Language Acquisition*, 19(2), 223–247. https://doi.org/10.1017/S0272263197002052

Robinson, P. (2001). Task complexity, task difficulty, and task production: Exploring interactions in a componential framework. *Applied Linguistics*, 22(1), 27–57. https://doi.org/10.1093/applin/22.1.27

Samuda, V. (2001). Guiding relationships betweem form and meaning during task performance: The role of the teacher. In M. Bygate, P. Skehan, & M. Swain (Eds.), *Researching pedagogic tasks: Second language learning teaching, and testing* (pp. 119–140). London: Longman.

Sanz, C., & Morgan-Short, K. (2004). Positive evidence versus explicit rule presentation and explicit negative feedback: A computer-assisted study. *Language Learning*, 54(1), 35–78. https://doi.org/10.1111/j.1467-9922.2004.00248.x

Shintani, N. (2016). *The role of input-based tasks in foreign language instruction for young learners*. Amsterdam: John Benjamins.

Shintani, N., Ellis, R., & Suzuki, W. (2014). Effects of written feedback and revision on learners' accuracy in using two English grammatical structures. *Language Learning*, 64(1), 103–131. https://doi.org/10.1111/lang.12029

VanPatten, B. (2009). Formal intervention and the development of proficiency: The role of explicit formation. In A. Benati (Ed.), *Issues in second language proficiency* (pp. 169–187). London: Continuum.

VanPatten, B., & Oikkenon, S. (1996). Explanation versus structured input in processing instruction. *Studies in Second Language Acquisition*, 18(4), 495–510. https://doi.org/10.1017/S0272263100015394

Appendix A. Metalinguistic Explanation Sheet

The Metalinguistic Explanation (ME) sheet

レッスン1
　〈仮定法過去完了〉とは、過去の事実や状況と異なることを表す時に使用します。
「あと5分早く起きていれば、遅刻せずに済んだのになぁ」と思うことはありませんか?
この文を仮定法過去完了を使って表すと
If I had gotten up five minutes earlier, I would not have been late for class.
となります。この学生は、実際には授業に遅刻してしまったのですが、もし早く起きて
いれば間に合ったのに、と事実とは異なった、仮の場合の話をしているわけです。
〜仮定法過去完了の公式〜
　　If + (主語) + had (過去分詞), S would have (過去分詞)
　　　「もし〜だったら...だったろうに」
　　※**would**以外にも、**could / might / should** でもよい。
では、練習問題を解きながら、上のルールを確認しましょう。
1. (　　　)に適するものを選びなさい。
　(1) If they had known your telephone number, they ( ) you up.
　　　　① have called ② had call　③ would have called　④ will call
　(2) If I ( ) about his illness, I would have visited him at the hospital.
　　　　① know　② have known　③ had known　④ might have known
2.　　次の文の下線部で文法的に間違っているものを選び、適する形にしなさい。
　(3) If I ① <u>have</u> known you ② <u>were</u> in Tokyo, I ③<u>would have</u> invited you out ④<u>to</u>
　　　dinner.

Translation:

Lesson 1

The "past conterfactual conditionals" express situations where an event differs from the fact or situation in the past. Have you ever said to yourself "I wouldn't have been late if I had gotten up five minutes earlier"? This statement can also be expressed as follows.

If I had gotten up five minutes earlier, I would not have been late for class.

This student was late for the class but referred to the hypothetical situation that he had gotten up earlier, which is against the fact.

〜**The fomula of past counterfactual conditionals**〜

　If + (subject) + had (past particle), S would have (past particle)

　　"If xx had 〜, xx would have …"

　※apart from would, could / might / should can also be used.

Now let's confirm the above rule by solving the following exercises.

1. Choose an appropriate choice for (　　　).
2. Identify the grammatical error out of the underlined parts and correct it with an appropriate form.

Appendix B. The Story Reconstruction (SR) Video File

Section	Length of the clip	Audio input	Computer screen
1	Approx. 20 sec.	–	Instruction (in Japanese)

今から英語の話を２回聞きます。１回目は画面に話が英文で表示されます。　２回目は話にあった絵が表示されます。

２回聴いたあと、この話をできるだけ詳しく英語で再現してますのでよく聴いてください。

質問がある場合は、このビデオを一時停止して手を上げてください。

Translation:

You will listen to an English story twice. For the first time, the transcript of the story will be shown on the screen. For the second time, some pictures describing the story will be shown.

Please listen carefully because after listening to the story twice, you will re-tell the story in as much detail as possible.

If you have any questions, please pause this video and raise your hand.

Section	Length of the clip	Audio input	Computer screen
2	Approx. 3 min.	Story narration	Script of the story

Ayaka's father was invited to a party. But he gave the ticket to Ayaka. It was organized by a famous musician. Many celebrities attended the party. The main hall was decorated with colorful tinsel, bells, and beautiful ribbons. Quiet music was played. Ayaka found her name card on one of the tables. On the stage, there was a space for the musician to sing. On the left side of the stage, was a big kitchen. When she sat down in her chair, the party began. A glass of champagne was served to everyone. She thought if her father hadn't worked for a TV company, she wouldn't have been able to experience the luxurious party.

Ayaka then heard an angry voice behind her. It was the manager of the party talking to a member of the volunteer staff. He was squabbling about the decorations. He looked up the ceiling of the stage. A big mirrored ball was hung in the middle of the stage. If you had put it on the left side of the stage, it would have shone better." The volunteer seemed unhappy to hear that and said, "A mirrored ball is always in the middle." The manager was becoming more frustrated. His voice became raspy, and he started to cry.

The performance started. Ayaka's favourite song was sung by the musician. But she couldn't stop thinking about the angry manager. She said to herself, "If I hadn't heard that angry conversation, I would have danced on the stage with the singer." Then suddenly, Ayaka saw the manager on the stage, acting like a chef. A big piece of meat was cut up in pieces by him. They were laid out nicely in a big pan.

Then the manager started to dance while he was cooking. A long cutting knife and a red spatula were tightly held in his hands. Soon the food was served to all the guests. When Ayaka was munching on her meat, the manager walked over to her and asked, "How is the food?" She answered, "It's scrumptious." She then said, "If the mirrored ball had been placed on the left side of the stage, your dancing would have been even more exciting."

Section	Length of the clip	Audio input	Computer screen
3	Approx. 3 min.	Story narration	6 descriptive pictures

Appendix C. Story reconstruction Sheet

1   **Instruction page**

今から先ほど聞いた英文をできるだけ詳しく正確に再現していただきます。

この画面を下にスクロールすると、さきほどの絵と文の一部が順番に表示され
ます。絵の横に文の一部や使われた単語（動詞は原型で表示）が示されていま
す。

絵とヒントを参考にして、さきほどの話をできるだけ正確に詳しく英語で話し
てください。

<u>自分の発話は録音してください。</u>

制限時間は１０分ですのですぐに録音を開始してください。

質問がある場合は、手を上げてください。

では、はじめてください。

Translation:
You will now re-construct the English sentences as accurately as you can.
Scroll down this screen, then you will see the pictures you saw and some parts of
the sentences in the same order. Parts of sentences and words used in sentences
(verbs are in the stem form) are shown next to each picture.
Referring to the pictures and the clues, re-tell the story as accurately as possible.
<u>Please record your production.</u>
You have 10 minutes. Please start recording immediately.
If you have any questions, raise your hand. Now please start.

2   **An example of picture cues with key words**

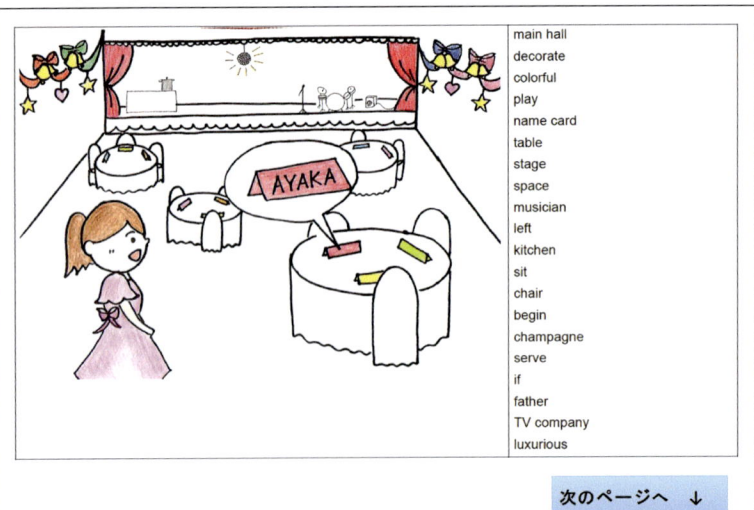

CHAPTER 6

The effects of recasts versus prompts on immediate uptake and learning of a complex target structure

Hossein Nassaji
University of Victoria

This study compared the effects of recasts and prompts on learning a complex target structure (English relative clauses). It also examined how these effects were mediated by learners' level of language proficiency. Fifty-four high- and low-proficiency ESL learners were assigned to three groups: recast ($n = 18$), prompt ($n = 18$), and control ($n = 18$). Both uptake and pretest-posttest measures were used to assess feedback effectiveness. Each learner met with a native-speaker interlocutor outside the classroom four times over a four-week period for the pretest, treatment, and immediate and delayed posttests. Picture-cued oral production tasks were developed and used to elicit the use of relative clauses. The findings revealed an advantage for recasts over prompts, and also showed that the two feedback types varied in their effects on uptake versus learning and also interacted differently with learners' levels of language proficiency. Although the study was conducted outside the classroom, the pedagogical relevance will be discussed.

Keywords: interactional feedback, recasts, prompts, complex target structures, English relative clauses

Introduction

The role that interactional feedback plays in language learning has been the focus of much theoretical and empirical investigation in the past two decades. Interactional feedback refers to "feedback generated in response to linguistically erroneous or communicatively inappropriate utterances that learners produce during conversational interaction" (Nassaji, 2014, p. 104). Such feedback can occur through various negotiation strategies, such as repetition, asking for clarifications, and checking

https://doi.org/10.1075/lllt.52.06nas

for confirmation. These strategies are assumed to contribute to L2 acquisition in important ways by highlighting the linguistic problems, helping learners notice the target form, or by pushing learners to modify their interlanguage and produce utterances that are more accurate and appropriate (e.g., Long, 1996; Pica, 1994). Since interactional feedback occurs during meaning-focused interaction, it is suggested that the feedback draws learners' attention to form at the point where learners' attention is on communicating meaning. Therefore, it provides learners with opportunities for form-meaning mapping, considered to be required for L2 development (e.g., Doughty, 2001).

Two major types of interactional feedback are recasts and prompts. Recasts are feedback strategies that correctly reformulate the whole or part of the learner's erroneous utterance. Therefore, they supply the learner with the correct form. Because such feedback provides the correct input, it has been described as input-providing feedback (Ellis, 2009). An example of recasts can be seen in the following exchange where a native speaker has reformulated a learner's non-targetlike utterance.

Example (1)
NNS: yeah and they're eat lunch [eat lunch]
NS: [yes] they're eating lunch
NNS: and finished its rain getting rain   Mackey & Philp (1998, p. 345)

Prompts are feedback strategies that do not reformulate but rather push the learner to rephrase their non-targetlike utterance. Thus, they have been described as output-pushing feedback (Ellis, 2009). Since prompts do not provide the correct form, they afford the learner with opportunities of self-repair. An example of a prompt can be seen in the following exchange in which the interlocutor has used a clarification request in response to the learner's erroneous utterance.

Example (2)
Student: . . . on the street there was a policeman, and she was skipping running.
Teacher: I am sorry, she was . . .?
Student: Skipping running, the thief.   Nassaji (2009, p. 429)

In the SLA literature, both types of feedback have been considered to be useful corrective strategies in meaning-focused interactions. Recasts provide the correct model of the language and thus they afford positive evidence. They may also signal to the learner that they have made an error. Therefore, they may provide opportunities for negative evidence (e.g., Doughty & Varela, 1998; Long & Robinson, 1998). Prompts afford opportunities for self-correction or modified output, and since they push the learners to correct the erroneous form, they may help them notice problems in their output. Prompts also assist learners to "reanalyze what they have already internalized at some level" (Lyster, 2002, p. 248), and consequently may contribute to the consolidation of already known interlanguage forms.

Despite the general agreement on the usefulness of both feedback types, there has been a debate in the SLA literature regarding which type is more effective (de Bot, 1996; Doughty, 2001; Goo & Mackey, 2013; Long, 2007; Lyster & Ranta, 2013). Doughty (2001), for example, pointed out that recasts help learners not only notice a gap in their interlanguage but also make the necessary form-meaning connection needed for acquisition. De Bot (1996), however, observed, "[m]y reading of the psycholinguistic literature on processing leads me to believe that there is never a direct comparison between input and output" (p. 228). Lyster (1998) argued, "recasts do not covey to learners what is unacceptable in the language," particularly in contexts where the primary focus is on content (Lyster, 1998, p. 75). Goo and Mackey (2013) contended that the argument by Lyster against recasts is not warranted as it is based on "a relatively small number of repairs following recasts evidenced in Lyster's observations of a specific context – namely, French immersion classrooms" (p. 135).

Due to the importance of interactional feedback in general and the debate around their role, an extensive body of empirical studies has examined its role (see Nassaji, 2015 for a review). In particular, a considerable body of research has examined recasts. These studies, conducted in both classroom and laboratory contexts, have reported different degrees of effectiveness for such feedback (e.g., Doughty & Varela, 1998; Goo, 2012; Han, 2002; Ishida, 2004; Iwashita, 2003; Leeman, 2003; Long, Inagaki, & Ortega, 1998; Mackey & Philp, 1998; Philp, 2003; Saito & Lyster, 2011). In this respect, studies that have compared recasts with no recasts have often provided positive evidence for recasts. However, those that have compared recasts with prompts or other feedback types have produced mixed results. For example, both Lyster's (2004) and Ammar and Spada's (2006) classroom studies reported more effectiveness for prompts than recasts when learners first received form-focused instruction on the target structure (see also Ammar, 2008). Lyster and Izquierdo (2009), however, which compared recasts and prompts in dyadic interaction outside the classroom following classroom instruction, found that the two were equally effective. Dilans (2010) also found similar effects for recasts and prompts (see also Nassaji, 2009). However, Yang and Lyster (2010), which compared the effect of prompts and recasts on the acquisition of regular and irregular English past tense among Chinese EFL learners, found more effects for prompts than recasts in both oral and written production although both feedback types had a similar effect on the use of irregular past tense.

Based on the results of these studies, it is difficult to conclude which type of feedback is more effective. It is quite possible that both are effective under certain circumstances. Laboratory studies have often produced more positive effects for recasts than meaning-focused classroom studies. However, classroom-based studies have also found significant facilitative effects for recasts (e.g., Doughty & Varela, 1998; Loewen & Philp, 2006; Lyster & Mori, 2006). There are a few other issues that need to be considered with respect to studies comparing recasts and prompts too. First most of them (e.g., Ammar, 2008; Ammar & Spada, 2006; Lyster, 2004; Lyster & Izquierdo, 2009; Yang & Lyster, 2010) have used these feedback types in conjunction with form-focused instruction or practice. In such cases, if feedback is shown to be effective, it is difficult to know whether it is because of the feedback or its combination with form-focused instruction. What these studies show is that if learners first receive instruction to the target structure, feedback that pushes them to produce the form may be more effective than feedback that simply provides the correct form. These studies have also compared one recast type, with multiple prompt types, some of which have been highly explicit such as metalinguistic cues. Therefore, the effects shown could be due to feedback explicitness rather than type of feedback. Finally, the advantage of prompts over recasts has been shown on only certain outcome measures. For example, in both Lyster (2004) and Ammar and Spada (2006), the benefit of prompt was mainly evident on written tests and not on oral tests, although Ammar and Spada (2006) reported some delayed effects of prompts on oral tests.

Another issue concerns the effect of the target structure. A number of studies have examined the role of interactional feedback on different target structures (e.g., Ammar, 2008; Ammar & Spada, 2006; Dilans, 2010; Ellis, 2007; Goo, 2012; Lyster, 2004; Lyster & Izquierdo, 2009; McDonough, 2007; Nabei & Swain, 2002; Sheen, 2007; Yang & Lyster, 2010). The findings of these studies suggest that the effectiveness of feedback depends on the nature of the target form. Some studies, for example, have found that recasts might be more accurately noticed in response to language forms that are more salient such as lexical or phonological than morphosyntactic forms (e.g., Mackey et al., 2000). There are also studies that have shown that while the nature of the target structure is an important factor in general, it may not mediate the effectiveness of different types of feedback. Yilmaz (2012), for example, did not find an interaction between the effect of salient versus less salient morphosyntactic forms and that of different feedback types.

One thing to note, however, is that most previous studies of the effect of target structures have categorized the target form in terms of their linguistic domain (i.e., grammatical, lexical, phonological, or morphosyntactic forms). They have also examined the role of feedback on linguistically simple target structures but not on more complex target structures. Yang and Lyster (2010), for example, which reported a superior effect for prompts, examined the effects of these two types of feedback on English past tense, for which learners had ample declarative knowledge. Ammar and Spada (2006), too, compared the effect of recasts versus prompts on a simple target structure (i.e., English third-person possessive determiners). Therefore, it is not clear whether these feedback types have similar effects on learning more complex target structures.

The effects of feedback have also been shown to vary depending on other variables such as the nature of the recasts, the context of recasts (e.g., Lyster & Mori, 2006; Sheen, 2004), learners' linguistic ability and developmental level (e.g., Ammar & Spada, 2006; Mackey & Philp, 1998), and various individual learner differences (e.g., Mackey, Philp, Fujii, Egi, & Tatsumi, 2002; Sheen, 2007, 2008; Trofimovich, Ammar, & Gatbonton, 2007). Characteristics of recasts such as length, number of changes, and linguistic mode (e.g., declarative versus interrogative) have all been found to impact the noticeability and effectiveness of recasts (e.g., Philp, 2003; Sheen, 2006). These findings confirm that the effects of feedback are multifaceted and should be interpreted with reference to the various mediating variables.

The present study

Although a few past studies have examined the differential effects of recasts and prompts, there is still a need to explore these effects with different learners, contexts, and target structures. As noted earlier, most previous studies have used simple target structures or those for which learners have already a great deal of prior knowledge. Furthermore, although previous research has examined the role of a number of mediating variables, more research is needed in this area to get a clearer understanding of what facilitates or constrains the efficacy of the feedback. In particular, research examining the effects of recasts should consider learners' level of language proficiency as this variable has been repeatedly shown to mediate the effect of such feedback across studies. The present study was designed to take these issues into account by examining the differential effects of recasts versus prompts on a complex target structure (i.e., English relative clauses), using one type of recast versus one type of prompts, and with no additional explicit instruction.

Both uptake, including learner immediate repair, and pretest-posttest measures were used to assess the effectiveness of the feedback. There are different definitions of uptake ranging from what leaners report they have learned from a lesson (e.g., Allwright, 1984)) to leaner's modification of their output (e.g., Nassaji, 2011) to any response made by the learner in reaction to feedback (Lyster & Ranta,

1997). Lyster and Ranta defined uptake as "a student's utterance that immediately follows the teacher's feedback and that constitutes a reaction in some way to the teacher's intention to draw attention to some aspect of the student's initial utterance" (p. 49). Uptake defined as such comprised any responses including even learners' acknowledgements or confirmation of the feedback. Lyster and Ranta then classified uptake into repair or needs repair. Following Lyster and Ranta (1997), most studies of corrective feedback have defined uptake as a learner response to feedback. To be consistent with previous research, the present study used the same definition and then analyzed learner responses in terms of immediate repair.

It should be noted that although uptake defined as such indicates a learner's reaction to the feedback, it does not indicate that any learning has taken place. However, it has been suggested that uptake may indicate that learners have noticed the feedback (Ellis et al., 2001; Mackey & Philp, 1998). Repair was defined as uptake that involved correct modification of the learner output. Repair may provide a better indication of learning. However, immediate repair may not always indicate that learning has taken place as repair may occur as a result of rote repetition of the feedback without understanding or processing it (Nassaji, 2011). In addition, immediate repair does not show that learners are able to retain the form. Therefore, in this study, in addition to uptake and repair, pretest-posttest measures were used to investigate whether learners are able to learn from the feedback.

Research questions

1. What is the effect of recasts versus prompts on learning English relative clauses?
2. Does the effect (if any) vary according to how it is measured: immediate uptake vs. pretest-posttest production measures?
3. Does the effect (if any) vary according to learners' level of language proficiency?

Participants

Participants were 54 adult ESL learners studying in an intensive ESL program in Canada and two native speaker interlocutors who interacted with the learners in dyadic interaction outside the classroom. Learners were from different language backgrounds including Arabic, Chinese, French, Japanese, Korean, Portuguese, Spanish and Thai. Of the participants, 21 were male and 33 were female and their ages ranged from 18 to 42 (*Mean* = 23.4). By the time of the study, they had been in Canada for 1 week to 10 months, and the length of time they had been studying

English in the program ranged from 1 week to 8 months. The two interlocutors were female English native speakers who were at the time completing a graduate degree in Applied Linguistics. Before the study, they were trained how to provide the intended feedback types involving a number of practice sessions.

The participants were randomly assigned to three groups: a recast (*n* = 18), a prompt (*n* = 18), and a control (*n* = 18) group. Prior to the group assignments, learners' language proficiency was determined based on a language proficiency test, which was an oral grammaticality judgment test, adapted from DeKeyser (2000). The test covered a wide range of grammatical structures including relative clauses. The students listened to 60 grammatical and ungrammatical sentences. They heard each sentence two times. After the second time, they decided whether it was correct or incorrect. They had six seconds to make their decision. Based on the median score of the test, half of the learners were classified as high-proficiency learners and the other half as low-proficiency learners. When assigning the participants to groups, half were randomly sampled from the advanced-level and the other half from the less-advanced level learners.

Target structure

The target structure was English relative clauses. One reason for choosing this target form was to examine whether feedback had any effects on learning a complex target structure. Relative clauses are linguistically complex because they involve structural embedding and also movement of a noun phrase within the embedded phrase (De López, Olsen, & Chondrogianni, 2014). Relative clauses are also highly frequent but at the same time well known areas of difficulty for many L2 learners; therefore, it is important to find out whether corrective feedback has any facilitative effects on their acquisition.

Procedures

Each learner met with the native speaker interlocutor outside the classroom four times over a four-week period: three times in the first week (for the background questionnaire, language proficiency test, pretests, treatment, immediate posttests) and then three weeks later for the delayed posttests. To elicit the target structures, I used oral picture-cued, elicited production tasks. Similar tasks have been used in previous research and have been shown to be successful in eliciting the different types of relative clauses. To design such tasks, I followed a procedure used by McDaniel and associates (McDaniel & Lech, 2003; McDaniel, McKee, & Bernstein,

1998). In this procedure, the learner participates in an elicited oral production task with an experimenter, involving sets of objects or pictures. The participant first listens to the description of the image or object and then responds to a question posed in a way to prompt the learner to produce a relative clause. More specifically, the elicitation task was designed in the form of a PowerPoint slideshow controlled by the researcher. The slide show consisted of 19 sets of 5 images (95 slides). Each set contained an image of two or more persons or animals doing some actions followed by four variations of the same image each eliciting a relative clause. First the interlocutor (experimenter) introduced the first image in each set with some introductory information. Then she asked a question that required the student to produce a relative clause (e.g., Which car is the boy touching?). If the student produced a correct relative clause, the interlocutor went to the next slide. If not, she provided the student with a recast (in the recast group), a prompt (in the prompt group) or no feedback (in the control group). The task, the questions, and the elicitation instruction were piloted before the study with a group of ESL students and necessary adjustments were made. All the tasks were conducted individually with each learner, audio-recorded, and then transcribed for analysis.

Recasts were operationalized as the interlocutor's reformulation of the learner's erroneous utterance. To make sure that all learners receive the same type of recasts, the kind of recast provided involved full recasts with no additional stress. The following provides an example of the kind of recast used.

Example (3)
Learner: The bear is watching the man whose his wife lives in a tent.
Interlocutor: Oh. The bear is watching the man whose wife lives in a tent.

Prompts were operationalized as feedback that did not provide the correct form but rather provided opportunities for self-repair. Again to ensure that all prompts were the same, they all involved different forms of clarification requests (e.g., What did you say?; Sorry what?; Pardon me?; Could you repeat that?, etc.). No explicit types of prompt such as metalinguistic cues were used. The following provides an example of the kind of prompt used.

Example (4)
Learner: The house turned green that she is walking to.
Interlocutor: Sorry, say that again.

Outcome measures

Two outcome measures were used: uptake involving learner repair in the course of interaction and pretest-posttest measures. Immediate repair was defined as an utterance following feedback that involved some modification of the learners' original output. For the pretest-posttest measures, elicited oral picture-cued production tasks similar to those used in treatment tasks were developed. Each task consisted of 65 images (13 sets of 5) that were designed to elicit the types of relative clauses that were the focus of the study. Three versions were prepared as a pretest, posttest, and delayed posttest. The versions were the same in terms of the kind of relative clauses assessed. However, they differed in the images used. The versions were piloted with a group of ESL students before the study and necessary amendments were made.

Analysis

Identification of uptake and repair

The audio-recorded data for the feedback groups were transcribed after the interaction, using normal orthography. The transcribed interaction data were then examined for identification of erroneous utterances, type of feedback, uptake, and the degree of learner repair. Uptake was defined as any learner response following feedback including those that modified or repaired the error and those that did not do so such as wrong modification, repetition of the error, acknowledgments, etc. These responses were then coded in terms of the degree of repair. Following Nassaji (2007, 2011), three categories were distinguished: no repair, partial repair, and successful repair. No repair included responses that did not correctly repair the error, those that ignored the feedback, and those that simply acknowledged the feedback; partial repair partially corrected the utterance and successful repair correctly repaired the error. The coding was conducted by trained research assistants and was verified with the researcher.

Scoring the pretest-posttest oral production measures

To score learners' responses in the pretest and the posttests, a strict coding criterion was used, in which the responses were scored as either correct or incorrect. To this end, each response to the test items was examined for (a) whether the learner attempted to produce a relative clause and (b) if so, whether the relative clause involved an error. An erroneous relative clause was defined as a clause that involved one of the following errors: Relative pronoun omission, incorrect relative pronoun, sentence structure, relative clause-related preposition omission, pronoun resumption, and relative pronoun in wrong position.

Results

Learner uptake and repair

Altogether, the elicitation tasks elicited 2736 utterances by the two groups. These included those the involved correct relative clauses, erroneous relative clauses, and utterances with no relative clauses. Out of these, 1648 (60%) involved erroneous relative clauses. Of the erroneous relative clauses, 702 (42%) received recasts in the recast group and 946 (48%) received prompts in the prompt group. The analysis first examined learner uptake following the two types of feedback, and revealed that of the 702 erroneous utterances that received recasts, 108 (15%) led to uptake whereas of the 946 utterances that received prompts, 562 (59%) led to uptake. The Chi-Square test showed that this difference was significant: ($\chi 2$ (2, $N = 1648) = 323.69, p < .001$).

The analysis that examined the nature of uptake in terms of learner repair showed that of the 108 instances of uptake following recasts, 80 (74%) involved successful and partially successful repair, but only 14% of uptake following prompts involved repair. A Chi-square test revealed a significant difference among the frequencies of learner repair in response to the two types of feedback: $\chi 2$ (2, $N = 670) = 180.31, p < .001$. Therefore, while prompts were significantly more successful in eliciting responses from the learners, recasts were significantly more effective in eliciting successful repair.

Table 1. Frequency of erroneous relative clauses and degree of uptake and repair

	Erroneous relative clauses	Uptake	Successful repair	Partial repair	No repair
Recasts	702	108 (15%)	30 (28%)	50 (46%)	28 (26%)
Prompts	946	562 (59%)	24 (4%)	56 (10%)	482 (86%)
Total	1648	670	54	106	510

Pretest-posttest results

Table 2 presents the results of the pretest-posttest measures including the means and standard deviations. First a one-way ANOVA was conducted and showed no significant difference among the three groups on the pretest. However, a significant difference was observed on the immediate posttest [$F(2, 53) = 8.97, p<.001$] and the delayed posttest [$F(2, 53) = 4.95, p<.05$]. The effect sizes using partial eta-squared (η_p^2) were .26 and .16 for the immediate and delayed posttests respectively, which represent large to moderate effect sizes.

Table 2. *Means* and standard deviations for the feedback groups

		n	*Mean*	*Std.*	*F*	*Sig.*
Pretest	Recast	18	12.56	12.29	.050	.951
	Prompts	18	11.94	9.54		
	Control	18	11.39	11.25		
	Total	54	11.96	10.88		
Posttest	Recast	18	30.94	14.34	8.97	.000
	Prompts	18	18.39	10.85		
	Control	18	13.72	12.39		
	Total	54	21.02	14.38		
Delayed posttest	Recast	18	27.83	14.25	4.95	.011
	Prompts	18	19.22	11.71		
	Control	18	13.50	15.04		
	Total	54	20.19	14.73		

To examine the extent to the effects of recasts and prompts and also the mediating effects of language proficiency, a two-way repeated measures ANOVA was conducted using feedback types and language proficiency as between-group variables and time of testing (pretest, posttest, delayed posttest) as a within-group variable. The means and standard deviations for low- and high- proficiency leaners across feedback groups are presented in Table 3, The results revealed a significant main effect for time, $F(2, 96) = 39.65$, $p = .000$, $\eta_p^2 = .45$, suggesting that the learners' performance improved from the pretest to the posttests irrespective of feedback type. It also showed a main effect for feedback, $F(2, 48) = 4.41$, $p = .017$, $\eta_p^2 = .15$, suggesting that there was a difference among the three feedback groups irrespective of time. In addition, they showed a significant time by feedback interaction, $F(4, 96) = 10.60$, $p = .000$, $\eta_p^2 = .31$, which suggests that the performance of the three group differed across the three testing times. The analysis also revealed a three-way interaction among time, group, and language proficiency, $F(4, 96) = 3.01, p = .022$, $\eta_p^2 = .11$, suggesting that the effect of different feedback types from the pretest to the posttests depended on the learners' level of language proficiency.

Table 3. Means and standard deviations for low- and high- proficiency leaners across feedback groups

		Pretest		Posttest		Delayed posttest	
		Mean	*Std.*	*Mean*	*Std.*	*Mean*	*Std.*
A. Low	Recast	11.00	11.86	22.67	15.89	22.11	15.35
	Prompts	8.30	7.21	16.90	9.55	15.00	7.95
	Control	10.78	10.42	10.11	7.73	11.67	12.75
	Total	9.96	9.63	16.57	12.22	16.21	12.58
B. High	Recast	14.11	13.22	39.22	5.51	33.56	11.06
	Prompts	16.50	10.56	20.25	12.71	24.50	13.93
	Control	12.00	12.62	17.33	15.40	15.33	17.62
	Total	14.12	11.90	25.81	15.21	24.46	15.90

To explore the interaction effects of feedback by time, post-hoc pairwise with Bonferroni adjustments were conducted. These analyses (Table 4) revealed that, on the immediate posttest, the recast group significantly outperformed both the control group ($p < .001$) and the prompt group ($p < .05$). No significant difference was found between the prompt group and the control group. On the delayed posttest, no significant difference was found between the recast and prompt groups but the recast group continued to outperform the control group ($p < .01$). The three-way integration among time, feedback, and language proficiency was examined by using pairwise comparisons of each feedback types (recasts vs. prompts) within each proficiency level. These analyses revealed that for low-proficiency learners, the recasts group scored higher than the prompt group at the time of the two posttests but the difference was not statistically significant. For high proficiency learners, however, the recast group significantly outperformed the prompt group on the immediate posttest ($p < .01$) and the control group ($p < .01$). On the delayed posttest, the recast group scored higher than the prompt group but the difference was not statistically significant (see Table 5. The means are also graphically presented in Figures 1 and 2). Overall, these results indicate that language proficiency mediated the effect of recasts but not prompts. They also show that this differential effect was more evident for high than low proficiency leaners.

Table 4. Pairwise comparison of feedback types

	Feedback	*Sig.*
Posttest	Recasts vs. Prompts	.012
	Recasts vs. Control	.000
	Prompts vs. Control	.512
Delayed posttest	Recasts vs. Prompts	.155
	Recasts vs. Control	.008
	Prompts vs. Control	.430

Table 5. Pairwise comparisons of different feedback types within each language proficiency level

	Test		Mean Difference	Sig.
Low	Posttest	Recasts vs. Prompts	5.76	.869
		Recasts vs. Control	12.55	.083
		Prompts vs. Control	6.78	.641
	Delayed Posttest	Recasts vs. Prompts	7.11	.759
		Recasts vs. Control	10.44	.312
		Prompts vs. Control	3.33	1.000
High	Posttest	Recasts vs. Prompts	18.97	.005
		Recasts vs. Control	21.88	.001
		Prompts vs. Control	2.91	1.000
	Delayed posttest	Recasts vs. Prompts	9.05	.510
		Recasts vs. Control	18.22	.017
		Prompts vs. Control	9.167	.494

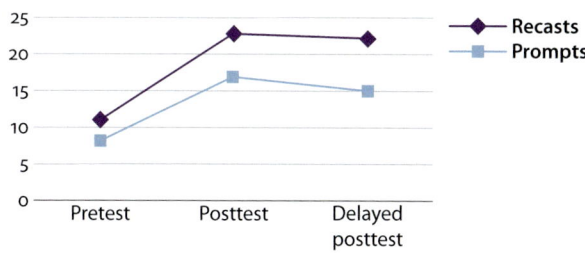

Figure 1. Low-proficiency learners' performance on the pretest-posttest measures

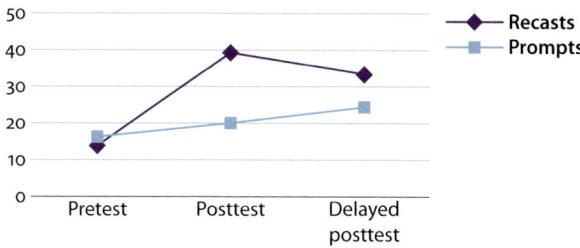

Figure 2. High-proficiency learners' performance on the pretest-posttest measures

Discussion

This study examined the differential effects of recasts versus prompts on learning English relative clauses, using immediate repair and pretest-posttest measures. The analysis that compared the two types of feedback in terms of uptake showed that while prompts led to a significantly higher rate of immediate responses to feedback, recasts led to a significantly higher rate of successful repair. Thus, while prompts were highly successful in pushing learners to produce a response, it was not successful in helping learners to correctly modify their erroneous output. This suggests that being pushed to produce output may not necessarily lead to successful modified output.

The pretest-posttest data showed that in both the immediate and the delayed posttests learners who received recasts outperformed those who did not (the control group). The recast group also outperformed the prompt group in the immediate posttests. No significant difference was found between the prompt and the control groups on either the immediate or delayed posttests.

These findings confirm those of previous studies that have shown facilitative effects for recasts. (e.g., Doughty & Varela, 1998; Han, 2002; Ishida, 2004; Mackey & Philp, 1998; Philp, 2003; Saito & Lyster, 2011). However, they also point to an advantage of recasts over prompts. One reason for this advantage could be that recasts provide positive evidence and also opportunities for negative evidence. Prompts provide opportunities for negative evidence only. Also learners may benefit more from recasts, particularly when the target structure is complex. Since in this study, the target structure was relative clauses, learners may not have as much declarative knowledge of the target form as those used in previous studies (such as English past -ed). This can explain why prompts did not lead to a high degree of repair as compared to recasts. For prompts to be successful, learners need to have some declarative knowledge of the target form, otherwise pushing them to correct their output may not lead to accurate output (Long, 2007). In such cases, they may benefit more from feedback that provides them with the target form and also possibly indicates to them how their interlanguage output differs from the targetlike input (Nassaji, 2016).

The findings of this study are different from those in Lyster's (2004) and Ammar and Spada's (2006) studies, which reported an advantage for prompts over recasts. Part of the reason could be that in those studies, as noted earlier, the feedback was used after form-focused instruction, and the kind of prompts was more explicit, involving metalinguistic cues. When feedback is associated with form-focused instruction and is also explicit, learners may better notice the corrective force of the feedback and hence benefit more from feedback.

As for the role of language proficiency, the findings showed that it mediated the effect of recasts but not prompts. In this study, more advanced level learners benefited significantly more from recasts than did less advanced level learners. But this was not true for the prompt group. Also, a significant difference was found between recasts and prompts for high-proficiency learners but not for low-proficiency learners. Thus, the differential effects of recasts over prompts were more evident for high- than low- proficiency leaners. The superior effects of recasts in more advanced level learners indicate that recasts might be more effective when learners have reached a certain level of language proficiency. Being more advanced, learners could have been more developmentally ready to learn from recasts. This finding is consistent with Mackey and Philp's (1998) study that found that the more advanced level learners benefited more from recasts on English question formation than less advanced level learners. However, the findings are different from those found in the Ammar and Spada (2006) study, which found that prompts and recasts were equally effective for high-proficiency learners and that prompts were more effective than recasts for low-proficiency learners. One reason for this difference could be related to the difference in the nature of prompts used in the two studies. As noted earlier, in Ammar and Spada, an implicit type of recasts was compared to multiple types of prompts, most of which were highly explicit. When learners are highly proficient, they benefit more from recasts because then they have the adequate level of language knowledge to notice and process implicit recasts. However, level of language proficiency may not mediate the effects of explicit feedback to the same extent. This is consistent with Nassaji' (2010) findings that showed that language proficiency was an important factor in learning from implicit feedback and not to the same degree in learning from explicit feedback.

Relevance for classroom instruction

The results of this study confirm that recasts facilitate language acquisition. They also provide evidence that recasts can be more effective than prompts when the target structure is complex and when the learners are not exposed to explicit instruction prior to feedback. Pedagogically, these findings suggest that, recasts can act as an effective strategy to draw learners' attention to form.

This study was conducted outside the classroom. Therefore, questions may be raised about the degree to which the findings can be relevant for classroom settings. Although we should be careful in drawing direct implications from laboratory studies to classroom contexts, the extent to which findings from such studies are applicable to classroom settings is an empirical question. Gass, Mackey, and Ross-Feldman (2005) analyzed and compared interactional patterns among dyads in a typical foreign language classroom context and interaction in a laboratory setting and found few differences between the two, particularly in terms of types of negotiation and feedback such as recasts. They did find differences, however, due to the type of task used. Based on their data, they concluded, "it is possible to suggest that interaction may not be as context-dependent as some researchers have claimed and may not vary depending on whether the participants are in the classroom or the laboratory." Therefore, they pointed out that it is inadvisable to make "the automatic assumption . . . that findings will be different in different settings." (p. 601). However, they also noted that there might be other factors that may determine the effectiveness of feedback in the classroom such as the kind of participant, the way they interact, and their social relations, which suggests the importance of replicating the results of laboratory research in classroom-based research.

The present study was experimental in nature. Although experimental studies allow for a systematic examination of the effect of feedback on L2 learning, it does so under controlled conditions. Thus, such studies are usually taken to be limited in terms of their ecological validity for naturalistic classroom settings. However, although classroom-based studies might be more ecologically valid, due to the many variables that cannot be controlled in naturalistic classroom research, it would be hard to tease apart the effect of feedback in these studies. Therefore, conducting experimental laboratory studies in such cases is helpful. An experimental research design allows a systematic examination of the effect of one or more independent variables (e.g., types of feedback and language proficiency in the present study) on a dependent variable (e.g., the learning of relative clauses in this study).

The present study addressed the role of oral corrective feedback, a highly frequent pedagogical strategy used by many teachers. It also concerned interactional feedback, a kind of feedback that occurs frequently during communicative interaction and has been shown to be useful for integrating attention to form and meaning in communicative settings. Because of that, although it was a laboratory study, the findings can be taken to be more relevant to classroom teaching than the findings of those studies that address theoretical questions. Of course, the study examined the effect of planned feedback that occurred intensively on a single target structure. This may be different from what often happens in classroom settings where most feedback may occur incidentally on a variety of language forms (e.g., Nassaji, 2010). However, in classroom settings, intensive feedback may also take place when teachers become selective and instead of addressing all errors, they focus on certain errors. Thus, the results of this study may have relevance for intensive classroom feedback.

Finally, in this study, feedback was provided during dyadic interaction. Most interactions in classroom settings may be whole-class interactions. However, dyadic interaction is also an important aspect of L2 classrooms. Research has indeed suggested that teachers do provide feedback on learners' errors when student work in small groups or when they interact with students one on one (Nassaji, 2013). Thus, although the dyadic focus of the study may limit the generalizability of the findings for whole-classroom interaction, it is likely that the findings are relevant for feedback that takes place in classroom dyadic interactions.

Conclusion

In the SLA literature both recasts and prompts have been proposed as a way of drawing learners' attention to form within communicative contexts. Most previous studies that have compared the two feedback types, and particularly those have reported evidence for the superiorly of prompts, have used the feedback in conjunction with explicit instruction. The present research compared the effects of the two feedback types in ways that did not conflate them with that of explicit instruction.

The results confirm that recasts facilitate language acquisition. They also suggest that, at least for complex target structures such as the one examined, learners may benefit more from recasts than prompts. Lyster and Ranta (2013) observed "[w]e would argue that good teaching should . . . place increased participatory demands on students, and one way to do so is by using [corrective feedback] types that push them to modify their output." (p. 174). While prompts can act as a useful strategy when learners have declarative knowledge or when the feedback is preceded with instruction (as prompts can provide opportunities for practice), it seems that recasts are also very effective particularly in facilitating target structures that are new to learners or for which learners do not yet have enough declarative knowledge. Recasts provide both positive evidence and opportunities for negative evidence. Due to this dual function, recasts can show learners the correct model of the target form and also how their interlanguage output differs from the target language. In so doing, recasts can act as a focus on form strategy on their own. However, given the various factors that may influence the effectiveness of both prompts and recasts, more research is needed to identify the conditions under which these feedback types are effective. In particular, further research is needed to compare the effective of these strategies in classroom contexts in ways their effects are not influenced by effects of form-focused instruction.

Acknowledgement

This research was supported by a research grant from the Social Sciences and Humanities Research Council of Canada (SSRCH). I would like to thank the students who participated in the study and the research assistants who helped with collecting the data.

References

Allwright, R. (1984). Why don't learners learn what teachers teach? The Interaction Hypothesis. In D. Singleton & D. Little (Eds.), *Language learning in formal and informal contexts* (pp. 3–18). Dublin: IRAL.

Ammar, A. (2008). Prompts and recasts: Differential effects on second language morphosyntax. *Language Teaching Research*, 12, 183–210. https://doi.org/10.1177/1362168807086287

Ammar, A., & Spada, N. (2006). One size fits all? Recasts, prompts, and L2 learning. *Studies in Second Language Acquisition*, 28, 543–574. https://doi.org/10.1017/S0272263106060268

De Bot, K. (1996). The psycholinguistics of the output hypothesis. *Language learning*, 46, 529–555. https://doi.org/10.1111/j.1467-1770.1996.tb01246.x

De López, K. J., Olsen, L. S., & Chondrogianni, V. (2014). Annoying Danish relatives: Comprehension and production of relative clauses by Danish children with and without SLI. *Journal of child language*, 41, 51–83. https://doi.org/10.1017/S0305000912000517

DeKeyser, R. (2000). The robustness of critical period effects in second language acquisition. *Studies in Second Language Acquisition*, 22, 499–533.

Dilans, G. (2010). Corrective feedback and L2 vocabulary development: Prompts and recasts in the adult ESL classroom. *Canadian Modern Language Review*, 66, 787–816. https://doi.org/10.3138/cmlr.66.6.787

Doughty, C. (2001). Cognitive underpinning of focus on form. In P. Robinson (Ed.), *Cognition and second language instruction* (pp. 206–257). Cambridge: Cambridge University Press. https://doi.org/10.1017/CBO9781139524780.010

Doughty, C., & Varela, E. (1998). Communicative focus on form. In C. Doughty & J. Williams (Eds.), *Focus on form in classroom second language acquisition* (pp. 114–138). Cambridge: Cambridge University Press.

Ellis, R. (2007). The differential effects of corrective feedback on two grammatical structures. In A. Mackey (Ed.), *Conversational interaction in second language acquisition: A collection of empirical studies* (pp. 339–360). Oxford: Oxford University Press.

Ellis, R. (2009). Corrective feedback and teacher development. *L2 journal*, 1, 3–18.

Fu, T. & Nassaji. H. (2016). Corrective feedback, learner uptake, and feedback perception in a Chinese as a foreign language classroom. *Studies in Second Language Learning and Teaching*, 6, 159–181.

Gass, S., Mackey, A., & Ross-Feldman, L. (2005). Task-based interactions in classroom and laboratory settings. *Language learning*, 55, 575–611. https://doi.org/10.1111/j.0023-8333.2005.00318.x

Goo, J. (2012). Corrective feedback and working memory capacity in interaction-driven L2 learning. *Studies in Second Language Acquisition*, 34, 445–474. https://doi.org/10.1017/S0272263112000149

Goo, J., & Mackey, A. (2013). The case against the case against recasts. *Studies in Second Language Acquisition*, 35, 127–165. https://doi.org/10.1017/S0272263112000708

Han, Z. (2002). A study of the impact of recasts on tense consistency in L2 output. *Tesol Quarterly*, 36, 543–572. https://doi.org/10.2307/3588240

Ishida, M. (2004). Effects of recasts on the acquisition of the aspectual form -te i- (ru) by learners of Japanese as a foreign language. *Language learning*, 54, 311–394. https://doi.org/10.1111/j.1467-9922.2004.00257.x

Iwashita, N. (2003). Negative feedback and positive evidence in task-based interaction: Differential effects on L2 development. *Studies in Second Language Acquisition*, 25, 1–36. https://doi.org/10.1017/S0272263103000019

Leeman, J. (2003). Recasts and second language development: Beyond negative evidence. *Studies in Second Language Acquisition, 25,* 37–63. https://doi.org/10.1017/S0272263103000020

Loewen, S., & Philp, J. (2006). Recasts in adults English L2 classrooms: Characteristics, explicitness, and effectiveness. *Modern Language Journal, 90,* 536–556. https://doi.org/10.1111/j.1540-4781.2006.00465.x

Long, M. (1996). The role of the linguistic environment in second language acquisition. In W. Ritchie & T. Bhatia (Eds.), *Handbook of second language acquisition* (pp. 413–468). San Diego, CA: Academic Press.

Long, M. (2007). *Problems in SLA.* Mahwah, NJ: Lawrence Erlbaum Associates.

Long, M., Inagaki, S., & Ortega, L. (1998). The role of implicit negative feedback in SLA: Models and recasts in Japanese and Spanish. *Modern Language Journal, 82,* 357–371. https://doi.org/10.1111/j.1540-4781.1998.tb01213.x

Long, M., & Robinson, P. (1998). Focus on form: Theory, research and practice. In C. Doughty & J. Williams (Eds.), *Focus on form in classroom language acquisition* (pp. 15–41). Cambridge: Cambridge University Press.

Lyster, R. (1998). Recasts, repetition, and ambiguity in L2 classroom discourse. *Studies in Second Language Acquisition, 20,* 51–81. https://doi.org/10.1017/S027226319800103X

Lyster, R. (2004). Differential effects of prompts and recasts in form-focused instruction. *Studies in Second Language Acquisition, 26,* 399–432. https://doi.org/10.1017/S0272263104263021

Lyster, R., & Izquierdo, J. (2009). Prompts versus recasts in dyadic interaction. *Language learning, 59,* 453–498. https://doi.org/10.1111/j.1467-9922.2009.00512.x

Lyster, R., & Mori, H. (2006). Interactional feedback and instructional counterbalance. *Studies in Second Language Acquisition, 28,* 269–300. https://doi.org/10.1017/S0272263106060128

Lyster, R., & Ranta, L. (2013). Counterpoint piece: The case for variety in corrective feedback research. *Studies in Second Language Acquisition, 35,* 167–184. https://doi.org/10.1017/S027226311200071X

Mackey, A., Gass, S., & McDonough, K. (2000). How do learners perceive interactional feedback? *Studies in Second Language Acquisition, 22,* 471–497. https://doi.org/10.1017/S0272263100004022

Mackey, A., & Philp, J. (1998). Conversational interaction and second language development: Recasts, responses, and red herrings? *Modern Language Journal, 82,* 338–356. https://doi.org/10.1111/j.1540-4781.1998.tb01211.x

Mackey, A., Philp, J., Fujii, A., Egi, T., & Tatsumi, T. (2002). Individual differences in working memory, noticing of interactional feedback and L2 development. In P. Robinson (Ed.), *Individual differences and instructed language learning* (pp. 181–208). Amsterdam: John Benjamins. https://doi.org/10.1075/lllt.2.12mac

McDaniel, D., & Lech, D. (2003). The production system's formulation of relative clause structures: Evidence from polish. *Language Acquisition, 11,* 63–97. https://doi.org/10.1207/s15327817la1102_1

McDaniel, D., McKee, C., & Bernstein, J. (1998). How children's relatives solve a problem for minimalism. *Language, 74,* 308–334. https://doi.org/10.1353/lan.1998.0177

McDonough, K. (2007). Interactional feedback and the emergence of simple past activity verbs in L2 English. In A. Mackey (Ed.), *Conversational interaction in second language acquisition: A collection of empirical studies* (pp. 323–338). Oxford: Oxford University Press.

Nabei, T., & Swain, M. (2002). Learner awareness of recasts in classroom interaction: A case study of an adult EFL student's second language learning. *Language Awareness, 11,* 43–63. https://doi.org/10.1080/09658410208667045

Nassaji, H. (2007). Elicitation and reformulation and their relationship with learner repair in dyadic interaction. *Language learning*, 57, 511–548. https://doi.org/10.1111/j.1467-9922.2007.00427.x

Nassaji, H. (2009). Effects of recasts and elicitations in dyadic interaction and the role of feedback explicitness. *Language Learning*, 59, 411–452.

Nassaji, H. (2010). The occurrence and effectiveness of spontaneous focus on form in adult ESL classrooms. *Canadian Modern Language Review*, 66, 907–933. https://doi.org/10.3138/cmlr.66.6.907

Nassaji, H. (2011). Immediate learner repair and its relationship with learning targeted forms in dyadic interaction. *System*, 39, 17–29. https://doi.org/10.1016/j.system.2011.01.016

Nassaji, H. (2014). Interactional feedback: Insights from theory and research. In A. Benati, C. Laval, & A. M. (Eds.), *The grammar dimension in instructed second language learning: Theory, research and practice* (pp. 103–123). London: Bloomsbury.

Nassaji, H. (2015). *Interactional feedback dimension in instructed second language learning*. London: Bloomsbury.

Nassaji, H. (2016). Anniversary article: Interactional feedback in second language teaching and learning: A synthesis and analysis of current research. *Language Teaching Research*, 20, 535–562. https://doi.org/10.1177/1362168816644940

Nassaji, H. (2017). The effectiveness of extensive versus intensive recasts for learning L2 grammar. *The Modern Language Journal*, 101, 353–368.

Philp, J. (2003). Constraints on 'noticing the gap': Nonnative speakers' noticing of recasts in ns-nns interaction. *Studies in Second Language Acquisition*, 25, 99–126.

Pica, T. (1994). Research on negotiation: What does it reveal about second-language learning conditions, processes, and outcomes? *Language learning*, 44, 493–527. https://doi.org/10.1111/j.1467-1770.1994.tb01115.x

Saito, K., & Lyster, R. (2011). Effects of form focused instruction and corrective feedback on L2 pronunciation development of /r/ by Japanese learners of English. *Language Learning*, 62, 595–633. https://doi.org/10.1111/j.1467-9922.2011.00639.x

Sheen, Y. (2004). Corrective feedback and learner uptake in communicative classrooms across instructional settings. *Language Teaching Research*, 8, 263–300. https://doi.org/10.1191/1362168804lr146oa

Sheen, Y. (2006). Exploring the relationship between characteristics of recasts and learner uptake. *Language Teaching Research*, 10, 361–392. https://doi.org/10.1191/1362168806lr203oa

Sheen, Y. (2007). The effects of corrective feedback, language aptitude, and learner attitudes on the acquisition of English articles. In A. Mackey (Ed.), *Conversational interaction in second language acquisition: A collection of empirical studies* (pp. 301–322). Oxford: Oxford University Press.

Sheen, Y. (2008). Recasts, language anxiety, modified output, and L2 learning. *Language learning*, 58, 835–874. https://doi.org/10.1111/j.1467-9922.2008.00480.x

Trofimovich, P., Ammar, A., & Gatbonton, E. (2007). How effective are recasts? The role of attention, memory, and analytical ability. In A. Mackey (Ed.), *Conversational interaction in second language acquisition: A series of empirical studies* (pp. 171–195). Oxford: Oxford University Press.

Yang, Y., & Lyster, R. (2010). Effects of form-focused practice and feedback on Chinese EFL learnersíacquisition of regular and irregular past tense forms. *Studies in Second Language Acquisition*, 32, 235–263. https://doi.org/10.1017/S0272263109990519

CHAPTER 7

The effects of multiple exposures to explicit information

Evidence from two types of learning problems and practice conditions

Goretti Prieto Botana and Robert DeKeyser
University of Southern California / University of Maryland

The role of explicit information (EI) has long been debated in second language acquisition. Numerous studies report null effects for EI (e.g., VanPatten and Oikennon, 1996) calling for its diminution, whereas just as many point to its facilitative potential (e.g., VanPatten et al., 2013 and others), suggesting it should remain part of instruction. Previous EI studies varied with respect to the targeted learning problem, practice conditions, and EI accessibility throughout the experiment, factors which could hold the key to the divergent results found in the literature. In order to address this, a study was conducted to assess the effects of (a) multiple vs. no exposure to EI when targeting (b) learnability problems of structural vs. semantic nature and (c) under task-essential (TE) and non-task-essential practice conditions. One hundred and thirty learners of Spanish were randomly assigned to eight experimental conditions and a control group. After treatment, participants completed picture-matching, fill-in-the-gap and sentence interpretation tasks. Immediate posttest results revealed that EI was crucial for benefits to obtain under non-TE conditions whereas under TE conditions it appeared to be expendable depending on the task.

Keywords: Explicit Information, inductive instruction, deductive instruction, Spanish *ser/estar*, Spanish *OVS*

Literature review

Various instructed SLA studies in the nineties called into question the so-called "traditional" classroom practices, of which explicit deductive information was generally a part. The first such study to isolate explicit deductive information as a variable was VanPatten and Oikkenon (1996), which sought to determine the role

https://doi.org/10.1075/lllt.52.07bot

of EI in the gains generated by processing instruction (PI), a grammar teaching approach that seeks to alter default and erroneous processing strategies promoting correct form-meaning mappings instead (e.g., VanPatten 1996, 2004). PI combines metalinguistic information with referential and affective structured input (SI). In the study, a group receiving explicit deductive information (dubbed EI Only) was compared to a group receiving referential and affective practice (SI), as well as a group receiving both of those elements combined (PI). Results revealed that the group receiving explicit deductive information did not improve, whereas the two groups receiving structured input practice improved significantly and to a similar degree. These results appeared to indicate that the gains for the practice groups could not have originated in explicit deductive information, which led to the conclusion that the latter was not beneficial for learning grammar.

VanPatten and Oikkenon (1996), whose target structure was Spanish Object-Verb-Sentences (OVS) spurred numerous replications in various languages. In Italian, Benati (2004a, 2004b), featured Italian gender agreement and future tense, respectively, as target linguistic units. They showed EI yielded no benefits, while both practice groups, whether they had received EI or not, made significant and comparable gains. In French, Wong (2004) focused on the French negative particle *de* and also reported significantly better results for SI and PI over EI and control groups. In line with VanPatten and Oikennon (1996), then, all three studies suggest explicit deductive information offers no benefit in grammar learning.

In German, Henry, Culman and VanPatten (2009) and Culman, Henry and VanPatten (2009) gauged the effects of EI in the acquisition of OVS. The first study featured two different groups, +EI and −EI. The data showed that the +EI group took significantly fewer trials to reach criterion, defined as the number of trials learners needed before they could process three target items and a distracter correctly (Henry et al., 2009, p. 570). This was also the case for Culman et al. (2009), where two PI groups of different proficiencies were also found to start processing OVS sentences faster than the analogous SI groups, suggesting that EI provision has a beneficial effect.

The majority of the replications were in Spanish, however. Farley (2004) set out to test whether PI benefits obtained with structures of greater complexity and with more semantic content (as opposed to the structural nature of OVS), such as the subjunctive. Results showed that both PI and SI groups made significant gains with the treatment, but they also revealed an interaction between time and treatment, which appeared to originate from the greater gains obtained by the PI group. This suggested that although SI was sufficient for gains to occur, the benefits obtained from that type of practice were not equal to those generated by the PI treatment, and invited speculation of a possible facilitative role for EI where form-meaning mapping is obscure.

Fernández (2008) conducted a study that tracked students' behavior online while engaged in practice. Featuring the classic explicit deductive information in isolation, versus affective and referential practice with and without EI, Fernández focused on OVS sentences as well as the Spanish subjunctive. Her data were analyzed to determine trials to criterion. While results aligned with VanPatten and Oikkenon (1996), revealing no difference between the two treatment groups in OVS processing, the EI group started to process the subjunctive forms significantly sooner than both practice groups, lending credence to Farley's (2004) claim that EI may be beneficial with certain linguistic phenomena.

Further evidence to the same effect comes from Russell (2012), yet another study on the subjunctive. Russell (2012) compared the effects of SI and PI alone to their effects when combined with visually enhanced input (VIE) and added a traditional instruction group to serve as control. In line with previous studies on the subjunctive, results offered some evidence of the facilitative effect of EI, manifested in this case by the superiority in interpretation of the +PI +VIE condition over +SI −VIE, and a lack of difference between +PI +VIE and +PI −VIE, or any other group.

White and DeMil (2013) explored the relative contribution of EI in the absence of strategies by way of a study featuring the classic PI and SI conditions in comparison to a group who received form-related explicit information (FREI), but no strategies. After receiving training in Spanish OVS sentences, results revealed only PI and SI groups made significant gains in interpretation tasks, and importantly, that PI retained significantly more gains than SI in the delayed posttest that was administered three weeks after treatment.

Finally, VanPatten et al. (2013) analyzed the correlation between grammatical sensitivity, and the outcomes for +EI and −EI (i.e., PI and SI) groups across four experiments involving French, German, Spanish, Russian. Three of the four experiments revolved around the OVS, with the fourth, for French, targeting the causative *faire*. Results varied across languages, with Spanish and Russian exhibiting parallel results and giving evidence of neither an effect for EI nor a substantial correlation with grammatical sensitivity. In the case of German, a beneficial EI effect was found, echoing Henry et al. (2009) and Culman et al. (2009), and accompanied by significant correlations for grammatical sensitivity for the +EI group only. The French learners who received EI started processing causative *faire* sentences correctly significantly sooner, but no significant correlation was found for grammatical sensitivity.

In general, these beg for the question as to whether semantically oriented processing problems may necessitate explicit deductive information, whereas for learnability problems of a structural nature providing practice of a certain type may suffice. As DeKeyser (2003) argues, it is possible that in the latter case the combination of relevant practice and feedback leads learners to infer themselves the rules that are simply provided as EI to PI groups. That being the case, it becomes interesting to determine under what circumstances EI may become necessary.

Crucially, when considering the null effects reported in the studies reviewed above, it should be born in mind that learners were given a single chance to review EI prior to commencing the treatment. This represents an important weakness with regard to ecological validity. Moreover, a single exposure would seem to make any positive effects that EI could have contingent upon the degree of attention participants paid during exposure and how much of the EI they remembered, factors that were never controlled for.

In addition to questions relating to the role of EI, as was mentioned at the outset of this paper, all the studies reviewed above featured designs that incorporated task-essential practice. Coined by Loschky and Bley-Vroman (1993), the term TE refers to practice conditions under which "not only the task cannot be completed without the grammatical point" but also "the grammatical point itself is the 'essence' of what is being attended to" (Loschky & Bley-Vroman 1993, p. 139). Loschky and Bley-Vroman (1993), as well as others after them, have claimed TE practice conditions facilitate development of grammatical knowledge through hypothesis testing and inferencing, due to the capacity of TE to raise learner consciousness of the target structure. Given that this condition appears to have invariably co-occurred with SI practice, examining whether the presence or absence of that TE component of SI in any way impacts EI expendability is in order. On the one hand, TE may allow for benefits attributed to SI to be explained more parsimoniously. On the other hand, if TE presence plays a part in EI expendability, such findings would allow for proper qualification of the role of metalinguistic information in grammar learning (structural or semantic).

The present study

In an attempt to find out whether the role of explicit deductive information may be moderated by the type of processing problem being addressed and/or the type of access students have to it, a pretest-posttest study featuring four experimental groups and a control was designed. The four experimental groups combined presence or absence of (a) explicit deductive information (henceforth +EI and −EI) and (b) practice with or without the task-essentialness that allows for induction of explicit knowledge (henceforth +TE and −TE).

Method

Participants

Participants for the present study were native speakers of English enrolled in first- and second-semester Spanish. A total of 132 took part[1]. Although students were randomly assigned to experimental conditions and control, all sessions required for the study took place within class time, either in the regular classroom or in a computer lab.

Procedure

Targeted structure

The linguistic phenomena targeted in our study are Object (O) Verb (V) Subject (S) sentences as well as the *ser/estar* distinction in Spanish. Although the canonical order in the target language is SVO, due to its rich morphology, Spanish exhibits a fairly flexible word order. Structures featuring the direct object pronoun in sentence initial position, and in which the subject appears post-verbally, are both grammatical and common in the language. It is a documented phenomenon that such structures are problematic for language learners both in L1 and L2 acquisition. Evidence from various studies indicates that both first (Bates et al., 1984; Bever, 1970) and second language learners (Gass, 1989; LoCoco, 1987) tend to interpret the first noun phrase (NP) in any sentence as the subject (VanPatten's First Noun Principle). When parsing OVS structures, the strategy of parsing the first NP as the subject results in the erroneous allocation of agent and theme roles. Thus, in a sentence such as "lo abraza María" (*Him embraces María*), learners tend to understand the sentence as "Él abraza a María" (*He embraces María*). Perhaps because they represent a departure from default processing strategies of NSs of English, OVS structures have been the target structure of choice for the vast majority of studies seeking to test the benefits of PI. In light of that fact, and in an attempt to obtain results that are interpretable within the existing research framework, the present study will also adopt OVS sentences as one of its target structures.

---

1.   Only the data from participants who completed the entire pretest, immediate posttest, de-layed posttest sequence was included in the analysis. However, In order to preserve as many participants as possible, elimination was done on a task-by-task basis. In other words, any participant who did not complete a session (i.e., the pre-, post-, or delayed posttest) of one of the tasks was eliminated from the analysis pertaining to that task, but kept for analysis of any other task where he/she had completed all testing sessions.

In addition to OVS, this study sought to examine the effects of EI and TE on the acquisition of a second linguistic phenomenon, namely, the *ser/estar* distinction in verb+adjective predicates. The rationale to include this second structure is that, given the preponderance of OVS structures in PI research, it is important to test whether benefits recorded for PI extend to structures that pose different processing problems. *Ser/estar* has been examined in one PI study, reported in Cheng (2002, 2004), which investigated the acquisition of this distinction from the pure TI vs. PI vantage point. The present study is an attempt to contribute to the rather scant evidence about the suitability of PI to address the processing problem this structure poses.

Indisputably a difficult distinction, *ser/estar* arguably constitutes a different processing problem from OVS. First, rather than drawing on word order or the First Noun Principle, the problematic nature of *ser/estar* presumably originates in the fact that it requires learners to perceive a difference not present in their NL. While correct OVS processing demands that learners refrain from automatically processing the first noun as the subject (thus allowing for the possibility that the theme may come first), in the case of the *ser/estar* distinction learners are faced with the need to separate a single element of their NL into two different representations and to learn the specific rules that govern the use of one as opposed to the other in different contexts. The task of identifying contexts that call for each of the two different copula manifestations is made particularly difficult by a number of factors. First, as already mentioned, both *ser* and *estar* map onto a single element – the verb 'to be' in English. Therefore, learners need to grasp which uses of the verb 'to be' should be mapped onto *ser* versus *estar*. In addition, although there are certain environments in which *ser* and *estar* occur in obligatory complementary distribution, the majority of predicates will allow both verbs with the choice of one versus the other resulting in semantic changes that range in subtlety. Thus, more often than not judgment of the linguistic context on a case-by-case basis becomes necessary, as application of a merely form-based rule or rote memorization of expressions that go with *ser* and *estar* are not viable options. This involves judging the nature of predicates and the adjectives contained in them in terms of dichotomous categories such as "inherent versus circumstantial" and "permanent vs. temporary". However, those distinctions only apply probabilistically, since additional contextual factors, including speakers' perception of perfectivity, are often decisive to deem a trait as inherent or permanent vs. circumstantial or temporary. This means that where object pronouns offer virtually no variation in terms of the meaning they map onto, copula choice is notorious for native speaker variation (Silva-Corvalán, 1994). Thus, one might argue that whereas, in the case of object pronouns integration into interlanguage (IL) grammars is hindered by constant connection to the wrong meaning, driven by a deeply ingrained processing strategy, the incorporation of *ser/estar* distinction into IL grammar is arrested by the inability to delineate the meaning that should be mapped to each of the copula verbs.

Unsurprisingly, research on the acquisition of *ser* and *estar* has shown that it is precisely those instances in which both *ser* and *estar* verbs are possible options that are acquired latest, suggesting that they are more difficult for learners to acquire (VanPatten, 1985; 1987). As it seems that it is in those predicates that the heart of the *ser/estar* problem lies, the present project investigated exclusively adjective predicates where both *ser* and *estar* could be correct, specifically the inherent vs. circumstantial distinction. Thus, we considered any instances of *ser/estar* utterances where copula choice could be successfully decided upon following the inherent vs. circumstantial rule suitable for inclusion in the study.

Materials

The present study featured materials consisting of two different elements: explicit information and practice tasks. EI was composed of two slides where the rules concerning the target structures were laid out and accompanied by examples (see Appendix A). The practice consisted of picture matching and sentence interpretation activities for each of the target structures. Two versions of each type of task were created. One version incorporated task-essentialness (see Appendix B) while the other one did not (see Appendix C). Both conditions depicted object pronouns in sentence initial position for OVS, and *ser* and *estar* in inherent versus circumstantial situations. However, in non-TE conditions the tasks could be solved by focusing on items other than the targeted linguistics units (either the number of objects, number agreement or the semantics of the verb). Thus, while in non-TE conditions, learners were exposed to the target items, not connecting them to their respective meanings did not result in the choice of the incorrect response and therefore the target form was never essential to complete the task. In the +TE items, learners were required to decide whether the object pronoun in sentence-initial position represented the agent or recipient of the action in order to successfully pick a response option. In *ser/estar* items, learners were required to correctly associate inherent situations with *ser* and circumstantial ones with *estar*. Thus, in +TE conditions, the target form was essential for successful task completion. In addition to the experimental practice described above, an additional picture-matching test targeting gender agreement was created for participants in the control group.

The presence or absence of the EI slides and the two versions of the picture-matching task were used to create the conditions [+/−TE] and [+/−EI] described above. As was mentioned previously, EI conditions (i.e., [+EI−TE] group and the [+EI + TE] group) in the present study encompassed exposure to EI not once, but five times throughout the course of the session. More specifically, participants were asked to review the EI right before starting the treatment, then again after item 1, (i.e., they had the chance to check their comprehension of the metalinguistic information), and three times more after target items 4, 8 and 16.

All efforts were made to use cognates and/or high frequency lexical items to prevent vocabulary comprehension issues from hindering the establishment of form-meaning connections that the practice intended to trigger. In addition, a gloss was provided for all verbs to ensure that vocabulary problems did not interfere with learner performance and learning. The treatment presented the 20 sentence-matching task items first and only then the 20 sentence interpretation task items.

A task corresponding to each of the outcome measures (a sentence-matching task, a sentence interpretation task and production task) was administered to participants in each of the three testing sessions: pretest, immediate posttest and delayed posttest.

Instruments

All three tasks were also administered prior to the treatment in order to gauge learners' pre-existing knowledge of the target structures. In the case of the picture matching and sentence interpretation tasks, the format and specifications were identical to those of the task-essential activities used during the treatment. Unlike the treatment, however, the picture matching and sentence interpretation tasks in the pretest (as well as the production task, for that matter) were all paper-based. The motivation not to adopt a computer-based delivery was one of convenience, as the paper format allowed us to rapidly administer testing instruments to intact classes.[2] Like the pretest, post-treatment tasks were also paper-based.

The picture-matching task comprised a total of 20 target items. Each item featured a sentence accompanied by two pictures. Participants were required to decide which of the two pictures corresponded to the sentence. For OVS, items were formed by a third-person singular object pronoun, a verb and a subject (in

---

2. Administering the testing instrument in paper-based format allowed us to be less disruptive in the classes where data were collected, though it did so at the expense of validity, since backtracking was an option. In addition to this, the language lab is in high demand; as a result the number of times that each class can have access to it is limited and fixed in accordance to the needs of all language courses. Conducting the five meetings that participation in this study required in the lab would have monopolized all lab hours from the courses involved in the research. For these and other reasons, it was deemed preferable to have all our outcome measures be paper-based, such that data collection for pretest and delayed posttest could be carried out in the regular classroom, while also keeping testing format as similar as possible from one session to another.

the third person as well). For *ser/estar* they comprised the verb in the third person singular followed by an adjective.

In the sentence interpretation task, distribution of target items was identical to the one featured in the picture matching task. In this case, however, learners were asked to match a sentence containing the target item to one of two interpretations. The interpretations were in English to ensure proper comprehension.

The fill-in-the-gap production task was included in order to test whether the benefits of PI extended beyond perception and whether they did so equally under TE and non-TE conditions. Production items featured a single picture, which was complemented by a prompt sentence featuring a gap where the target item should go. In order to prevent learners from providing answers that would be difficult to interpret, each item in the production task was preceded by a line prompting participants to fill in the gap with *lo* or *la*, in OVS items, and *es* or *está*, *ser/estar* items. Although providing two options made this task as close to a multiple-choice task as a production task can be, it was still informative in a way that neither picture matching nor sentence interpretation tasks could (a claim that was supported by our results).

As was the case with the picture-matching task, the production task included a total of 20 OVS target items and 40 gender-agreement-based distracters. No feedback was given during the pretest.

Immediately after the treatment session for each of the target structures learners were administered a posttest in the form of paper-based sentence-matching, sentence-interpretation, and production posttests. The posttest was an alternative version of the pretest[3].

Results

Pretest scores for both target units were submitted to a one-way ANOVA to confirm that groups were comparable at pretest. Posttest scores for each condition were submitted to ANCOVAs, with pretest scores as the covariate. Scores for each task were submitted to a separate analysis, for the posttest and delayed posttest scores.

---

3.   An ad-hoc examination using Rasch analysis revealed means of difficulty of 49.77 and 50.90 logits for the pretest and posttest respectively.

Production task

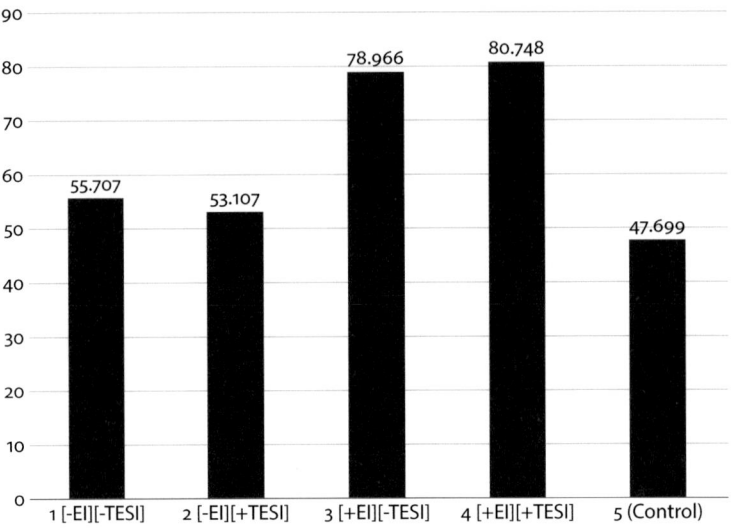

Figure 1. OVS production

As Figure 1 shows, for OVS both [+EI] groups emerged as the highest-scoring groups in production, followed by [−EI] groups and finally the control group.

After submitting the scores to an ANCOVA, a main effect for Group emerged, $F(4,122) = 9.19$; $p < .001$. A Bonferroni post-test revealed that this main effect was due to the differences between the control group and [+EI] groups, as well as differences between [−EI] and [+EI] groups. The fact that [+EI] groups were superior whether with TE or not, suggests that the gains are due to the EI (as opposed to TE). This is further confirmed by the significant difference recorded between the [−EI +TE] and the [+EI +TE].

In the case of *ser/estar* (Figure 2), the analysis also yielded a main effect for Group, $F(4,121) = 12.88$; $p < .001$. A Bonferroni correction revealed that those differences were located between Group 1 [−EI −TE] and all other experimental groups, as well as between the control group and all four experimental groups. These results seem to suggest that for *ser/estar*, both [+TE] and [+EI] alone result in significant gains. That is, combining [+TE] and [+EI] does not seem to result in greater gains than exposure to one of them alone, in the absence of EI.

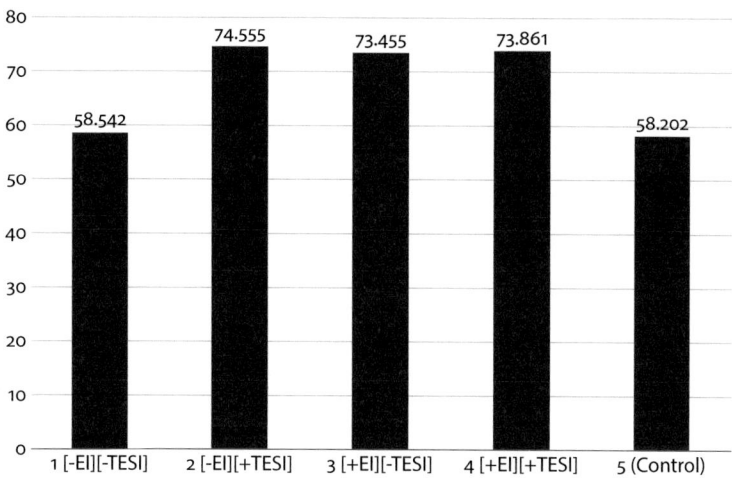

Figure 2. *Ser/estar* production

Sentence matching task

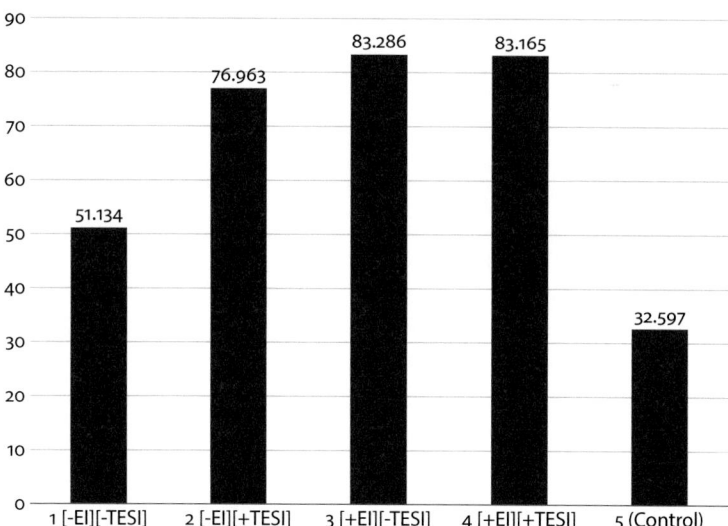

Figure 3. OVS picture matching

Results for OVS sentence matching (Figure 3), were similar to those in production in as much as the control group and [−EI −TE] exhibited the lowest performance, with [+TE] and [+EI] groups scoring much higher. Analysis of the scores yielded a main effect for Group, $F(4,120) = 11.69$, $p < .01$. A post-hoc test located the difference in means between Group 1 [–EI –TE] and all other experimental groups. These results are suggestive of the superiority of treatments that include EI or TE. Further, lack of difference between [+TE] and [+EI] groups suggest that while receiving either EI or TE practice results in comparable significant gains, combining EI and TE does not offer an additional benefit. There were also differences between the control group and Groups 2 [–EI +TE], 3 [+EI –TE] and 4 [+EI+TE]. No difference was found between the performance of the control group and [–EI –TE], which would indicate that receiving non-Task-Essential practice but no EI is as good as not receiving any treatment at all.

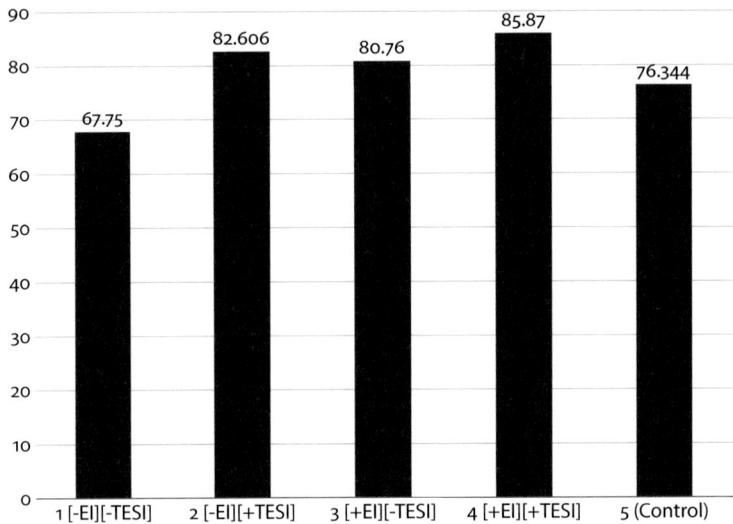

Figure 4. *Ser/estar* picture matching

The pattern of results in *ser/estar* picture matching mirrored that of OVS, with [+EI] and [+TE] groups scoring highest (Figure 4). The differences in scores yielded a significant effect for Group, $F(4,121) = 7.65$; $p < .001$. Pairwise comparisons revealed that the differences, once again, originated in the contrast between Group 1 [–EI –TE] and all other experimental groups, again suggesting superiority of [+TE] and [+EI] treatments. Importantly, however, in this case the control group was not different from any of the experimental groups. This seems to indicate that none of the groups learned very much, as shown by the fact that none of the treatments yielded an effect significantly larger than the practice effect in the control group.

Sentence interpretation task

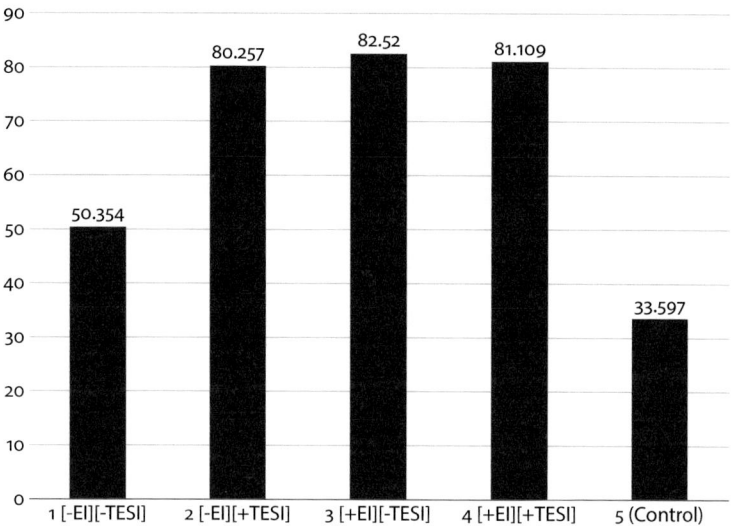

Figure 5. OVS sentence interpretation

As Figures 5 and 6 show, Sentence Interpretation also yielded superiority for [+EI] and [+TE] groups.

After analysis of OVS results, a group effect emerged, $F(4,120) = 17.57$; $p < .001$. Results from the Bonferroni post-hoc test revealed that the differences were between [−EI][−TE SI] and all other experimental groups. There was also a difference between Group 5 (Control) and Groups 2 [−EI +TE], 3[+EI][−TE SI] and 4 [+EI] [+TE SI] but no difference between control and [−EI −TE]. This means that for OVS, results in Sentence Matching and Sentence Interpretation are identical.

Lastly, for *ser/estar*, analysis of the adjusted means yielded a main effect for Group, $F(4,123) = 14.082$; $p < .001$. Post-hoc analyses showed the usual differences between Group 1 [−EI −TE] and all other experimental groups. In this case, the difference between Groups 1 [−EI −TE] and 5 (Control) also appeared to be marginally significant. In addition, although no difference was found between [+EI] groups (Groups 3 and 4), scores for Groups 2 [−EI +TE] and 4 [+EI +TE] were significantly different. This would indicate that in sentence interpretation for *ser/ estar*, receiving EI in addition to TE practice did result in additional gains.

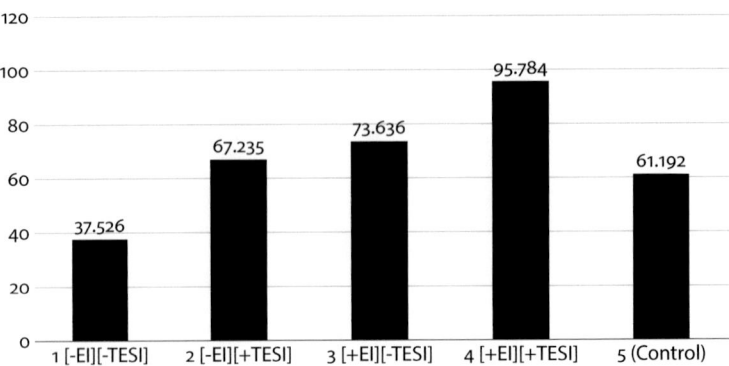

Figure 6. *Ser/estar* sentence interpretation

Discussion

In general, results from this study appear to suggest that given ample access to review it, EI has a facilitative effect for both OVS, a structural learnability problem, and *ser/estar*, a semantic learnability problem. This is shown by the fact that conditions receiving EI and conditions receiving practice under TE conditions improved from pre to posttest for bother linguistic targets and all tasks.

With the exception of OVS production, where TE alone yielded gains that were inferior to those obtained by groups receiving EI, the benefits generated by EI provision and TE practice were comparable. Further, in general, it would appear that so long as TE practice is present, EI does not have an additional facilitative effect. That said, in the case of OVS production and *ser/estar* Sentence Interpretation combining TE practice and EI did lead to greater learning as compared to groups who received either TE practice or EI only. This finding is particularly interesting in that is appears to indicate that different learnability problems or even different tasks may call for a different type of instruction, with some requiring approaches that include overt provision of EI, as well as TE practice. Perhaps our most important finding would be that, with the exception of *ser/estar* Sentence Interpretation, groups receiving non-Task-Essential practice and no EI performed in parallel to the control group, which received no treatment at all. We interpret these findings to mean that unless rules governing a phenomenon are available to the learner, whether deductively by way of overt EI or inductively by way of a practice environment such as TE, which allows the learner to derive them, no learning can be expected.

Structure	Immediate posttest	Group effect?	Location of statistical differences
OVS	Production	YES	G1 [−EI −TE]≠ G3[+EI −TE] & G4[+EI +TE] G2 [−EI+TE] ≠ G3[+EI −TE] & G4[+EI +TE] G5 (Control) ≠ G3[+EI −TE] & G4[+EI +TE]
	Picture Matching	YES	G1 [−EI −TE]≠ G2[−EI +TE], G3[+EI −TE] & G4[+EI +TE] G5 (Control) ≠ G2[−EI +TE], G3[+EI −TE] & G4[+EI +TE]
	Sentence Interpretation	YES	G1 [−EI −TE]≠ G2[−EI +TE], G3[+EI −TE] & G4[+EI +TE] G5 (Control) ≠ G2[−EI +TE], G3[+EI −TE] & G4[+EI +TE]
Ser/estar	Production	YES	G1 [−EI −TE]≠ G2[−EI +TE], G3[+EI −TE] & G4[+EI +TE] G5 (Control) ≠ G2[−EI +TE], G3[+EI −TE] & G4[+EI +TE]
	Picture Matching	YES	G1 [−EI −TE]≠ G2[−EI +TE], G3[+EI −TE] & G4[+EI +TE]
	Sentence Interpretation	YES	G1 [−EI −TE]≠ G2[−EI +TE], G3[+EI −TE], G4[+EI +TE] & G5 (Control) G2 [−EI+TE] ≠ G4[+EI +TE] G5 (Control) ≠ G1 [−EI −TE]& G4[+EI +TE]

Figure 7. Summary of results

Pedagogical implications

While it is certainly not the case that all SLA research should inform the language classroom, given the nature of its inquiries and the many millions of formal language learners and teachers worldwide, it seems only logical that a portion SLA research should focus on how languages are learned, so that they can ultimately be taught better. Undeniably, a sizeable number of studies that fall under the umbrella of SLA indeed set out to address classroom issues and, of course, it is also the case that a subset of those studies revolves around cognitive questions, as opposed to matters of affect. In concert with the study presented earlier in the chapter, in this section we would like to limit our claims precisely to the body of SLA research that addresses issues of cognition.

Although it is widely accepted that cognitive SLA research does and should embrace an experimental research design, no such common understanding seems to exist around cognitively-oriented, instructed SLA research. In fact, instructed SLA research rather seems to be characterized by a tension between experimental and descriptive designs with the former often being criticized for lacking applicability in the real classroom, and the latter being dismissed for lack of validity.

Based on the findings from the empirical study presented earlier in the chapter, the present paper would like to advance that (a) these two types of research design are not in a dichotomous relationship, and (b) adopting an experimental design does not necessarily jeopardize relevance to the classroom.

Pertaining to the first item, the argument of the present paper would be that the experiment reported on in this chapter stemmed directly from hundreds of hours in the classroom setting, largely as practitioners but occasionally as observers as well. As it often happens, then, descriptive, observational research was necessary in order to identify key hypotheses about language acquisition. While our descriptive observations were never formally drafted into a research paper, it remains that in the context of instructed SLA, in order for experimental research to be of any value, it must rest on the findings of descriptive research. As Sato and Loewen (2016) argued, if you want to generate a theory, do observational research, if you want to test the theory, turn to experimental research. The notion that descriptive research should suffice is untenable: in the absence of variable control, we cannot trace any gains (or lack thereof) observed in learning to a particular mode of practice. Conversely, the notion that instructed SLA can stand without descriptive research obviates the fact that any experimental study rests on the outcome from our observations. Thus, the idea that instructed SLA should be limited to one of those two designs in order to be relevant appears thoroughly misguided.

Regarding point (b) above, we think that pedagogical implications that follow from our findings are directly relevant to practitioners. First, our results suggest that explicit deductive information can help students, and therefore should not be eliminated from instructed settings just yet. As per our results, deductive EI can facilitate acquisition, both on its own and when combined with practice that in itself is conducive to gleaning the rules governing the target unit inductively. Equally relevant to the classroom is the fact that deductive EI may not always be needed, with certain grammatical structures allowing and perhaps even benefitting from an inductive approach. In particular, our research suggests that it is especially learnability problems that are semantic in nature that may require the additional help of deductive EI if practice conditions do not favor induction. While our treatments were delivered in a computer lab, and not in a classroom, we consider the present results sound and valid for classroom application. On the one hand, the types of exercises our participants carried out were the same kinds that are often present in the classroom today and, in addition, virtually all language classes these days include an online component that requires learners to practice autonomously through their computers in a fashion similar, if not identical to the way they practiced during our treatment. Furthermore, our results suggest that activities of the kind featured in our treatment are effective for grammar instruction when they allow rule induction, which seems to be most likely when the structures to be learned do not convey meaning distinctions that are themselves new to the learner. Finally, we would argue that implementing our research in a classroom context would have obscured these results, as it would have been impossible to disentangle a lack of effect from a lack of attention, for example. Thus, it is our feeling that in this particular case, adopting an experimental design did not come at the expense of ecological validity but rather, it increased the likelihood that our findings may actually be replicable in a regular classroom.

Takeaways for research methodology

Cost and participant availability

The study reported on in this paper leads us to some important methodological considerations. First and foremost, there is the issue of cost, which in our case was primarily tied to subject availability. In order to try and shed light on the interaction of two variables that may hold the key to the differing results reported in the literature, the present paper featured four experimental groups, as well as a control. This decision, made in a deliberate effort to obtain data that could help advance the field, had the downside of requiring a very large pool of participants. This meant various challenges; the first was finding enough participants to populate each condition with at least 20 subjects. The second was to find funds to compensate all of them for their participation in the experiment. Further, in an attempt to obtain data directly comparable to that in previous studies, while still contributing new data to our research questions, our study targeted two linguistic structures, which doubled the participation time required from our subjects.

The issue of access is a well-known problem in SLA, with small *n* sizes and their corresponding impact on reliability and validity persisting as a common shortcoming in many SLA studies. Our experiment was made possible thanks to the invaluable help of our gatekeeper, a language program director, who after reviewing the proposal for the study granted us access to all of the sections of first and second semester Spanish in a large university. Quite exceptionally, we were allowed not only to advertise our research, but also to recruit and administer our study during class time. Persuading students to participate in the study was considerably easier this way and, importantly, since students were not asked to make a time investment outside of class hours, their participation did not have to be compensated monetarily (only with course credit). Our initial pool of participants included 232 students. Crucially, even with the unusually ample access to participants, attrition was a factor that posed great risk for the project. At the end of our study, approximately

130 participants remained, with the remaining 100 needing to be dropped from the study for failing to complete a task, missing a testing phase or leaving the language course they were enrolled in.

On this point, the importance of collaboration between researchers, program directors and practitioners cannot be stressed enough. Needless to say, such collaboration is more likely to take place when all parties involved can derive meaningful information from the research being conducted, which only further underscores the importance of addressing questions that may be informative to practitioners.

Ethics – randomization, stages and disruption to the class

In addition to presenting a challenge with regard to cost, a multi-phase, experimental study in instructed SLA of pretest, posttest, delayed posttest design also poses some important ethical questions. Principally, any experimental study will require random assignment of participants to their respective conditions in order to prevent factors such as student preference to impact the data. From the moment a research endeavor commits to randomization, the possibility of administering treatments as part of the regular class is out of the question, since students within the same classroom will practice under different conditions. Thus, while random assignment is a must in order to increase the likelihood that our sample is representative of the entire population, it is highly intrusive. Even with brief treatments such as ours, in essence it means that at least three to five class periods will need to be devoted to data collection. One might argue that, if the research questions address issues of relevance for the classroom, this could arguably justify the disruption. Yet, in our particular case, this was a point where negotiation with the program director was required. Even after the researchers and the director had agreed on how many classes the study could claim, the time commitment also endangered collaboration with practitioners, who typically already struggle to cover the content included in their syllabi as it is. Their reservations were well justified too. For one, not only were students deprived of a week's worth of class time at their own cost, both financially and academically, but also, instructors are asked to make adjustments as needed so as not to compromise the content of the syllabus as a result of the research. In addition, these days practitioners also often worry that students' attitudes towards items beyond their control, from departmental policy on make-ups to excessive research collaboration demands, may negatively impact course evaluations, a tool commonly used to make promotion decisions. In our particular case, the majority of the instructors were willing to collaborate as long as we had the director's approval and the students were willing to participate during class time. However, the project did face resistance from one instructor, who was responsible for two classes of about 20 students each. Thanks to the directors' intervention, this resulted in neither participant attrition nor data loss. However, the mere prospect of problems of this nature can and often stop classroom research at its inception.

Technology – stimulus presentation software vs. authoring systems

An important issue when conducting lab-oriented, instructed SLA research is the choice of software for the delivery of the materials. In the more cognitive SLA tradition, commercially available software for designing and running experiments, such as Superlab or E-prime, is favored. Such software tends to offer greater functionality when it comes to recording participant performance, saving the response to every individual item comprised in the treatment, as well as the overall score in a task. In addition, it offers different types of measures to gauge learning, such as reaction time or trials to criterion. While those features are certainly desirable for their contribution to the rigor of the research, the software is not always user-friendly and may require an important time investment on the part of the researcher for stimulus preparation. Technical difficulties aside, such software often requires expensive licensing for each computer where the experiment will be run. This has direct implications of cost and hugely impacts the rate at which data can be collected, as funding often only allows licensing of a few computers, at best.

Authoring systems sometimes also require individual computer licensing, but there are options that will allow for the experiment to be run on multiple computers with a single-license purchase. For our present study, we used one such option, Respondus StudyMate. This tool had the obvious advantage of lowering the cost, and was, as authoring systems tends to be, intended for users with modest computer skills. The system, however, required the support of a learning management system (in our case Blackboard), where the files containing the stimuli could be hosted. Creating our treatment by way of an authoring system was beneficial in terms of ecological validity, as our final product looked very much like an activity in an online homework system, which students are very familiar with these days. However, because they are not designed with experiments or data collection in mind, authoring systems present a series of important deficiencies. In our case, Respondus 4.0 offered two different practice modalities. One resembled a test situation, which meant students would not receive feedback during the exercise, not finding out how they did and what items they got right and wrong till the end of the task. The other practice modality, Respondus StudyMate, was intended for students to prepare for tests. As such, it did offer feedback after every response, but since it was not a test, no final score was given at the end. For our purposes, we wanted participants to receive feedback after every item, but we also wanted a final score to be issued. For lack of a better option, we decided to use StudyMate to deliver the treatment, following up with paper-based outcome measures. In doing so, we lost any opportunity of conducting item analysis or seeing how participants performed during the treatment itself. In addition, paper-based tests meant a concession in terms of internal validity, since we could not exert any control over backtracking.

Finally, as with any computer-delivered treatment to be administered during class-time, our study demanded access to computer facilities that could accommodate about two dozen students simultaneously. This posed an additional challenge in that our computer lab was shared by other classes, often from other programs, which made scheduling all testing phases for all participating course sections complicated.

Student motivation – identifying erratic behavior

As we mentioned earlier in the chapter, any study featuring a pretest, posttest, delayed posttest design will impose considerable time demands on its participants. Particularly in cases such as the present study, where participants were not compensated, the time commitment may contribute to attrition or, at the very least, result in an increased risk of maturational effects. For the experiment we report on in this chapter, the possibility that a poor performance due to lack of motivation may be attributed to a given treatment may pose a threat to the validity of our findings. One way to address this problem is to incorporate items intended to gauge participant attention throughout the outcome measures. These could take the form of questions requiring participants to judge the plausibility of an item's propositional content, for example. Alternatively, one may resort to analyzing the data by way of mathematical models that can identify the kind of erratic behavior that comes from guessing. One such option is Rasch analysis, a model that relies on the notion that a person answering an item of a given difficulty correctly, overall should have a higher score (logit) than those who answer that same item incorrectly. Submitting data to Rasch analysis will yield, amongst other things, two indexes, infit and outfit, for every participant to help identify subjects whose responses are not aligned with their ability, as suggested by their overall score. Rasch analysis, therefore, offers a way eliminate from the data pool individual scores that are not representative of the effectiveness of treatments, thus increasing the validity of our results and the overall quality of our research. For the present study, data were submitted to Rasch analysis and misfitting participants were eliminated from the pool. To our surprise, misfitting participants were in the single digits in each testing phase and spread across conditions (surely thanks to randomization), which suggested that their impact may not have posed such a large threat after all.

Generalizability of the findings

A large subset of instructed SLA research focuses on practice, generally seeking to inform what approach may be most appropriate for teaching a particular skill or aspect of language. In our case, our study sought to compare the relative merits of practice conditions that allowed for rule induction alone and/or in combination with deductive explicit information. While we aimed to contribute valuable information to a long-standing debate about the role of explicit deductive information, we only targeted two linguistic structures. Thus, the scope of our study was rather limited, as is often the case in SLA. As our results suggest, the question of what practice condition is more appropriate depends on the particular learning goal we may be targeting. In the strictest sense, our findings provide evidence in support of the fact that practice environments that allow for rule induction may suffice for OVS, with explicit deductive treatments facilitating acquisition for both *ser/estar* and OVS, beyond what was learned inductively. From a slightly broader perspective, our *ser/estar* results lend credence to previous research with other semantically based learnability problems, such as the subjunctive, which also found that explicit deductive information was beneficial for learning (Farley 2004; Fernández 2008; Russell 2012). In truth, at this point we can only very cautiously suggest that our results may generalize to other semantically based learnability problems, such as the preterit/imperfect distinction, for example. Further research is needed to replicate previous findings and to test whether they extend to other structures.

Regarding OVS, our results mostly align with previous research. Given the number of studies that have targeted this structure, we can propose with certain level of confidence that OVS does not require explicit deductive information. In terms of how much these results may obtain with other structural learnability problems, studies targeting other structures, such as contrary-to-fact conditionals, other researchers also found explicit inductive instruction to be sufficient (Rosa and O'Neill 1999; Rosa and Leow 2004) and explicit deductive information to be beneficial (Rosa and O'Neill 1999; Rosa and Leow 2004). Unfortunately, research on two structures is hardly sufficient. Much as was the case with *ser/estar*, we are far from being able to make strong claims about the appropriateness of explicit inductive approaches to the instruction of grammar items of that nature. Yet, we would argue that in both cases (*ser/estar* and the subjunctive) the results do point in that direction.

Finally, one might argue that the generalizability of our findings is further limited by the fact that our study was conducted in a lab setting. That said, and as we mentioned earlier in the chapter, the present lab setting very closely mirrors practice situations that language learners face regularly these days. While it is certainly not the case that students are asked to review explicit information and answer questions on it while completing language exercises, given that online homework is generally graded for accuracy, it seems reasonable to assume the student may complete these exercises with access to EI. It is certainly the case that they have access to EI in several forms when practicing in class. In all, then, although some compromises were made, we would argue that our study shows lab research can be designed in such a way that it remains directly relevant to instructed language contexts.

Conclusion

Our carefully controlled experimental study was designed to answer a question that is of crucial importance to language teachers: how much explicit information should be given to the students, and does that depend on the structure or the kind of practice they get? Our findings show that for structures that do not require any new semantic distinctions, only new form-meaning mappings, as is the case for the OVS structure, learners can induce the explicit knowledge they need from task-essential practice. For structures involving new semantic distinctions, however, such as *ser/estar*, it appears that deductively presented explicit information is required, even though task-essential practice is useful.

We think that the fairly tight control our design provided greatly benefited the internal validity of the study without compromising its ecological validity: in many of today's classrooms, the students will encounter presentation and practice very similar to the ones in this study. In order to maintain strict control, however, we had to compromise in terms of linguistic generalizability. Further research is definitely needed to replicate our study with different structures.

References

Bates, E. (1994). Modularity, domain specificity and the development of language. *Discussions in Neuroscience*, 10, 136–149.

Benati, A. (2001). A comparative study of the effects of processing instruction and output- based instruction on the acquisition of the Italian future tense. *Language Teaching Research*, 5, 95–127. https://doi.org/10.1177/136216880100500202

Bates, E., B. MacWhinney, C. Caselli, A. Devescovi, F. Natale, and V. Venza. (1984). 'A cross- linguistic study of the development of sentence interpretation strategies.' *Child Development*, 55, 341–54.

Benati, A. (2004). The effects of structured input activities and explicit information on the acquisition of the Italian future tense. In B. VanPatten (Ed.), *Processing Instruction: Theory, research, and commentary* (pp. 207–225). Mahwah, NJ: Lawrence Erlbaum Associates.

Benati, A. (2004a). 'The effects of processing instruction and its components on the acquisition of gender agreement in Italian.' *Language Awareness* 13(2), 67–80.

Benati, A. (2004b). 'The effects of structured input activities and explicit information on the acquisition of the Italian future tense' in B. VanPatten (ed.): *Processing Instruction: Theory, Research, and Commentary*. Laurence Erlbaum Associates, 207–26.

Berkovits, I., Hancock, G., & Nevvitt, J. (2000). Bootstrap resampling approaches for repeated measures designs: Relative robustness to sphericity and normality violations. *Educational and Psychological Measurement*, 60, 877–892. https://doi.org/10.1177/00131640021970961

Bever, T. G. (1970). The cognitive basis for linguistic structures. In J. R. Hayes (Ed.), *Cognition and the development of language* (pp.279–362). New York, NY: Wiley.

Briscoe, G. (1995). The acquisition of ser and estar by nonnative speakers of Spanish (Unpublished dissertation), University of Pennsylvania.

Cheng, A. C. (2002). The effects of processing instruction on the acquisition of ser and estar. *Hispania*, 85, 308–323. https://doi.org/10.2307/4141092

Cheng, A. C. (2004). Processing instruction and semantic ser and estar: Forms withsemantic aspectual values. In B. VanPatten (Ed.), *Processing instruction: Theory, research, and commentary* (pp. 119–141) Mahwah, NJ: Lawrence Erlbaum Associates.

Culman, H., Henry, N., VanPatten, B. (2009) The Role of Explicit Information in Instructed SLA: An On-Line Study with Processing Instruction and German Accusative Case Inflections. *The Unterrichtpraxis/Teaching German*. 42(1), 19–31.

Culman, H., Henry, N., and VanPatten, B. (2009). 'The role of explicit information in instructed SLA: An on-line study with processing 90 instruction and German accusative case inflections.' *Die Unterrichtspraxis/Teaching German* 42(1), 19–31.

de Graaff, R. (1997). The eXperanto experiment: Effects of explicit instruction on language acquisition. *Studies in Second Language Acquisition*, 19, 249–276. https://doi.org/10.1017/S0272263197002064

DeKeyser, R. (1995). Learning second language grammar rules: An experiment with a miniature linguistic system. *Studies in Second Language Acquisition*, 17, 379–410. https://doi.org/10.1017/S027226310001425X

DeKeyser, R. (2003). Implicit and explicit learning. In M. Long & C. Doughty (Eds.), *The handbook of second language acquisition* (pp. 313–348). Malden, MA: Blackwell. https://doi.org/10.1002/9780470756492.ch11

Ellis, N. (1993). Rule and instances in foreign language learning: Interactions of explicit and implicit knowledge. *European Journal of Cognitive Psychology*, 5, 289–318. https://doi.org/10.1080/09541449308520120

Farley, A. (2004). Processing instruction and the Spanish subjunctive: Is explicit information needed? In B. VanPatten (Ed.), *Processing instruction: Theory, research, and commentary* (pp. 227–239), Mahwah, NJ: Lawrence Erlbaum Associates.

Fernández, C. (2008). Reexamining the role of explicit information in processing instruction. *Studies in Second Language Acquisition*, 30, 277–305. https://doi.org/10.1017/S0272263108080467

Gass, S. M. (1989). How do learners resolve linguistic conflicts? In S. Gass & J. Schacter (Eds.), *Linguistic perspectives on second language acquisition* (pp. 183–199). Cambridge: Cambridge University Press. https://doi.org/10.1017/CBO9781139524544.013

Geeslin, Kimberly L. (2000). A new approach to the second language acquisition of copula choice in Spanish. In R. P. Leow & C. Sanz (Eds.), *Spanish applied linguistics at the turn of the millennium: Papers from the 1999 Conference on the L1 and L2 Acquisition of Spanish and Portuguese* (pp. 50–66). Somerville, MA: Cascadilla.

Guntermann, G. (1992). An analysis of interlanguage development over time, part II: Ser and estar. *Hispania*, 75, 1294–1303. https://doi.org/10.2307/344396

Henry, N., Culman, H., & VanPatten, B. (2009). More on the effects of explicit information in SLA. *Studies in Second Language Acquisition*, 31, 559–575. https://doi.org/10.1017/S0272263109990027

Ho, R. (2006). *Handbook of univariate and multivariate data analysis and interpretation with SPSS*. New York, NY: Taylor & Francis. https://doi.org/10.1201/9781420011111

Hettmansperger, T. P., & McKean, J. (2012). *Robust non-parametric statistical methods* (2nd ed.). New York, NY: Taylor & Francis.

Huitema, B. (2012). *The analysis of covariance and alternatives.* New York, NY: John Wiley & Sons.

Lee, J. F., & VanPatten, B. (1995). *Making communicative language teaching happen.* San Francisco, CA: McGraw-Hill

LoCoco, V. (1987). Learner comprehension of oral and written sentences in German and Spanish: The importance of word order. In B. VanPatten, T. R. Dovrak, & J. F. Lee (Eds.), *Foreign language learning: A research perspective* (pp. 116–129). Rowley, MA: Newbury House.

Lomax, R. G. (2007). *An introduction to statistical concepts for education and behavioral sciences* (2nd ed.). Mahwah, NJ: Lawrence Erlbaum Associates.

Lomax, R. G. (2007). *Statistical concepts: A second course for education and the behavioral sciences* (3rd ed.). Mahwah, NJ: Lawrence Erlbaum Associates.

Loschky, L., & Bley-Vroman, R. (1993). Grammar and task-based learning. In G. Crookes & S. Gass (Eds.), *Tasks and language learning: Integrating theory and practice* (pp. 123–167). Clevedon: Multilingual Matters.

Paulston, C. (1972). Structural pattern drills: A classification. In H. Allen & R. Campbell (Eds.), *Teaching English as a second language* (pp. 129–138). New York, NY: McGraw-Hill.

Robinson, P. (1996). Learning simple and complex second language rules under implicit, incidental, rule-search and instructed conditions. *Studies in Second Language Acquisition, 18,* 27–67. https://doi.org/10.1017/S0272263100014674

Robinson, P. (1997). Generalizability and automaticity of second language learning under implicit, incidental, enhanced, and instructed conditions. *Studies in Second Language Acquisition, 19,* 223–247. https://doi.org/10.1017/S0272263197002052

Rosa, E., & Leow, R. (2004). Awareness, different learning conditions and second language development. *Applied Psycholinguistics, 25,* 269–292. https://doi.org/10.1017/S0142716404001134

Rosa, E., & O'Neill, M. (1999). Explicitness, intake, and the issue of awareness: Another piece to the puzzle. *Studies in Second Language Acquisition, 21,* 511–556. https://doi.org/10.1017/S0272263199004015

Russell, V. (2012). Learning Complex Grammar in the Virtual Classroom: A Comparison of Processing Instruction, Structured Input, Computerized Visual Input Enhancement, and Traditional Instruction. *Foreign Language Annals.* 45(1), 42–71.

Ryan, J., & Lafford, B. (1992). The acquisition of lexical meaning in a study abroad environment: Ser + estar and the Granada experience. *Hispania, 75,* 714–722. https://doi.org/10.2307/344152

Sanz, C. (2004). Computer delivered implicit versus explicit feedback in processing instruction. In B. VanPatten (Ed.), *Processing instruction: Theory, research, and commentary* (pp. 241–257). Mahwah, NJ: Lawrence Erlbaum Associates.

Sanz, C., & Morgan-Short, K. (2004). Positive evidence versus explicit rule presentation and explicit negative feedback: A computer-assisted study. *Language Learning, 54,* 35–78. https://doi.org/10.1111/j.1467-9922.2004.00248.X

Sato, M. & Loewen, S. (2016). A quasi-experimental study of corrective feedback and metacognitive instruction in intact English L2 classes. Paper presented at the American Association of Applied Linguistics, in Orlando.

Silvá-Corvalán, C. (1986). Bilingualism and language change: The extension of estar in Los Angeles Spanish. *Language, 62,* 587–608 https://doi.org/10.1353/lan.1986.0023

Silvá-Corvalán, C. (1994). *Language contact and change: Spanish in Los Angeles.* Oxford: Clarendon Press.

VanPatten, B. (1984). Learners' comprehension of clitic pronouns: More evidence for a word order strategy. *Hispanic Linguistics, 1,* 57–67.

VanPatten, B. (1993) Grammar teaching for the acquisition-rich classroom. *Foreign Language Annals*, 26, 435–450. https://doi.org/10.1111/j.1944-9720.1993.tb01179.x

VanPatten, B. (1996). *Input processing and grammar instruction: Theory and research.* Westport, CT: Ablex.

VanPatten, B. (2002). Processing instruction: An update. *Language Learning*, 52(4), 755–803. https://doi.org/10.1111/1467-9922.00203

VanPatten, B. (2004). Input processing in SLA. In B. VanPatten (Ed.), *Processing instruction: Theory, research, and commentary* (pp. 5–31). Mahwah, NJ: Lawrence Erlbaum Associates.

VanPatten, B. (2007). Input processing in adult second language acquisition. In B. VanPatten & J. Williams (Eds.), *Theories in second language acquisition* (pp. 115–135). Mahwah, NJ: Lawrence Erlbaum Associates.

VanPatten, B., & Cadierno, T. (1993). Explicit instruction and input processing. *Studies in Second Language Acquisition*, 15, 225–244. https://doi.org/10.1017/S0272263100011979

VanPatten, B., & Oikkenon, S. (1996). Explanation vs. structured input in processing instruction. *Studies in Second Language Acquisition*, 18, 495–510. https://doi.org/10.1017/S0272263100015394

VanPatten, B. (2010). Some verbs are more perfect than others: Why learners have difficulty with ser and estar and what it means for instruction. *Hispania*, 91, 29–38.

VanPatten, B. (1985). "The Acquisition of Ser and Estar by Adult Learners of Spanish: A Preliminary Investigation of Transitional Stages of Competence." *Hispania* 68(2), 399–406.

VanPatten, B. (1987). "Classroom Learners' Acquisition of Ser and Estar: Accounting for Developmental Patterns." *Foreign Language Learning*. Ed. Bill VanPatten, Trisha R. Dvorak, and James F. Lee. Rowley: Newbury. 19–32. Print.

VanPatten, B., Collopy, E., Price, J. E., Borst, S., and Qualin., A., (2013). 'Explicit information, grammatical sensitivity, and the first-noun principle: a cross-linguistic study in 45 processing instruction.' *The Modern Language Journal*, 97(2), 506–27.

White, J. and A. DeMil. (2013). 'Transfer of nontraining effects in processing instruction,' *Studies in Second Language Acquisition* 35, 519–44.

Wilcox, R. (2005). An approach to Ancova that allows multiple covariates, nonlinearity, and heteroscedasticity. *Educational Psychology and Measurement*, 65, 442–450. https://doi.org/10.1177/0013164404268670

Wong, W. (2004). Processing instruction in French: The roles of explicit information and structured input. In B. VanPatten (Ed.), *Processing instruction: Theory, research, and commentary* (pp. 187–205). Mahwah, NJ: Lawrence Erlbaum Associates.

Appendix

Appendix A   Sample of EI for SER/ESTAR and OVS ([+EI] conditions)

ser/estar –EI **(Slide 1 of 2) administered immediately before the treatment and after practice items 1, 4, 8 and 16)**
PLEASE READ THIS INFORMATION TO BE ABLE TO COMPLETE THE TAKS IN THIS EXPERIMENT.

English verb 'to be' has several equivalents in Spanish: Among them are SER and ESTAR. Generally, we use SER when we talk about inherent qualities. By inherent qualities we mean traits that are built-in, ingrained, an essential part of how someone or something really is. For example:
"El hombre <u>ES</u> serio"

The usage of SER in the example above indicates that the man is a serious individual. This is a part of his personality. This person is not prone to being boisterous, or frivolous. Rather, his usual demeanor is sober and stern.

ser/estar –EI (Slide 2 of 2) administered immediately before the treatment and after practice items 1, 4, 8 and 16)

In contrast to SER, ESTAR is used to express traits that are true in a particular circumstance. Although the trait may not be a part of the personality of the individual at hand, it happens to describe the state of the person under a particular circumstance. For example:

"El hombre ESTÁ serio"

The usage of ESTAR in the example above indicates that the man is serious under the present circumstances. Thus, ESTAR is generally used to describe circumstantial states, not a defining or inherent quality.

IMPORTANTLY ... because in English the verb to be is used for both inherent and circumstantial conditions, American leaners of Spanish often tend to confuse the two. In the following activities it will be very important for you to look at the verb (ES or ESTÁ) in order to know whether the sentences you read refer to an inherent (ES) or circumstantial (ESTÁ) trait.

OVS –EI (Slide 1 of 2) administered immediately before the treatment and after practice items 1, 4, 8 and 16)

PLEASE READ THIS INFORMATION. There is a question on it in the next slide.

Consider sentence (1) below:

(1) Mónica compra un perro

In that sentence we could replace 'un perro' the following way:

(2) Mónica LO compra

Because Spanish has flexible word order we can also have the following sentence:

(3) LO compra Mónica

HIM buys Mónica (or *Mónica buys him*, if put in the English order)

As you can see, 'LO compra Mónica' literally means '*HIM buys Mónica*' (NOT '*HE buys Mónica*', mind you!) and although this sentence is not possible in English it is both possible and very common in Spanish.

PLEASE NOTE that while in (2) 'Mónica LO compra' the first word in the sentence (i.e., Mónica) is the DOER of the action of buying, sentence (3) 'LO compra Mónica' starts with the VICTIM of the buying. In grammar we refer to the DOER as the SUBJECT and the VICTIM as the OBJECT.

OVS –EI (Slide 2 of 2) administered immediately before the treatment, and after practice items 1, 4, 8 and 16)

IMPORTANTLY because sentences in English can start with the DOER (subject) only, Americans tend to process sentences such as (4) incorrectly as shown below:

(4) 'LA visita Juan' is processed as ... *She visits Juan* ** WRONG

'*She visits Juan*' would be 'Ella visita a Juan'. Note that (4) says 'LA visita' and NOT 'Ella'

(3) 'LO compra Mónica' is processed as ... *He buys Mónica* ** WRONG

'*He buys Mónica*' would be 'Él compra a Mónica' and as you see (3) says 'LO compra' and NOT 'Él'.

In the next tasks it will be crucial to remember that LO is different from ÉL and LA is different from ELLA. LO and LA stand for the VICTIM/OBJECT of buying, visiting or whatever the verb, whereas ÉL and ELLA designate who does the buying, visiting, etc.

Appendix B   Target items for [+TE SI] condition

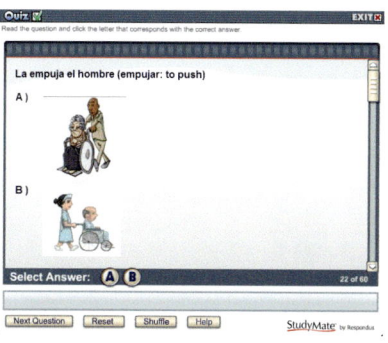

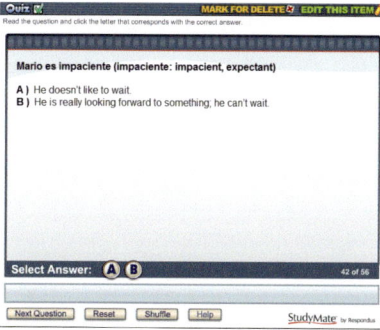

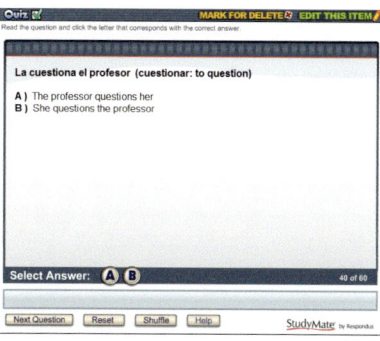

Appendix C   Target items for [–TE] condition

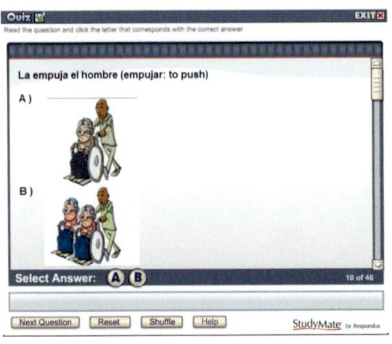

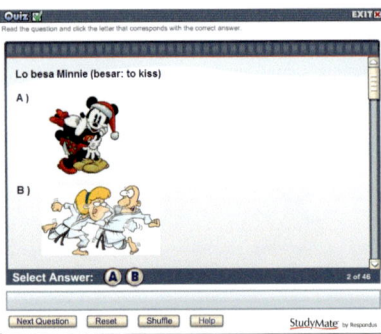

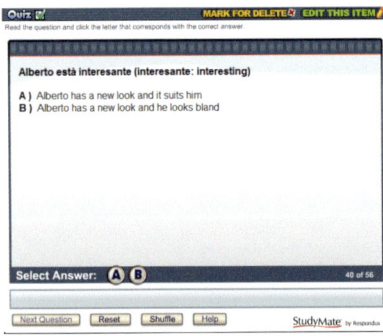

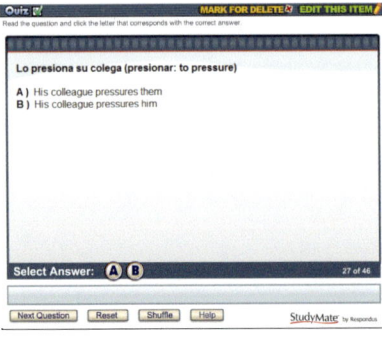

CHAPTER 8

CALL in ISLA

Promoting depth of processing of complex
L2 Spanish *"Para/Por"* prepositions

Ronald P. Leow[1], Luis Cerezo[2], Allison Caras[1] and Gorky Cruz[2]
[1]Georgetown University / [2]American University

Despite the current curricular push for hybridization in language programs, research on ISLA provides little guidance as to what and how syllabus content can be migrated online. Cerezo, Caras, and Leow (2016) recently showed that videogames using guided induction (GI) can successfully promote robust learning outcomes and deep processing of a complex L2 grammatical structure, Spanish *gustar* constructions. This study addressed Cerezo et al.'s various limitations by comparing the effects of two videogame versions (GI vs. deductive instruction or DI) on both learning outcomes and processes of a lexically-driven, L2 form (Spanish *para* and *por* prepositions). Different from Cerezo et al. (2016), results showed no significant edge of GI over DI, suggesting that type of linguistic item might moderate the effectiveness of GI and that "one size may not fit all" in the hybridization of syllabus content. Beyond pedagogical and curricular implications, our discussion also focuses on the advantages and challenges of incorporating CALL in ISLA research.

Keywords: CALL, curricular approach, guided induction, deductive instruction, videogames, cognitive processes, Spanish *para/por*

Introduction

The already vast research on computer assisted language learning (CALL) has evolved in different directions, investigating how CALL compares to traditional instructional treatments without technology or which types of CALL are most effective and why (Heift & Chapelle, 2012; Reinders & Stockwell, 2017). However, while these research avenues are all informative, to really make an impact on the burgeoning field of instructed second language acquisition (ISLA), CALL researchers need to arguably follow "a curricular approach" (Leow & Cerezo, 2016). A curricular approach addresses the context (naturalistic vs. classroom), type of

https://doi.org/10.1075/lllt.52.08leo

processing (explicit learning), and *where* the learning context resides, namely, within the language curriculum with its specified learning outcomes, policies, and procedures, together with the affordances that technology may provide for promoting deeper processing and potential migration of syllabus content to an online platform to maximize language practice in the instructed setting.

Following this curricular approach, Cerezo et al. (2016) recently showed that a videogame using guided induction (GI) – an instructional approach halfway between deductive and inductive instruction – successfully engaged learners in rule discovery, promoting deep processing and robust learning outcomes of a structurally and cognitively complex second/foreign language (L2) grammatical structure (Spanish *gustar* constructions), and helping them outperform participants who attended a traditional deductive instruction (DI) lesson. However, as Cerezo et al. acknowledged (pp. 288–289), their experimental design presented a number of limitations, including the conflation of instructional types and settings (GI and DI were, respectively, videogame-based and face-to-face, FTF), the lack of recorded online information in the DI group, and the specificity of the targeted L2 feature, which questions the generalizability of GI's reported edge. To address these limitations, the present study compared both the learning outcomes and processes of GI and DI in the same setting via videogames that targeted a complex L2 feature that is lexically- rather than structurally-driven, Spanish *para* and *por* prepositions. We also addressed, in addition to pedagogical and curricular implications, the advantages and challenges of incorporating CALL in ISLA research.

Review of the literature

The CALL-ISLA interface

The potential role of CALL in ISLA is reflected in the 30 plus research syntheses and meta-analyses that have compared the effectiveness of non-CALL instruction against CALL technologies in general (Grgurović, Chapelle, & Shelley, 2013) and specific types, such as electronic glosses (Taylor, 2013), e-tutors (Cerezo, 2016; Cerezo, Baralt, Suh, & Leow, 2014), and synchronous computer-mediated communication (Ziegler, 2016). Plonsky and Ziegler's (2016) recent "second-order synthesis" pooled together 14 of these meta-analyses, including 408 primary studies and over 14,000 learners total, and found nearly 70% of groups in CALL contexts achieving higher learning outcomes than those in non-CALL environments, albeit with a small positive effect for technology. Benefits were found for different linguistic areas, including pronunciation, reading comprehension, grammar, and vocabulary, although to different degrees and depending on the type of technology used.

At the same time, the creation of e-tutors (computer software that allows learners to practice independently, without the help of a teacher or a peer) has proven successful in the ISLA literature in not only promoting deeper learning but also allowing researchers the additional advantage of specifically manipulating *how* students process the L2 input while performing the tasks (e.g., Cerezo et al., 2016; Leow, 2001). These studies, in addition to others that have employed technology-based tasks (e.g., Adrada Rafael, 2017; de la Fuente, 2016; Gurzynski-Weiss, Al Khalil, Baralt, & Leow, 2016) have reported important roles for levels of awareness, depth of processing or amount of mental or cognitive effort employed, metacognition, and activation of prior knowledge (for one model that incorporates the roles of these processes in the L2 learning process, see Leow, 2015).

Given that technology has made huge inroads into education and several institutions have already embraced hybrid or fully online language curricula (Allen, Seaman, & Garrett, 2007; Allen, Seaman, Poulin, & Straut, 2016), the time is clearly ripe to maximize the use of CALL in ISLA, as suggested by Leow (2007):

> it may be advantageous to incorporate technology, in both research designs and instructional exposure, by means of carefully designed activities founded on theoretical SLA underpinnings to help learners process L2 structures and establish form-function relationships. There may also be the need for further research on learners' cognitive processes during practice in order to determine whether the external conditions created by each given task or activity prompted the types of processes that had been initially predicted by the researchers.   (p. 47)

Similarly, this more focused use of CALL in ISLA research and pedagogy has tremendous potential to address recent definitions of ISLA (e.g., Loewen, 2015) that underscore the need to investigate not only the manipulation of how learners learn but also the conditions under which such learning occurs. According to Loewen (2015), ISLA is

> a theoretically and empirically based field of academic inquiry that aims to understand *how* the systematic manipulation of the *mechanisms of learning* and/or the *conditions* under which they occur enable or facilitate the *development and acquisition* of a language other than one's own.   (p. 2, emphases added)

However, to really make an impact on ISLA, CALL researchers need to arguably follow "a curricular approach" (Leow & Cerezo, 2016) that seriously takes into account the context of learning (naturalistic vs. instructed), type of processing (explicit learning), and the language curriculum with its learning goals, passing grades etc. In other words, we need to acknowledge the fact that most ISLA occurs in classroom settings with stringent curricular objectives where time is of the essence, and as a result, both instruction and learning are largely explicit. In addition, the superiority of explicit/intentional over implicit/incidental learning is well documented in the ISLA literature (Leow, in press a; Leow & Zamora, 2017). This does not mean that ISLA research should not investigate more implicit and/or time-consuming forms of instruction; it means, though, that without situating learning outcomes and processes in a real context, ISLA research will fail to do its job (Leow, in press b). In addition, the proliferation of technology in the instructed setting cannot be ignored. To this end, current theoretical postulations of the roles of cognitive processes together with empirical support can guide ISLA researchers, language program directors, and teachers to take advantage of technology to create hybrid curricula with regard to what and how real syllabus-content can be migrated online to maximize classroom time for communicative practice. The next section reports one study situated within this curricular approach and the use of CALL in ISLA.

Guided induction in videogames: Cerezo, Caras, and Leow (2016)[1]

This study addressed the feasibility of establishing a partial hybrid curriculum that would shift the formal classroom-based presentation of a problematic grammatical structure in Spanish to an online component. Allowing students to be cognitively engaged in performing psycholinguistics-based tasks, which would provide them the opportunity to process these points at a deeper level outside the classroom setting, would logically free up time in the instructed setting to maximize their exposure to and interaction with the L2. Building also on the inconclusive findings of the literature comparing deductive and inductive instruction – where grammar rules are respectively provided or elicited – and inspired by Leow's (2015) model of the L2 learning process in ISLA, Cerezo et al. developed a videogame that implemented "guided induction" to successfully instruct complex grammar online.

Guided induction is an instructional approach in which teachers help learners co-construct grammar rules by directing their attention to relevant aspects in the input, asking guiding questions, or both. Unlike previous studies on guided induction (e.g., Toth, Wagner, & Moranski, 2013; Vogel, Herron, Cole, & York, 2011), until Cerezo et al. (2016) no known study had jointly investigated the effects of GI on both learning outcomes and processes, or whether it could be successfully implemented in videogames, where teacher mediation is not possible. In Cerezo et al., 70 English-speaking learners of beginning Spanish were divided into three groups. The GI group played *The Gustar Maze* videogame. To exit a maze, participants had to correctly translate a sentence with Spanish *gustar*, one constituent at a time, by sequentially choosing from two or three options. These options included the correct response but also L1 transfers that are not correct in the L2. For example, to translate

---

1.   For corroboration of Cerezo et al.'s (2016) study, see Zhuang's (in press) replication study,

the sentence "I like Spanish" (*A mí* [DAT-to me] *me* [DAT CL 1st Sg.] *gusta* [pleases] *el español* [Spanish]) the composition path was **Yo/A mí > me/*Ø > *gusto/gusta > el español*. The treatment consisted of 20 sentences, scaffolded into 4 levels of increasing complexity. Upon each selection, participants received right/wrong feedback with guiding questions and prompts. For example, when selecting the verb form, the videogame asked, "Is the verb agreeing with *a mí* or *el español*?". As opposed to GI, participants in the DI group attended a typical deductive classroom lesson. A teacher wrote a sentence on the blackboard, asked students to translate it, wrote the correct translation, and explained the rules for each constituent, repeating this process for the same 20 exemplars in the videogame. Finally, participants in the control group simply performed the assessment tasks without any formal exposure to the targeted structure. Assessments included two controlled production tasks (written and oral sentence translation) and one receptive task (multiple-choice written recognition), immediately after the treatment and 2 weeks later. Results revealed that while both instruction groups improved across time, outperforming the control group, GI achieved higher learning outcomes on most productive posttests and experienced greater retention. To investigate cognitive processes, Cerezo et al. transcribed and coded think-aloud protocols of participants in the GI group. Results revealed that most of the participants verbalized the highest level of processing (formulation of the correct rule) followed by metacognition (comments about participants' progress), activation of prior knowledge (using prior knowledge to encode or decode the targeted structure), and hypothesis formulation.

Based on the participants' deep processing and robust learning outcomes, Cerezo et al. concluded that GI could be successfully implemented in videogame-based instruction, illustrating a productive way of migrating complex L2 material online to free up classroom time for communicative practice. However, as Cerezo et al. acknowledged (pp. 288–289), they (a) conflated type of instruction (GI, DI) with instructional setting (videogame, FTF), (b) did not investigate the cognitive processes of the DI group due to logistical reasons, and (c) targeted only one linguistic feature, a grammatical structure.

Spanish *para* and *por* prepositions

Spanish prepositions are a challenge to most English-speaking learners and a particularly frequent source of errors for beginners (Galloway, 1980). Two of these prepositions, *para* and *por*, pose particular interpretation and production problems. First, like most other Spanish prepositions, they are short and unstressed, which makes them minimally salient or hard to notice. Second, neither has a one-to-one equivalence in English. *Para* can be translated as *for, to, in order to, toward, by,* or can even be omitted, while *por* can be translated as *for, because of, over the course of, during, throughout, all over, around, in exchange for*, and *by*. Third, each preposition has many semantic values. Guntermann (1992), for example, listed eight uses of *para* and 15 of *por*. Among other uses, *para* can express purpose, opinion, movement toward a destination, a future deadline, or the recipient of something. *Por*, in turn, can express reason, duration, approximate location, an exchange or substitution, and the passive voice. While there have been several attempts to connect these semantic values conceptually using, for example, cognitive linguistics (Delbecque, 1996; Lam, 2009; Lunn, 1987), they are more intuitive for some uses than others. For example, Lam's (2009) prototypical meaning of *para* as "an object aimed towards another object" can be an effective mnemonic when *para* expresses destination (*Iba para la escuela cuando ...* ["I was going towards the school when ..."]) or recipient (*Había comprado un pastel para su abuela* ["She had bought a cake for her grandmother"]). However, it may be harder to apply in *El incidente fue muy trágico para la niña* ("The incident was very tragic for the girl") or *Me parecía muy simpática para una niña de su edad* ("She seemed very nice for a girl her age"), which Lam explains, respectively, as a "judgment [being] 'aimed at' the person," or "a standard of comparison that one aims to be like" (pp. 6–7). Finally, a last factor contributing to the complexity of *para* and *por* is that their use is not entirely reliant on the context, as they may express a "grammaticized concept" (Delbecque, 1996, p. 252). For example, *por* appears in Spanish adverbial expressions such as *por supuesto, por lo general, por eso, por fin, por lo menos*, or *por ejemplo*. In sum, the difficulty of fully learning all the uses of these two Spanish prepositions has been well established for English-speaking students of Spanish.

To probe further into the feasibility of CALL as part of a hybrid curriculum and extend Cerezo et al.'s study in relation to its limitations, the present study investigated the effects of DI and GI in only one medium (CALL) via videogames targeting a complex L2 feature that is lexically- rather than structurally-driven: Spanish *para* and *por* prepositions.

Research questions

The following research questions guided the present study:

1. Learning outcomes. Does type of instruction (GI vs. DI) delivered via a video game have differential effects on the development of a lexically-driven complex L2 feature (Spanish *para* and *por* prepositions)? If so, do these effects hold after one week?
2. Cognitive processes. Does type of instruction (GI vs. DI) delivered via a video game have differential effects on the cognitive processes verbalized while processing a lexically-driven complex L2 feature (Spanish *para* and *por* prepositions)?

Method

Participants

Participants, drawn from three sections in one of the two institutions associated with this study, were originally 39 college-level students of beginning Spanish. In this research-based institution, at the beginning of the academic year the teaching staff's cooperation in data-collection procedures is solicited by the Language Program Director. To maximize participation, we incorporated the instruction of the targeted items as part of the syllabus (as opposed to the usual custom of seeking volunteers outside classroom time and syllabus content) and felt that this number (39) to be appropriate for both statistical analyses and adequate power in the study. In addition, given the current daily use of technology among our students, we invited participants to take part in the experiment not only as language learners but also as videogame evaluators via feedback after the study. This invitation potentially promoted some personal investment in the participation. We gathered data from the students in the three sections late in the semester for both comparative purposes with the original study (Cerezo et al., 2016) and to allow participants to have a working knowledge of Spanish to adequately play the videogame and perform the assessment task. Consequently, participants had received formal exposure to Spanish under a communicative approach for a period of approximately ten weeks (ca. 25 hours) before participating in the study. The course textbook used was *Vistazos*, 3rd edition (McGraw-Hill).

Like Cerezo et al., we originally established three criteria for participants' inclusion: (1) little or no prior knowledge of the prepositions and especially no productive ability, (2) no exposure to, or practice with, the targeted items during the study (both inside and outside of class), and (3) completion of all three experimental sessions. However, we ran into two major problems: First, the treatment session fell on the day before Thanksgiving and, while we were aware that some of the participants would not attend the treatment session in preference for an early trip back home, one third of the participants opted not to attend classes that day.[2] Second, the pretest scores of the remaining 26 participants revealed that several participants already possessed prior knowledge (most likely from high school) of some of the prepositional uses. We had to make a decision to raise the cutoff point for inclusion (40% for recognition and 20% for production) and lost a further 11 (42%) of the remaining 26 participants. Out of an original sample of 39 participants, we eliminated 24 (61.5%), due mostly to these two problems raising the caveat that experimental sessions should not be scheduled near major holidays.

---

2.   We did upload the two videogames on Blackboard after the completion of the study for these students to play.

Treatments

To deliver the two experimental treatments, GI and DI, two versions of a videogame, *The Para/Por Trip to Nicaragua*, were developed using Zaption <http://zaption.com>, a publicly available game development platform. We fortunately did not incur any cost in the designing of the videogame given that one of the co-authors is well versed in computer programming although we are aware that the development of videogames can be costly. At the same time, it is important to report that Zaption ceased to exist shortly after this study was conducted so any potential fine-tuning or modification of the videogame has been lost. Relying on free online platforms may be a risk factor to consider when incorporating CALL in ISLA research.

In this videogame, each participant played the role of a student whose goal was to drive a boat across Lake Nicaragua from Chontales to Granada. To collect the required gallons of gas, participants had to take part in a conversation with the boat captain by correctly selecting the prepositions *por* or *para* in a series of fill-in-the-blanks (FITBs). These FITBs successively composed a storyline and included trivia about Nicaraguan culture, history, and geography. There were 30 FITBs total. The first 20 introduced 5 different uses of *por* and 5 uses of *para*, in blocks of 2 consecutive items per use. The remaining 10 items elicited only one use, adding up to a total of 3 elicitations per use (see *Targeted items* below). Participants received right/wrong feedback with every selection (see Figure 1 for an example). Irrespective of selection (right or wrong), they continued to the next step in the game. To win the game, they had to collect at least 20 of the 30 gallons available. In other words, they had to select the correct preposition on their first attempt on at least 20 FITBs. If they failed to do so, the boat sank and they became shark bait (the image of a shark was occasionally visually presented during the game).

In the DI group, the videogame began by displaying a rule that explained a specific use of *por* or *para*, along with two model sentences that illustrated the rule at hand. Participants had to complete a FITB in the storyline by selecting the preposition that had just been explained and modelled. After each answer, the videogame displayed right/wrong feedback and a reiteration of the rule.

The videogame in the GI group first displayed two model sentences, one with *por* and one with *para*, and participants were asked to determine which of these was most similar to the FITB in the storyline, selecting the preposition accordingly. Then, they received right/wrong feedback, the correctly solved FITB, and the matching model from the two presented earlier, followed by the question, "What do you think these two sentences have in common?" This question was aimed at pushing participants to formulate hypotheses and rules (Figure 1).

Given that GI differs from traditional inductive instruction in that it provides additional support to learners, thus allowing more of them to infer correct

Figure 1. GI version of *The Para/Por Trip to Nicaragua*: FIB, corrective feedback, and question

hypotheses and rules, the video game also included "recap screens", similar to those employed in Cerezo et al. to promote deeper processing. These screens were interspersed after each block of 2 consecutive items per use, for items 1–20. They included the previously seen models and a list of possible rules, asking participants to select the rule they thought applied. Like in Cerezo et al., whether their selection was accurate or not, they continued playing the game. There were no recap screens for items 20–30 (Figure 2).

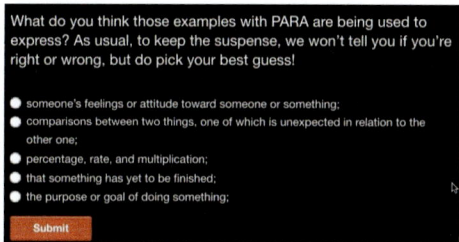

Figure 2. GI version of *The Para/Por Trip to Nicaragua*: Recap screen

To ensure that all participants were exposed to the same L2 input, the game was not over until they had completed all 30 FITBs. Both DI and GI groups were exposed to the same model sentences, although their order varied (the DI group received two models of either *por* or *para* before every FITB, whereas GI received one of both). All text was written in Spanish, but English translations were made available to minimize the possibility of incorrect selections due to comprehension problems.

Targeted items

The present study focused on five popular uses of *para* (purpose, recipient, destination, deadline, opinion) and *por* (reason, duration, passive voice, approximate
location, exchange or substitution). To minimize potential formal exposure to these
targeted forms, all references to both prepositions were removed from the syllabus and homework assignments, and instructors were requested not to entertain
questions or elaborate on the prepositions in class before and during the entire
three-week experimental period. This does not mean that participants were not, in
some way, exposed to the targeted prepositions in their textbook, but a debriefing
questionnaire administered after the delayed posttest assisted in controlling for
any potential data contamination due to additional exposure during and outside
the experimental period. Tables 1 and 2 below include each preposition use, the
rules provided to the DI group, examples from the treatment, and their location
in the treatment.

Table 1. *Para*: Uses, item number in treatment, DI rule, FITB exemplar

Use	Item	DI rule	FITB exemplar
Purpose	01	We use *PARA* to express the	*Vamos a usar esta lancha* ___
	02	PURPOSE or goal of doing	*llegar a la Ciudad de Granada.*
	21	something, usually equivalent to "in	["We'll be using this boat to get
		order to", "to", or "for" + a verb.	to Granada City."]
Recipient	03	We use *PARA* to express the	*Necesitamos gasolina* ___ *la*
	04	RECIPIENT of something. In other	*lancha.* ["We need gas for the
	29	words, the person or thing that	boat."]
		something is for.	
Destination	05	We use *PARA* to express motion or	*¡Salimos* ___ *la Ciudad de*
	06	movement toward a DESTINATION.	*Granada ahora mismo!* ["We're
	24		leaving for Granada City
			now!"]
Deadline	11	We use *PARA* to express a future	*¿Cree que podemos llegar a la*
	12	DEADLINE. In other words, by	*Ciudad de Granada* ___ *las dos?*
	22	when something is needed.	["Do you think we can get to
			Granada City by 2 PM?"]
Opinion	15	We use *PARA* to express OPINION.	___ *los nicaragüenses, el gallo*
	16	In other words, what someone thinks	*pinto es el mejor almuerzo.*
	25	of or feels about something.	["For Nicaraguans, gallo pinto
			is the best lunch."]

Table 2. *Por*: Uses, item number in treatment, DI rule, FITB exemplar

Use	Item	DI rule	FIB exemplar
Reason	07 08 23	We use *POR* to express REASON or motivation. In other words, the reason(s) why something happens.	*Nicaragua destaca ___ sus lagos y volcanes.* ["Nicaragua stands out for its lakes and volcanoes."]
Duration	09 10 28	We use *POR* to express DURATION. In other words, how long someone does something for.	*El volcán Momotombo ha estado dormido ___ treinta años.* ["The Momotombo volcano has been dormant for thirty years."]
Passive voice	13 14 30	We use *POR* to express the PASSIVE VOICE. In other words, "by whom" something was done.	*Violeta Chamorro fue la primera mujer elegida presidente ___ un país centroamericano.* ["Violeta Chamorro was the first woman to be elected president by a Central American country."]
Approximate location	17 18 27	We use *POR* to express APPROXIMATE LOCATION: the place "around", "through", "along", or "by" which something is located or happens.	*Al llegar a Granada podemos pasear ___ las calles hasta encontrar un buen restaurante.* ["When we get to Granada City we can walk through the streets until we get to a good restaurant."]
Exchange or substitution	19 20 26	We use *POR* to express EXCHANGE, SUBSTITUTION, and PRICE. In other words, what someone gives for something.	*Ahora necesitamos más gasolina como premio ___ tu conocimiento de* por *y* para. ["Now we need more gas in exchange for your knowledge of *por* and *para*."]

Assessment task

To address the potential of a 50% chance response for the written production assessment task if administered separately, both the multiple-choice recognition and controlled written production assessment tasks were combined into one assessment task eliciting either recognition or controlled written productive ability. Participants were provided with an incomplete sentence with the targeted translation in parenthesis followed by six options. If they recognized the appropriate preposition, they selected options (a) through (d), which would count as recognition. If the appropriate preposition was not listed, they needed to write it in (e), which would score as production. If they did not know for sure, they were asked to select (f). The instructions and one productive exemplar are provided below:

Please select one option to complete the following sentences ONLY when you are positive that you know the answer. Please do not guess! If you do not know the answer, simply select "I don't know". ☺

1.   El cumpleaños de mi madre es mañana y voy a comprar un regalo _____ (for) ella.
    ["My mother's birthday is tomorrow and I am going to buy a gift _____ (for) her."]
    a.   por
    b.   hasta
    c.   hacia
    d.   Ø
    e.   None of the above (write the correct word _____)
    f.   I don't know

In this exemplar, the answer is *para* and the participant would need to write this preposition in (e), indicating that s/he knew the use of *para* as compared to *por*. This item would constitute one point for the controlled written production assessment task.

This task was employed at all three testing stages (pretest, immediate posttest, delayed posttest). Items on the pretest were randomly re-ordered for each posttest. There were 10 critical items on the multiple-choice recognition component (1 item per preposition use) and 20 on the written production component (2 items per preposition use). In addition, there were 16 distractors eliciting prepositions other than *para* and *por*, for a total of 46 items.

Procedure

On the first day of the experiment, participants read and signed the Institutional Review Board (IRB) form and completed the pretest in their classrooms. Two weeks later, they reported to the language laboratory, where they were randomly assigned to either the GI (*n* = 7) or DI (*n* = 8) group. Participants were trained in thinking aloud non-metacognitively, that is, to simply say aloud what they were thinking without explaining their thoughts, with a mathematical problem. They then proceeded to play *The Para/Por Trip to Nicaragua* while thinking aloud. The think aloud protocols were recorded on QuickTime. The treatment sessions lasted an average of 28:30 minutes (GI: 30 minutes; DI: 27 minutes). Directly after, participants performed the immediate posttest and, one week later, the delayed posttest in their respective classrooms.

Scoring

All critical items on the assessment task were scored one point or zero. The maximum score was 10 for multiple-choice recognition and 20 for controlled written production.

Analysis

Before addressing the research questions, Cronbach's alphas on all test items were performed. These alphas were high (.918 and .885 on immediate and delayed posttests, respectively), proving the reliability of the assessment instruments.

The first research question asked whether type of instruction had any differential effects on the development of a Spanish *para* and *por* prepositions. Given the small sample size of this pilot study, and to avoid incurring a Type II error (i.e., wrongly concluding that a treatment has no effects), a two-pronged analysis was performed, triangulating the results of tests of significance with standardized mean difference effect sizes (Neill, 2008). Separate *t*-tests on pretest scores revealed a non-significant difference between groups at the outset of the study, either for recognition, $t(13) = .44$, $p = .664$, or production $t(13) = 1.31$, $p = .211$. Visual inspection of the distribution of the data in the Q-Q plots and acceptable skewness and kurtosis values ($<$ absolute 1) suggested that the recognition and production scores in the two experimental groups were normally distributed. In light of this, the data were analyzed via separate repeated-measures ANOVAs, entering Type of instruction (GI, DI) and Time (pretest, posttest, delayed posttest) as between- and within-subject factors, respectively, with the alpha level set at 0.05. An observed power (OP) of .8 was considered acceptable. Cohen's *d* values of .40, .70, and 1.00 were considered small, medium, and large, respectively (Oswald & Plonsky, 2010).

The second research question asked whether type of instruction had any differential effects on the cognitive processes verbalized while processing Spanish *para* and *por* prepositions. To address this, participants' think-aloud protocols obtained during the treatment were transcribed. Two of the authors highlighted and coded, based on Cerezo et al. (2016) four types of cognitive processes, namely, hypothesis and rule formulations, activation of prior knowledge, and metacognition (see Cerezo et al., 2016, for details). Interrater reliability was 100%.

Results

Research Question 1: Learning outcomes

Since our assessment tests included a very limited number of items per preposition use (10 for recognition, 1 item for each of 10 uses taught, and 20 for controlled written production, 2 items for each of 10 uses taught), we ran our analyses on composite scores of *para* and *por*. Table 3 provides descriptive statistics of accuracy for all uses of *para* and *por* by type of instruction, assessment task, and testing stage.

Table 3. Descriptive statistics: All groups, tests, and items

	Pretest *mean* (SD)	Posttest *mean* (SD)	Delayed *mean* (SD)
Multiple choice recognition			
GI (*n* = 7)	2.57 (1.27)	6.43 (2.51)	5.57 (2.07)
DI (*n* = 8)	2.88 (1.36)	6.75 (2.25)	5.63 (2.26)
Controlled written production			
GI (*n* = 7)	.14 (.38)	10.57 (6.19)	7.43 (5.22)
DI (*n* = 8)	.75 (1.16)	12.75 (6.36)	10.50 (6.30)

Multiple-choice recognition

The ANOVA performed on the recognition scores yielded a significant main effect for time, $F(2, 26) = 16.72$, $p = .000$, $\eta_p^2 = .56$, $OP = .99$, a non-significant main effect for type of instruction, $F(1, 13) = .12$, $p = .738$, $\eta_p^2 = .01$, $OP = .06$, and a non-significant interaction between time and type of instruction, $F(2, 26) = .23$, $p = .977$, $\eta_p^2 = .002$, $OP = .05$. These results are best interpreted in conjunction with their visual representation in Figure 3.

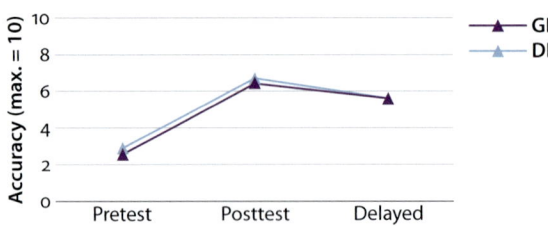

Figure 3. Multiple choice recognition accuracy by group

While the interaction between time and type of instruction was non-significant, given the small sample size and low *OP*, the standardized mean difference effect sizes between the two experimental groups were computed. The resulting effect sizes were negligible, both on the immediate (d = .13) and delayed (d =.02) posttests.

Given the significant main effect found for Time, separate paired sample t-tests were computed. Results revealed that participants in both groups experienced significant gains from pretest to immediate posttest [GI: $t(6)$ = 3.37, p = .015; DI: $t(7)$ = 4.33, p = .003] and retained those gains one week later [GI: $t(6)$ = .68, p = .52; DI: $t(7)$ = 1.51, p = .174].

Controlled written production

The ANOVA on the controlled written production scores also yielded a significant main effect for Time, $F(2, 26)$ = 35.48, p = .000, η_p^2 = .73, OP = 1, a non-significant main effect for Type of instruction, $F(1, 13)$ = .94, p = .35, η_p^2 = .07, OP = .15, and a non-significant interaction between Type of instruction and Time, $F(2, 26)$ = .4, p = .672, η_p^2 = .03, OP = .11. Figure 4 provides a visual representation.

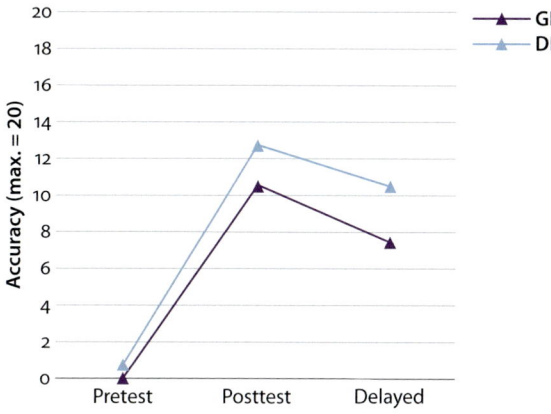

Figure 4. Controlled written production accuracy by group

To triangulate these results with tests of non-significance, the standardized mean difference effect sizes were computed. Cohen's d values were .35 and .53 on the immediate and delayed posttests, respectively, which are indicative of a small effect size.

To address the significant main effect found for Time, separate t-tests revealed that participants in both groups experienced significant gains from pretest to immediate posttest [GI: $t(6)$ = 4.54, p = .004; DI: $t(7)$ = 3.63, p = .008]. However, while GI retained those gains, $t(6)$ = 1.55, p = .172, DI experienced a significant decrease, $t(7)$ = 3.63, p = .008.

Research Question 2: Cognitive processes

As reported above, the four cognitive processes, namely, hypothesis and rule formulations, activation of prior knowledge, and metacognition identified in Cerezo et al. (2016) served as a basis for our coding scheme.

DI group

Since rules were already provided in the DI group, opportunities for hypothesis and rule formulations were at best limited unless participants failed to understand the rules correctly. Indeed, the predominant strategy was repetition and execution of the rules provided, which could be interpreted as activation of prior (just learned) knowledge or, at a more shallow level, regurgitation of such rules without much deep processing (Hsieh, Moreno, & Leow, 2016). We did not find instances of metacognition. Anecdotally, one participant systematically recalled all previous rules, which was associated with substantial learning. He was the top scorer overall, with 80% on recognition and 90% on production, both immediately after the treatment and one week later. Below is a transcript of this cognitive process, which we call *comprehensive recall*.

> *Comprehensive recall*
> Ok let's go through all this. *Para* is for an opinion. *Para* is for a deadline. *Para* is for someone or something and *para* is in order to. And *para* is... Oh sh*t there is another one. *Por* is for the passive voice. *Por* is for duration. *Para* is opinion. *Para* is in order to *para* is for someone or something *para* is by a deadline. *Por* is for passive voice. *Por* is... for duration.

GI group

In contrast to the DI group, participants in GI performed similarly to those in Cerezo et al.'s study, that is, they all engaged in rule and hypothesis formulations, activation of recent prior knowledge, and metacognition. Below are some exemplars:

Rule formulation

> So it's going to be um ... *para* because it's like a date or time. So if it's a date or time– *para*. And I think what the rule here is ... a deadline or something is needed.

Activation of recent knowledge

> so here *por* is the same as the central park example uh where it's like through... so that HAS to be *por* through the streets. Because it's through the same as walking through your house or central park.

Metacognition

> I am a little confused about the infinitive following *por* or *para*, just as a general rule.

Hypothesis formulation

> It seems that *para* comes before a verb ... a *regalo* is a present ... so *para* maybe can come before a person as well.

Participants' feedback

Participants expressed satisfaction with the videogame (DI or GI) they played. Below are some samples of their feedback.

DI

- Maybe make it slightly harder. But I liked it, nice videos and music
- My only suggestion would be to make it a little less easy, and have the players of the game have to recall on knowledge they had just learned more often
- A bit repetitive
- The game was easy because of the prompting of information between turns, but also interesting and funny. Seeing the examples helped a lot, in terms of reinforcing the rules for *por* and *para*. I also learned new vocabulary. I did like it for the reasons above and I have no suggestions for improvement
- I like it as a game / for fun, but for studying, I would categorize which sentences that use *para* and which sentences that use *por*. I think that would be easier for me to understand the difference. Perhaps, you can also observe students' reaction visually by using camera, etc. so that you also can see their reaction through body language

GI

- I liked the game! While it was a little repetitive, this really helped show the difference between "*por*" & "*para*" when used in different contexts. I kind of wish the game would tell you which rule was correct after we choose it. It would also put the progress level somewhere in the corner, so people can see how far they have come. I feel like I have a much better grasp on *por* & *para*, even if I'm still not 100% certain. Overall, I liked the scenario, dialogue, imagery and music!
- At first the game was confusing but I began to understand it after a few examples. I really like the game because the examples were relatable and they helped me draw connections between similar examples. The similarities present helped me to understand *por* and *para* better. I would have liked to play the game for longer period of time because I found it very helpful

– I think the game was good because it showed me the differences between *por* and *para* by letting me look at examples and feedback so that I could figure it out for myself. A few of the examples/translations left me confused about why it was *por* or *para* but for the most part I could figure it out quickly enough to answer the question correctly. I thought the game was interesting enough to keep me engaged with the material. I did like the game because I liked seeing examples of what *por* and *para* mean without just being told of their specific uses.

Discussion

The first research question asked whether type of instruction (DI vs. GI) would have a differential effect on the development of 10 uses of the Spanish prepositions *para* and *por*. The results revealed that both GI and DI led to notable improvement in form recognition (range: 55%–67%) and controlled written production (range: 37%–63%) (see Table 4 for details); in addition, the learning trajectories of both groups were not statistically different.

These results both replicate and contradict the findings of Cerezo et al. (2016) comparing the effects of GI and DI via videogames. On the one hand, as Table 4 shows, both types of instruction were able to promote significant learning of *para* and *por* in this study and *gustar* in Cerezo et al., proving that DI and GI can be successfully implemented in online environment to promote learning of both semantically and structurally complex L2 forms.

Table 4. Learning outcomes: *Para/por* (this study), *gustar* (Cerezo et al., 2016)

	Para/Por			Gustar			[Gustar] – [Para/Por]		
	Pre	Post	Delayed	Pre	Post	Delayed	Pre	Post	Delayed
Recognition									
GI	25%	64%	55%	15%	90%	83%	−10%	+26%	+28%
DI	28%	67%	56%	12%	84%	81%	−16%	+17%	+25%
Production									
GI	1%	53%	37%	0%	91%	82%	−1%	+38%	+45%
DI	4%	64%	52%	0%	60%	40%	−4%	−4%	−12%

On the other hand, the learning gains in this study were generally much lower. Cerezo et al.'s GI group outperformed our GI group by up to 28% on multiple choice recognition and 45% on controlled written production. The results for the DI group, however, were mixed, with Cerezo et al.'s DI group outperforming our group by up to 25% on recognition and underperforming by up to 12% on controlled written production. In addition, in Cerezo et al., GI outperformed DI in controlled written production, both on the immediate and delayed posttests, while in our study both groups performed comparably in all cases, and pairwise comparisons actually suggest that, were any significant differences to arise, they would favor DI with a small-sized lead.

Several factors may explain the lower effectiveness of the *Para/por* videogame in general, and the GI version in particular. The first one relates to quantitative and qualitative differences in the underlying rules. The *Gustar* game instructed four rules that fed into each other, while the *Para/por* game instructed 10 discrete, unrelated, rules. For example, to play level 4 in the *Gustar* video game, in which the goal was to translate sentences like "Mary and John like the house" (*A María y a Juan les gusta la casa*), participants had to activate the three previously learned rules. They had to process the thing liked as the subject (*la casa*), make the experiencer the indirect object (*María y Juan*), and conjugate the verb in agreement with the thing liked (*gusta*) (Rule 1); they also had to produce the dative pronoun *les*, which is typically confused with its direct object pronoun counterpart *los* due to its similarity and low saliency (Rule 2); they had to preface the indirect object with a redundant preposition *a* because it was a noun phrase, rather than a pronominal phrase (*A María y Juan*) (Rule 3); and finally, they had to duplicate this redundant preposition for the second noun (*A María y a Juan*) (Rule 4). As a result, participants were constantly activating their recently learned knowledge. In contrast, the current study involved 10 discrete, disconnected rules, five for *para* and *por* each, which resulted in a larger amount of linguistic information to be processed and learned.

The second factor has to do with the amount of practice provided. In the *gustar* videogame, participants were exposed to 20 practice items, divided as follows: 10 items for Rule 1, 4 items for Rule 2, and 3 items for Rules 3 and 4 each. In the present study, participants were exposed to 30 practice items, which came to 3 items per preposition use. Arguably, this lower amount of practice may explain the overall lower learning in this study. At the same time, it may explain while contrary to Cerezo et al., our GI group did not have an edge over DI. The protocols appear to suggest the following: (1) three items per preposition use may not have provided enough contexts and opportunities for some participants to figure out all the underlying rules and/or (2) attempting to formulate 10 discrete rules within a limited period of time may have been for some participants cognitively overloading.

A third factor resides in the nature of our task. Due to design considerations and space constraints, the *Para/por* videogame did not display the model sentences (one with *por*, one with *para*) in the same screen as the FITB, but rather, on the previous screen. Hence, participants had to rely on memory to find similarities between the model sentences and the FITB. Perhaps if the model sentences and the FITB had been on the same screen our results would have differed.

Finally, a fourth factor may be differences in the medium. In the *gustar* study, the DI was FTF, while in the present study, both groups were videogame-based. Arguably, individual practice with a videogame may result in more cognitive engagement than attending a teacher-centered lesson. This could explain why the DI group in Cerezo et al. (2016) performed worse than GI, contrary to the present study.

The second research question investigated which cognitive processes were employed during the learning of complex *para/por* prepositions in both instructional conditions. The protocols revealed that the DI group overwhelmingly verbalized repetition and activation of recent knowledge, that is, the rule just provided. On the other hand, similarly to Cerezo et al. (2016), our GI group verbalized a wide array of cognitive processes, namely, hypothesis and rule formulations, activation of recent prior knowledge, and metacognition. While at first glance this study suggests no link between greater depth of processing and L2 development, the fact that the DI group experienced a significant decrease after just one week, replicating Cerezo et al.'s DI's productive performances after two weeks, suggests that the effects of deeper processing may not appear immediately, but rather, over time (e.g., Hsieh, et al., 2016; Rott, 2005). This, of course, warrants further investigation. Finally, participants' feedback on the videogames was overall positive with more enthusiasm demonstrated for the GI videogame.

Conclusion

The present study sought to address how technology can be used to enhance explicit L2 learning in a prototypical language classroom with stringent curricular goals and time constraints. Our results showed that an instructional approach such as GI can be successfully implemented in videogame-based instruction to promote robust learning of a lexically-driven complex L2 form such as Spanish *para/por* prepositions. From a curricular perspective, this study thus joins Cerezo et al. (2016) in demonstrating that CALL can clearly play an important role in not only promoting deeper processing and more robust learning but also providing language program directors and teachers the option of creating hybrid curricula to free up important time in the instructed setting for communicative practice. In addition, the relatively strong gain scores of both studies augur well for pedagogical extrapolations and curricular considerations given that students are required to earn a passing grade to succeed in a language program: (Leow, in press b).

At the same time, this study suggests that the effectiveness of GI may be moderated by a number of variables, including the nature of the targeted form and its underlying rules, the amount of practice provided, task-design considerations, and the learning environment. To address some of these variables, we are currently redesigning our *Para/por* videogame, taking into account the results and limitations of this study and the feedback from our participants. In particular, we felt that the amount of 10 discrete uses of the two prepositions in such a short period of time was cognitively challenging and will only include six uses in a follow-up study. For pedagogical purposes, the other four uses can be included in a similar but different videogame. In addition, we will increase the sample number and incorporate measures of language aptitude and memory to uncover whether different components such as language analytic ability or rote memory correlate with the learning of structurally and lexically driven L2 forms such as *gustar* and *para/por* prepositions. ISLA researchers are also urged, where feasible, to employ concurrent data elicitation procedures (e.g., think aloud protocols, eye-tracking) in any attempt to gather concurrent data as L2 learners process the L2 data. A better understanding of such processing and processes holds tremendous potential for the creation of cognitively engaging tasks that do promote robust learning in instructed settings.

Unfortunately, CALL comes with some caveats. Using CALL requires two types of knowledges: (1) an adequate understanding of the L2 learning process if researchers desire to achieve a "systematic manipulation of the mechanisms of learning and/or the conditions under which they occur" (Loewen, 2015: 2) and (2) some expertise in computer programming, without which the use of CALL can be an expensive enterprise involving the cost of paying for technological expertise and/or the use of a technology-based platform. We addressed the first type of knowledge by heavily relying on the empirical findings of studies that reported concurrent data on the roles of learner processes and the postulations of Leow's (2015) model. We avoided the technological expense due to the cross-institutional nature of this project (two researchers each at two institutions) that fostered colleague collaboration and helped enormously to develop the videogame, all the way from script writing to software programming at one institution to data collection and coding at the other institution. Unfortunately, the platform (Zaption) we used for our videogame ceased to exist underscoring one of the potential risks of CALL in ISLA, namely, a reliance on free online platforms in ISLA research, pedagogy, and curricula.

On the brighter side, incorporating CALL in ISLA research can have several advantages for researchers, teachers, and language program directors. For researchers, some advantages include (1) the manipulation of learners' depth of processing when the technology-based task or activity is grounded within a theoretically-driven and empirically supported approach, (2) the affordance technology provides for the collection of concurrent data of learner performance and cognitive processes employed during practice, (3) the provision of computer-delivered feedback to deliver concurrent, immediate, and/or individualized feedback, (4) the methodological rigor of tightly controlling several experimental variables (such as type, amount, and timing of input and/or feedback), and (5) via the use of concurrent think aloud protocols, promoting internal validity by ensuring that participants faithfully follow instructions in the experimental condition, thus accurately representing the experimental cell to which they were assigned (cf. Hulstijn, 2000; Leow, 2015). For teachers and language program directors, CALL provides the opportunity to supplement in-class activities with more online focused tasks that promote deeper processing and cognitive engagement, especially related to complex grammatical or lexical L2 items, and create hybrid curricula that free up valuable in-class activities that are designed to promote more communicative practice with the L2. Grounding the creation or designing of CALL activities, tasks, or videogames that are theoretically-driven and empirically supported has tremendous potential for the successful promotion of robust learning in the instructed setting that ultimately falls within stated curricular goals.

References

Adrada-Rafael, S. (2017). Processing the Spanish imperfect subjunctive: Depth of processing under different instructional conditions. *Applied Psycholinguistics*, 38, 477–508. https://doi.org/10.1017/S0142716416000308

Allen, I. E., Seaman, J., Poulin, R., & Straut, T. T. (2016). *Online report card: Tracking online education in the United States*. Babson Park, MA: Babson Survey Research Group and Quahog Research Group, LLC.

Allen, I. E., Seaman, J., & Garrett, R. (2007). *Blending in: The extent and promise of blended education in the United States*. Sloan-C.

Cerezo, L. (2012). Beyond hybrid learning: A synthesis of research on e-tutors under the lens of SLA theory. In F. Rubio & J. J. Thoms (Eds.), *Hybrid language teaching and learning: Exploring theoretical, pedagogical and curricular issues* (pp. 50–66). Boston, MA: Heinle/ Cengage Learning.

Cerezo, L. (2016). Theoretical approaches to CALL research: Toward a psycholinguistic perspective. In R. P. Leow, L. Cerezo & M. Baralt (Eds.), *A psycholinguistic approach to technology and language learning.* (pp. 23–46). Berlin, Germany; Boston, MA: De Gruyter Mouton.

Cerezo, L., Baralt, M., Suh, B-R., & Leow, R. P. (2014). Does the medium really matter in L2 development? The validity of CALL research designs. *Computer Assisted Language Learning*, 27(4), 294–310. https://doi.org/10.1080/09588221.2013.839569

Cerezo, L., Caras, A., & Leow, R. P. (2016). The effectiveness of guided induction versus deductive instruction on the development of complex Spanish *gustar* structures: An analysis of learning outcomes and processes. *Studies in Second Language Acquisition*, 3(2), 265–291. https://doi.org/10.1017/S0272263116000139

De la Fuente, M. J. (2016). Explicit corrective feedback and computer-based, form-focused instruction: The role of L1 in promoting awareness of L2 forms. In R. P. Leow, L. Cerezo, & M. Baralt (Eds.), *A psycholinguistic approach to technology and language learning* (pp. 171–197). Berlin: De Gruyter Mouton.

Delbecque, N. (1996). Towards a cognitive account of the use of the prepositions por and para in Spanish. In E. Casad (Ed.), *Cognitive linguistics in the redwoods: The expansion of a new paradigm in linguistics* (pp. 249–318). Berlin: Mouton de Gruyter. https://doi.org/10.1515/9783110811421.249

Galloway, V. (1980). Perceptions of the communicative efforts of American students of Spanish. *Modern Language Journal*, 64(4), 428–433. https://doi.org/10.1111/j.1540-4781.1980.tb05218.x

Grgurović, M., Chapelle, C. A., & Shelley, M. (2013). A meta-analysis of effectiveness studies on computer technology-supported language learning. *ReCALL Journal*, 25(2), 165–198. https://doi.org/10.1017/S0958344013000013

Guntermann, G. (1992). An analysis of interlanguage development over time: Part I, por and para. *Hispania*, 75(1), 177–187. https://doi.org/10.2307/344777

Gurzynski-Weiss, L., Al Khalil, M., Baralt, M., & Leow, R. P. (2016). Levels of awareness in relation to type of recast and type of linguistic item in computer-mediated communication: A concurrent investigation. In R. P. Leow, L. Cerezo, & M. Baralt (Eds.), *A psycholinguistic approach to technology and language learning* (pp. 151–170). Berlin: De Gruyter Mouton.

Heift, T., & Chapelle, C. A. (2012). Language learning through technology. In S. M. Gass & A. Mackey (Eds.), *The Routledge handbook of second language acquisition*. London: Routledge.

Hsieh, H-C., Moreno, N., & Leow, R. P. (2016). Awareness, type of medium, and L2 development: Revisiting Hsieh (2008). In R. P. Leow, L. Cerezo, & M. Baralt (Eds.), *A psycholinguistic approach to technology and L2 learning*. Berlin: De Gruyter Mouton.

Hulstijn, J. H. (2000). The use of computer technology in experimental studies of second language acquisition: A survey of some techniques and some ongoing studies. *Language Learning & Technology*, 3(2), 32–43.

Lam, Y. (2009). Applying cognitive linguistics to teaching the Spanish prepositions por and para. *Language awareness*, 18(1), 2–18. https://doi.org/10.1080/09658410802147345

Leow, R. P. (2001). Attention, awareness, and foreign language behavior. *Language Learning*, 51, 113–155. https://doi.org/10.1111/j.1467-1770.2001.tb00016.x

Leow, R. P. (2007). Input in the L2 classroom: An attentional perspective on receptive practice. In R. M. DeKeyser (Ed.), *Practice in a second language: Perspectives from applied linguistics and cognitive psychology* (pp. 21–50). Cambridge: Cambridge University Press. https://doi.org/10.1017/CBO9780511667275.004

Leow, R. P. (2015). *Explicit learning in the L2 Classroom: A student-centered approach*: New York, NY: Routledge.

Leow, R. P. (in press a). Explicit learning and depth of processing in the instructed setting: Theory, research, and practice. *Studies in English Education* 23 (4).

Leow, R. P. & Cerezo, L. (2016). Deconstructing the I and SLA in ISLA: One curricular approach. *Studies in Second Language Learning and Teaching*, 6(1), 43–63. https://doi.org/10.14746/ssllt.2016.6.1.3

Leow, R. P., & Zamora, C. (2017). Intentional and incidental learning. In S. Loewen & M. Sato (Eds.), *Routledge Handbook of Instructed Second Language Acquisition* (pp. 33–49). New York, NY: Routledge.

Loewen, S. (2015). *Introduction to instructed second language acquisition*. New York, NY: Routledge.

Lunn, P. V. (1987). *The Semantics of por and para*. Bloomington, IN: Indiana University Linguistics Club.

Neill, J. (2008). Why use effect sizes instead of significance testing in program evaluation. Retrieved from <http://wilderdom.com/research/effectsizes.html> (20 July 20, 2014).

Oswald, F. L., & Plonsky, L. (2010). Meta-analysis in second language research: Choices and challenges. *Annual Review of Applied Linguistics*, 30, 85–110. https://doi.org/10.1017/S0267190510000115

Plonsky, L. & Ziegler, N. (2016). The CALL–SLA interface: Insights from a second-order synthesis. *Language Learning & Technology*, 20(2), 17–37.

Reinders, H., & Stockwell, G. (2017). Computer-assisted SLA. In S. Loewen & M. Sato (Eds.), *The Routledge handbook of instructed second language acquisition* (pp. 361–375). New York, NY: Routledge.

Rott, S. (2005). Processing glosses: A qualitative exploration of how form-meaning connections are established and strengthened. *Reading in a Foreign Language*, 17(2), 95–124.

Taylor, A. M. (2013). CALL versus paper: In which context are L1 glosses more effective? *CALICO Journal*, 30, 63–81. https://doi.org/10.11139/cj.30.1.63-81

Toth, P. D., Wagner, E., & Moranski, K. (2013). 'Co-constructing' explicit L2 knowledge with high school Spanish learners through guided induction. *Applied Linguistics*, 34, 279–303. https://doi.org/10.1093/applin/ams049

VanPatten, B., Lee, J., & Ballman, A. (2010). *Vistazos: Un curso breve* (3rd ed.). New York, NY: McGraw-Hill.

Vogel, S., Herron, C., Cole, S. P., & York, H. (2011). Effectiveness of a guided inductive versus a deductive approach on the learning of grammar in the intermediate level college French classroom. *Foreign Language Annals*, 44(2), 353–380. https://doi.org/10.1111/j.1944-9720.2011.01133.x

White, C. & Reinders, H. (2010). *The theory and practice of technology in materials development and task design*. Cambridge: Cambridge University Press.

Zhuang, J. (in press). Computer-assisted guided induction and deductive instruction on the development of complex Chinese ba structures: Extending Cerezo et al. (2016) To appear in R. P. Leow (Ed.), *The Routledge Handbook of second language research in classroom learning*. New York, NY: Routledge.

Ziegler, N. (2016). Synchronous computer-mediated communication and interaction. *Studies in Second Language Acquisition*, 38(3), 553–586. https://doi.org/10.1017/S027226311500025X

CHAPTER 9

Lexical development in the writing of intensive English program students

Alan Juffs[1]
University of Pittsburgh

This paper focuses on vocabulary development in intensive English program (IEP) students, comparing free writing data from an IEP to previous research in more controlled contexts. These free writing data derive from writing assignments collected from students with three language backgrounds: Arabic ($n = 22$), Chinese ($n = 20$) and Korean ($n = 19$), who studied at the intermediate and subsequently the advanced levels of an IEP in the USA. The main finding was that a purely text-based measure of diversity, vocD, did not capture gains in lexical development, whereas a measure of lexical sophistication, Advanced Guiraud (AG), did show measureable improvement. Discussion focuses on a more theoretically complex conceptualization of lexical development, how experimental methods compare with 'messy' classroom corpus data, and the problem of text length. Specific pedagogical recommendations include more focus more on lexical quality (Perfetti & Hart, 2002) and words at lower frequency bands (3000–9000).

Keywords: lexical diversity, vocD, lexical sophistication, Advanced Guiraud, intensive English programs

---

1. I would like to thank the teachers and students of the English Language Institute at the University of Pittsburgh for their participation in the project reported in this paper. This research was supported in part by a grant from the Pittsburgh Science of Learning Center <www.learnlab. org> to Alan Juffs. I am also grateful to the editors, an external reviewer, and especially Yoon Hyung Joo for suggestions on an earlier draft. All errors are mine. The Pittsburgh Science of Learning Center was funded by the United States National Science Foundation award number SBE-0836012. Previously, it was NSF award number SBE-0354420.

https://doi.org/10.1075/lllt.52.09juf
© 2019 John Benjamins Publishing Company

Introduction

The stated goal of this volume is to investigate the pros and cons of SLA research methods and evaluate their relevance for real world classroom applications. In this context, this paper presents a study documenting the development of productive vocabulary use with naturally occurring classroom data. The paper uses methods for analyzing lexical development that are common in experimental SLA studies and considers which of these measures can provide teachers and learners with the best insights into their teaching practice and learning outcomes at the advanced level. SLA research methods that focus on lexical development frequently use corpora that are carefully constructed (e.g., papers in Jarvis & Daller (2013)) or from commercial proficiency tests (e.g., Murakami & Alexopolou, 2016, Yu, 2010). In such controlled research, the corpus is often strictly constrained by topic and/or time allowed for writing. These constraints, while necessary in experimental research, may not reflect how learners actually behave when they have more time, open access to learning aids, and freedom to choose the topics they write about. (See Hamp-Lyons (2007) for more discussion of broader issues on this topic). In contrast to these experimental studies, the data for this paper were collected over a period of several years, and neither the time students had to write nor the topics were controlled. In addition, students had access to dictionaries, feedback from teachers, and other resources as they chose. The teachers also varied over the data collection period. Thus, these data lack the focus of a typical experimental intervention or data collection that is typical in SLA research. However, the data do reflect what actually happened in an institute where teachers change and where students are free to write with the help of feedback and learning tools. While some researchers have analyzed more naturally occurring data (e.g., Crossley et al. 2011), SLA researchers value the control of independent variables to isolate their effects on a dependent measure and development is often measured through constrained tasks or tests rather than less controlled production data. For this reason, the developmental stages discovered in controlled corpora and formal tests may not reflect how learners actually develop in classroom contexts. This tension is a familiar one in discussions of internal and external validity (Brown, 1988, pp. 36–40) because by controlling the internal validity of such corpora, the ecological validity for instructed learning can be threatened. The paper begins by considering how lexical development is defined before proceeding to the data and results of the corpus analysis. Pedagogical implications are discussed in the final section.

Lexical development has been an increasingly important topic of SLA research since seminal work by Laufer & Nation (1995). Nation (2001) pointed out mastery of the 'basic' 2000 words (e.g., West's (1953) General Service List or the most frequent 2000 words from frequency counts such as the British National Corpus

(BNC)) is a threshold for vocabulary development. However, for more advanced learners, especially in English for Academic Purposes (EAP), a large range of formal vocabulary above this level is needed. For this reason, more specialized word lists, such as Coxhead's (2000) academic word list (AWL; 570 word families) have also guided curriculum development and instruction. The AWL is thus a special focus in many IEPs that prepare students to study in English-medium graduate and undergraduate programs.[2] A core component of this preparation is a focus on a broad range of vocabulary.

Before considering range of vocabulary, it is worth reviewing the definition of 'word'. A *lemma* is considered the basic word form, often the headword in a dictionary, whereas a *lexeme* is a specific form of a lemma. A set of lexemes makes up a word family. For example, 'ignore' is a lemma, with 'ignores, ignored, 'ignoring' as associated *inflected* lexemes and 'ignorance' and 'ignorant' *derived* lexemes. All these forms constitute the 'word family'. A well-known problem that arises with derived forms is that of semantic drift (Gardner & Davies (2014, p. 307) reemphasized this point). Thus, the base meaning of 'ignore' = 'not pay attention to' is not quite the same as its derived forms 'ignorance' = 'lacking knowledge' or 'ignorant', which can mean 'impolite' for some (American) speakers. English morphology can also be misleading: for example, 'compete' and 'competent' are only distantly related while 'corn' and 'corner' not are related at all. Partly for these reasons, Nation (2007) stated that the lemma is better for describing production data rather than word families. Moreover, research on students typical of the IEP in this study has shown that they struggle to identify words related by derivation (Friedline, 2011). Thus, this paper will calculate measures of development based on a range of lexeme types rather than lemmas or word families in order to evaluate lexical development.

Lexical development can encompass increases in *lexical diversity, lexical sophistication*, and *lexical depth* (Bulté & Housen, 2014; Jarvis, 2013; Siskova, 2012; van Hout & Vermeer, 2007). Lexical diversity refers to the relationship among words in a text expressed by different ratios of types and tokens; in this approach, texts are analyzed independently of frequencies in corpora. Lexical sophistication refers to the proportion of less frequent words in a text, using frequencies from corpora for comparison (e.g., the British National Corpus (BNC) or the Corpus of Contemporary American English (COCA)). Finally, lexical depth deals with the thoroughness with which a word is known – including its forms, collocations, register and usage. Lexical diversity and lexical sophistication are developed more fully in the following paragraphs.

---

2. Although some weaknesses in the AWL have been pointed out and alternatives proposed (Gardner & Davis, 2014; Todd, 2017), when these data were collected these publications were not available to the curriculum supervisors in the IEP.

Lexical diversity is a mathematical description of type/token ratios in a text in which various forms, e.g., 'run', 'runs', 'running', and 'ran', are all separate types as well as separate tokens. A widely used measure to describe diversity is a calculation known as 'VocD', which presents a statistic called 'D'. One advantage of D as a lexical richness measure is that it supposed not to be a function of sample size and is capable of demonstrating developmental trends independently of text length. McCarthy and Jarvis (2010, p. 383) summarize the procedure to calculate D thus: 100 random samples of 35 words are taken and a type/token ratio (TTR) calculated. This process is repeated twice again with a larger sample of words, producing a TTR curve that results in a final score, which usually ranges from 10 to 100.[3] Although some research has indicated that D is in fact sensitive to length (McCarthy & Jarvis, 2007), because previous research has shown vocD to be a robust measure and because computer programs such as CLAN (MacWhinney, 2000) and websites (e.g., www.textinspector.com) provide vocD, this paper will use this measure for lexical diversity. Another less complex measure that has been used is a simple Guiraud Index, which is the number of types divided by the square root of the total number of tokens. This procedure is also said to control for text length (Daller, Turlik & Weir, 2013.

In contrast to lexical diversity, lexical sophistication compares the range of words in learners' texts with word frequency lists (Bulté & Housen, 2014; Daller, Turlik & Weir, 2013). These lists consist of bands of words grouped into frequencies of 1000. Examples of words in the BNC most frequent bands, from most to less frequent, are:

1000	the, and, language, show, study
2000	accurate, focus, reaction, variable
3000	compromise, grammar, mask, visual
5000	inhibitory, retrieve, verb, parallel
10000	decompose, lexicon, neural, paradigm, prefix,
13–20k	impervious, orthography, neuroscience, connectionist

Because of dialect differences, (e.g., the frequency of 'lorry' in British English vs. 'truck' in American English), Cobb's website <http://lextutor.ca/> for analyzing corpora provides a combined list of BNC-COCA 1–25K bands. Daller, Turlik & Weir (2013) and Bulté and Housen (2014) both use lexical sophistication in their studies in addition to vocD. The measure of lexical sophistication that they used was the 'Advanced Guiraud' (AG), which is the number of types above the 2000 frequency band divided by the square root of total tokens.

---

3.   Complete details of the calculation are reported in Malvern et al. (2004).

Related to the issue of lower frequency words, Schmitt and Schmitt (2014, p. 496) pointed out that an instructional focus on the 3000 to the 9000 frequency bands is very important because they contain crucial words for students whose goal is to study and for a range of 'authentic purposes'. For example, the following words appear in those bands:

3,001–4,000:	academic, consist, exploit, rapid, vocabulary
4,001–5,000:	agricultural, contemporary, dense, insight, particle
5,001–6,000:	cumulative, default, penguin, rigorous, schoolchildren
6,001–7,000:	axis, comprehension, peripheral, sinister, taper
7,001–8,000:	authentic, conversely, latitude, mediation, undergraduate,
8,001–9,000:	anthropology, fruitful, hypothesis, semester, virulent

Thus, statistical measures that do and do not refer to word frequencies have been important in research on lexical development.

While this paper will concentrate on lexical diversity and lexical sophistication, approaches to lexical development have evolved over the past several years. For example, Jarvis (2013, pp. 24–25) considers lexical diversity based on the field of biodiversity in ecology. He includes not just mathematical ratio definitions, but also includes other (more subjective) elements of variability, volume, evenness, rarity, dispersion, and disparity. Second, words used in multiword expressions have increasingly been seen as important (e.g., Ellis & Simpson-Vallach, 2009; Hsu, 2014). Moreover, lexical diversity from the point of view of the learner has to be considered because predictions of difficulty based on frequency may not always turn out to be correct, possibly due to differences in learning styles (Booth, 2013). Booth also notes that a very important limitation of the focus on vocabulary size is that insufficient attention is paid to lexical depth and students' understanding of appropriate usage. Brown (2013) compared lexical frequency lists with words that learners actually reported knowing in articles; while he did find support for frequency approaches, learners did not know word families well. This result supports the point made by Booth (2013) that knowing one form-meaning mapping may not equal accurate 'knowledge'. Hence, while these aspects are important, it is beyond the focus of the current study to deeply investigate complex usage and collocations as the main focus.

With this background in mind, the goal of this paper is to investigate the lexical development in the writing assignments of intermediate to high intermediate/advanced students in an IEP in the United States over two semesters. It is important to reiterate that the data are not the result of a direct instructional intervention specific to this study, nor were the data specifically collected to target lexical development. Instead, the data are naturally occurring from work the students completed as part of their studies. As indicated in the introduction, this approach differs from other corpus-based approaches that restrict topic, time on task, and access to study aids.

The entire corpus contains data from spoken assignments, reading reports, grammar assignments and writing, including revisions collected via an on-line submission system that was created by the IEP to provide electronic feedback to students and to track development. Students were strongly encouraged to submit work via the on-line system, but not all teachers and not all students systematically used on-line submission. In addition, students could opt out of having their work included in research based on informed consent that was obtained.

At the time of data collection, the IEP offered three levels of instruction based on placement testing of entering students' proficiency: low intermediate ('level 3'), intermediate ('level 4') and advanced ('level 5'). The curriculum is divided into a traditional skills-based curriculum, with reading, writing, listening and speaking having separate rather than combined classes. In addition, students take a grammar class. The IEP has a clearly articulated curriculum, both horizontally across one level and vertically from one level to another. This study focuses on levels 4 and 5 because insufficient participants contributed data to compare learners from different language backgrounds across all three levels.

Of direct relevance to the topic of this paper is the focus in all levels and all classes on words from the AWL (Coxhead, 2000). IEP 'Core Vocabulary' lists had been created for weeks 2–12 of the semester, 5–8 words for each week for a total of up to 55 to 80 lexemes per week. Level 3 words (55) ranged only from BNC-COCA frequency 1000–4000, Level 4 words (93) from frequency bands 1–6, with most being BNC-COCA level 3000, and level 5 words (122) again concentrated in the BNC-COCA 3000 range. Hence, the maximum number of words students were consistently instructed on over three semesters would have been 270. Students at each level are provided with a list of words for that level to study.

In all classes in the IEP, teachers were encouraged to write the words on a word wall in class and elicit definitions, examples, and morphological variants for about the first five minutes of each class. Despite these curriculum guidelines, not every teacher in every class took the time to do this activity over the course of the period that the data were collected, whereas some teachers took much more than five minutes. Thus, no guarantee exists that these activities took place in each class every day in the same way. While this characteristic may be seen as a deficit in an experimental study, these conditions in fact reflect the day-to-day operation of an IEP. It can be said that instruction sought to raise awareness of lexical development and the correct usage of different forms of a word.

The writing curriculum at the intermediate level (level 4) stated that 'Students will produce medium-length, original written texts (≤ 500 words) responding to information on personal, practical, social, and general academic topics.' The goal of the program was also to ensure that students would be able to 'use core vocabulary selected from the Coxhead list and that also appear on the BNC 3000–4000 word lists and additional targeted vocabulary in written texts on personal, practical, social, and general academic topics.' The topics in the database from level 4 reflect this approach. Essay types were labeled 'Process' (common examples were 'recipes' and 'how to find an apartment'); 'Classification' (e.g., types of doctors, festivals, jobs, lists of reasons). 'Cause-effect': one frequent topic was of 'Causes of Happiness'. Thus, while the types of essay were set, students were free to choose their own topics. For example, the topic of classification (festivals) predictably elicited descriptions of the lunar New Year for students from China and Korea and Eid Al-Fitr for Arabic-speaking students, which included descriptions of food and different customs from those cultures.

The advanced (level 5) writing curriculum goals stated that: 'Students will produce medium-length and long, original written texts (500- 2,000 words) on personal, practical, social, and general academic topics.' In addition, in terms of vocabulary targets, the objectives stated that 'Students will use core vocabulary selected from the Coxhead list and that also appear on the BNC 5,000 + word lists and additional targeted vocabulary in written texts on personal, practical, social, and general academic topics.' Essays topics included: 'Explanation' (e.g., 'how to learn English', 'how to stay healthy', 'the effects of a bad diet'); 'Narratives'; 'Argument/ persuasive essay' that presents a point of view and supports it (e.g., 'euthanasia', 'the death penalty', 'pollution', 'same-sex marriage'); 'Comparison/contrast essay' (e.g., 'town or city living', 'your home town vs. Pittsburgh', 'Macintosh vs. PC computers'). 'Example Essay' – illustrate a case, e.g., 'education in the ELI', etc.

Thus, the writing classes, and indeed the program as a whole, specifically targeted words that have been the focus of research in vocabulary in the context of academic topics and rhetorical patterns common in ESL writing instruction. At issue is whether the instruction contributes to lexical development as intended by the curriculum. The research questions in this paper were thus as follows: using naturally occurring corpus data, is it possible to answer these questions:

1. Do students improve the lexical diversity in their writing based on a list independent measure (VocD)?
2. Do students improve the lexical sophistication in their writing based on the AG (using the BNC-COCA 1–25k list for frequency).
3. Is there an effect of proficiency on entering the IEP in lexical development?
4. Is there an effect of first language, such that students from one language group improve more than another over the course of two semesters?

Method

The data are a subset of the data from students in writing classes over two semesters, but not necessarily the same two semesters for all students because the data could come from any consecutive semesters from 2006 to 2013. As the data were produced in the course of students' studies and not for an experiment or an examination, the data are 'naturalistic' and truly reflect variability and real-world behaviors of students and teachers in IEPs over time. Another issue is one of proficiency in a level. On arrival at the IEP, some students place directly into the intermediate level 4 based on their test scores. Other students may have already been in the IEP for a semester and have moved up to intermediate level 4 from low intermediate level 3. Teachers often suggest that those students who move up from level 3 are less proficient than students who place directly into the intermediate level 4 on arrival. These differences are noted in the description of the participants. Unlike the scheduled and monitored data collection reported in many studies (e.g., Daller, Turlik & Weir, 2013), the numbers of assignments submitted to the corpus varied according to the instructor and individual students. Such variability is normally considered a threat to internal validity and thus could potentially make measures of lexical development used in experiments inapplicable.

Participants

The participants, who had provided written informed consent, were from the language backgrounds that represented the major first languages of in the IEP: Arabic, Chinese, and Korean. (Other L1s do not constitute large enough samples). Records from 64 Arabic speakers, 47 Korean speakers and 41 Chinese speakers were downloaded from the database and automatically marked up in CLAN (MacWhinney, 2000) for the level and class the assignment had been completed for. In order to be included in the corpus for this paper, students had to meet certain criteria for amount of data contributed to the database. Although students may remain in the IEP for three semesters, not enough Chinese-speaking and Korean-speaking students had contributed enough data to track over three semesters. Therefore, data from a minimum of two semesters were used. Each student had to have enough data from at least two texts from each semester with a minimum sample per student of 500 words. These criteria decreased the pool to 61 students.

Table 1 shows the proficiency placement test scores, with the differences among the scores noted. The data show that the Arabic speakers were reliably less proficient based on Michigan Test of English Language Proficiency (MTELP) scores and the in-house listening placement test, but not on the in-house writing placement test.

Table 1. Mean placement scores by first language

Test	Arabic $n = 22\ (6)$	Chinese $n = 20\ (15)$	Korean $n = 19\ (10)$	F	p ≤	η^2
Listening	16.62[a,b]* (3.70)	20.20[a] (4.48)	20.16[b] (4.77)	(2, 58) = 3.81	= .028	.116
MTELP	49.36 [a,b]* (7.98)	60.65[a] (9.29)	60.42[b] (10.75)	(2, 58) = 10.08	= .0001	.258
Writing	3.08 (0.82)	3.41 (0.85)	3.19 (0.78)	(2, 58) = 1.6	= .321	.038

* Means that are co-superscripted in each row are reliably different.

The numbers for each language group indicate the total *n* with the number of students who placed directly into level 4 in parentheses. Thus, it is clear that most Chinese-speaking and Korean-speaking students started at a higher proficiency level than the Arabic-speaking students. All but six Arabic-speaking students had spent the previous semester in the IEP, whereas over 50% of the other two groups had placed directly into level 4.

Materials and procedure

The CLAN files for each participant were searched for assignments in level 4 and level 5 writing and these assignments were copied and pasted into a word document for each participant and level, resulting in two word files per participant. After participant data were screened for meeting the minimum text and word counts, the resulting word document files were submitted to a spell check to eliminate chance misspellings, e.g., 'feild' for 'field'. However, it was not possible to correct words that were not the ones intended by the students, but were actually words that exist in English. Such word choice errors were often based on mispronunciations. For example, an Arabic-speaking learner produced 'defferent' instead of 'different'; a Chinese-speaking learner produced errors such as 'In mordant society, people who cannot handle the pressures well could cause some mental problems', instead of 'modern'. An example of Korean-speaking learner's errors was 'For the following reasons, Oishi is my favorite restraint for lunch in Okland' instead of 'restaurant'. After spell checking, each assignment from each participant was copied and pasted separately into the website 'Text Inspector' at <http://www.textinspector.com/>. The number of words in each text was recorded in an excel file along with the vocD lexical diversity score provided by the website.

The procedure for calculating Advanced Guiraud (AG) was different. The base Guiraud (total types/√tokens) is supposedly robust for texts from 1000 to 100,000 words. However, many of the texts in the data are shorter than 1000 words. To avoid the problem of short texts for AG it was decided to run the AG measure on the whole set of texts for each participant, rather than for each individual text. This was justified after a test case with the Korean level 4 data was carried out: all the texts from the Korean speakers' level 4 output were first analyzed *separately* for AG, resulting in a mean and SD for each student text produced (*AG* = 0.81(0.31). Then AG statistics (mean and SDs) were calculated for each Korean student's *combined* texts (*AG* = 1.38 (0.68)). These two measures correlated at Pearson *r* = .89, p≤.0001, showing that AG for all texts is related to a mean of separate texts. Conforming to the original Guiraud text length requirement as closely as possible, the entire file of sample texts for each student at level 4 and level 5 were entered into the BNC-COCA analysis at Cobb's <http://www.lextutor.ca/vp/comp/>. The frequency bands selected was the BNC-COCA 1–25 listing. As Cobb <http://www.lextutor.ca/vp/comp/CCL_blurb.htm> emphasizes that: 'The goals of refining these lists include as usual to drain the swamp [sic!] of 'off-list' items, to get more text coverage for fewer items, to get a better fix on what Norbert Schmitt is now calling 'mid-frequency vocabulary,'[4] to get a baseline for potential 'technical' or 'domain specific' items, and to do more on Lextutor for the advanced learner (a growing constituency)'. All types for each student above the BNC-COCA 2000 list were calculated and subsequently divided by the square root of total tokens in the sample = 'AG' statistic. The essays in the database vary considerably in length as a function of how and why the students participated in the data collection, so this procedure made text length less of a variable for the calculation of AG.

Results

Descriptive statistics for the samples from each language group at both IEP levels are displayed in Tables 2 and 3. The numbers of participants, texts, and tokens are roughly equal, with the Arabic speakers providing slightly more data at level 5.

Table 2. Text counts, token counts and vocD by language and by level

	Total tokens overall: 254,055 Total texts: 632	Arabic (*n* = 22)	Chinese (*n* = 20)	Korean (*n* = 19)
Level 4	Total tokens: 100,292	31,357	37,404	31,531
	Total texts	97	110	91
	Average texts per participant	4.41 (2.22)	5.5 (2.64)	4.79 (2.35)
	Mean VocD per text	69.06 (9.53)	77.48 (14.34)	72.45 (13.24)
Level 5	Total tokens: 153,763	60,522	49,987	43,254
	Total texts	130	107	97
	Average texts per participant	5.9 (2.09)	5.35 (2.18)	5.11 (2.33)
	Mean VocD per text	74.72 (12.61)	80.94 (16.16)	77.01 (13.27)

---

4. Schmitt & Schmitt (2014)

Table 2 shows that the average vocD score per text increases slightly from level 4 to level 5. The placement test MTELP score did not correlate with average text vocD measure at level 4 for any language group; however, for the Chinese-speaking learners MTELP at placement did correlate with the level 5 average vocD, $r = .47$, $p = .04$; for the Korean-speaking learners MTELP at placement correlated with the level 5 average vocD, $r = .58$, $p = .01$. No reliable correlation was found for the Arabic-speaking learners. To control for placement proficiency scores, a repeated measures General Linear Model procedure was performed in SPSS with first language as the between participants variable, mean scores for vocD in level 4 and level 5 as the within participants variable, using placement MTELP as a covariate. The results of the RMANCOVA showed no reliable effect for vocD increase ($F1,55)= .53$, $p = .41$), no interaction between in vocD and initial proficiency MTELP score ($F(1,57)= 1.41$, $p = .240$); there was no interaction of vocD and MTELP, ($F(1,57)= 1.14$, $p = .24$), and no interaction between time and first language with vocD as the dependent variable ($F(2, 57) = 0.57, p = .57$). This latter pattern is illustrated in Figure 1.

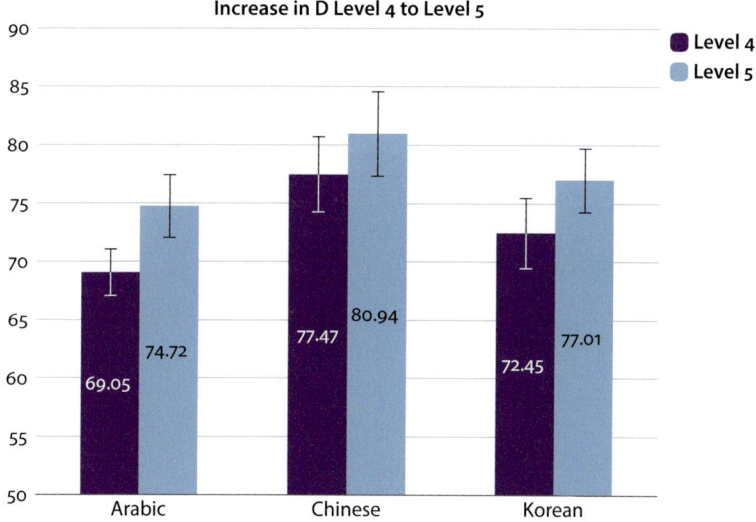

Figure 1. Interaction of increase in mean vocD level 4 and vocD level 5 for the three language groups. (Error bars represent standard error).

If the analysis is run without MTELP as a covariate, there is a reliable increase from level 4 to level 5; however, even in this case the average gain in vocDs is only 4.56 from level 4 to level 5. The Chinese learners in particular, most of whom were placed into level 4 on entry to the program, develop very little in the vocD measure.

The descriptive statistics of the Guiraud and AG by level and language are displayed in Table 3.

Table 3. Measures related to guiraud and AG analysis by IEP level and first language

	Arabic	Chinese	Korean
Level 4 Guiraud (Total types/√Tokens)	11.69 (1.51)	13.16 (2.33)	12.07 (2.04)
Level 5 Guiraud (Total types/√Tokens)	13.68 (2.45)	14.33 (3.49)	13.66 (3.09)
Level 4 Mean Types > 2000 (Per total student contribution)	51.50 (28.23)	67.10 (46.51)	56.68 (39.20)
Level 5 Mean Types > 2000 (Per total student contribution)	120.32 (78.00)	107.95 (86.54)	95.11 (73.29)
Level 4 Advanced Guiraud Types > 2000/√tokens	1.32 (0.55)	1.53 (0.79)	1.38 (0.68)
Level 5 Advanced Guiraud Types > 2000/√tokens	2.12 (1.07)	2.07 (1.22)	1.90 (1.07)

The changes in AG from level 4 to level 5 are illustrated in Figure 2.

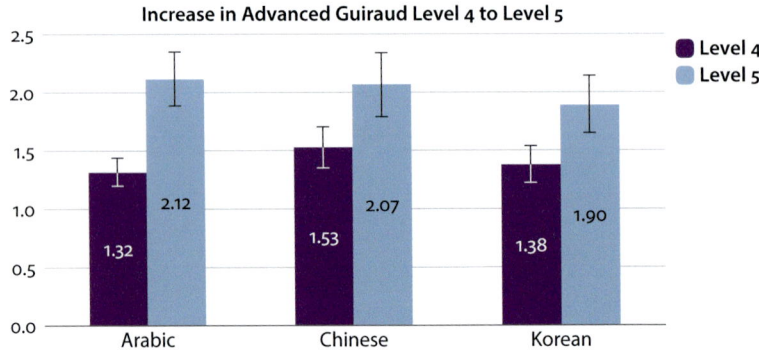

Figure 2. Increase in mean advanced guiraud from level 4 and level 5 for the three language groups. (Error bars represent standard error).

The Guiraud index (all types/√tokens) can used as a measure of lexical diversity. The figures are reported here for comparison in the discussion, but controlling for proficiency and token count, no reliable change from level 4 to level 5 (F(1,55) = 2.72, p = .105) was found.

Daller, Turlik and Weir (2013, pp. 196–197) reported that token count does not influence Guiraud in texts from 1000 to 100,000 words and that for learner texts Guiraud is robust in controlling for text length. However, token counts in these data are positively correlated with the related measure AG at both level 4 (r (61) = .51, p ≤.0001) and level 5 (r (61) = .81, p ≤. 0001). Scatterplot analysis showed that the correlation was not due to the inclusion of a few student samples below 1000 words. We have already noted the potential effect of placement proficiency scores. Therefore, a repeated-measures General Linear Model with MTELP and token counts for level 4 and level 5 as co-variates was carried out. The analysis confirms the pattern in Figure 2 in that between subjects results showed no effect for first language and no language by level interaction with AG as the dependent variable. In the within subjects' analysis, an effect of level with AG as the dependent varia-ble ($F(1,55)$ = 3.71, p = .059; η_p^2 = .063) closely approached significance even with MTELP and token counts accounted for. This effect size is moderate (Yoon & Polio, 2016, p. 12; Norouzian & Plonsky, 2018, p. 267).

Discussion

We now return to the research questions posed at the end of the introduction.

(1) *Do students improve the lexical diversity in their writing based on a list-independent measure (vocD)?*

The answer to this question is that although a small increase occurs, the analysis was not able to detect an improvement based on vocD, which has been useful for tracking development at earlier stages in development (Duràn et al., 2004, p. 238). The small amount of growth in the students' vocD scores was not independent of placement score proficiency measures, a finding consistent with Yu's (2010, p. 251) cross-sectional study. The fact that placement proficiency is related to gain scores evokes the 'Matthew effect' (Penno, Wilkinson & Moore, 2002; Stanovich, 1986); this effect is that learners who already have better proficiency are able to build on that advantage more rapidly during the course of further study. The conclusion should not be that vocD is a not a useful measure, but rather that at the advanced level in an IEP, it ceases to provide the grain size of measurement that can distin-guish growth. Durán et al. (2004, p. 238) reported that vocD ranges from 70 to 120 in native speakers' academic writing, with a mean of about 90. These students are approaching this native speaker level in some level 4 texts, which is an indication that their vocD scores are reaching a high plateau, with little room for progress to be made on this particular measure. Comparison of the D scores (70+) and Guiraud scores (12+) in level 4 with those reported by Daller, Turlik & Weir (2013, p. 203) also suggests that these learners have reached a very high level, exceeding the scores reached by their participants, who averaged a D score of over 60 and a Guiraud score of over 7 at the last data collection point at the end of 2 years instruction. Of note here is that the last three topics out of 7 that the participants of in the Daller,

Turlik & Weir (2013, p. 199) study were similar to the kinds of topic in level 4 and 5, namely 'cause and effect in damage to the environment', 'employment related issues in globalization', and 'causes of internet addiction'. This result also replicates Bulté & Housen's (2014) and Yoon & Polio (2016)'s failure to find increases in D in their studies of similar IEP students to the ones in this study, although it should be noted that the tracking of students in both their data sets was over only one semester rather than two in this paper.

This finding reminds us of Jarvis' caution when using mathematical formulae alone to define a construct:

> For most existing measures of lexical diversity, the underlying construct definition is essentially just the equation that is used to calculate the index. While existing equations do have roots in empirical observations, the practice of adopting a mathematical formalization as a yardstick for future observations is almost certainly not what Bachmann (1990) had in mind regarding the development of valid and maximally useful measures. Jarvis (2013, pp. 17–18)

These data appear to support a view that lexical diversity at the advanced level must be theoretically more than a text-internal statistical measure and should include a more qualitative approach.

(2)   *Do students improve the lexical sophistication in their writing based on the AG (using the BNC-COCA 1–25k list for frequency)?*

The answer to this question is affirmative based on the data analyzed. Descriptively, the number of advanced types in students' texts increased dramatically from level 4 to level 5. Moreover, the AG increased based on level regardless of first language. This result appears robust even when controlling for the extreme variability in text length in the data and for topic variability. While the gains are not large, at level 4 these students already exceed AG reported by Daller, Turlik and Weir (2013, p. 204) for their participants, who reached an average AG score of approximate 0.3 at the last data collection, with even the outliers in their data not exceeding a score of 1.0. It would appear that their finding could be related to the controlled task and length of text, as advanced types averaged only 5 in the Daller study, compared to over 50 at level 4 in this study. In the current study, students had time to consult learning tools and to revise, whereas in the Daller, Turlik & Weir (2013) study (as with many research studies) time was limited to 1 hour and 15 minutes. This difference in scoring points to an advantage students who can submit longer texts. Under experimental or test conditions, learners are forced to rely on their own memory and are constrained by time, producing texts well below the original 1000-word Guiraud reliability threshold. It is entirely possible that the participants in the Daller, Turlik & Weir (2013) study did not show their true lexical knowledge, whereas the learners in this study were able to rely on resources of time and learning tools that are available in classroom and homework conditions. Such resources are clearly available in real world academic tasks. The scores in this IEP data set also exceed the level of 0.65 (0.40) for the sample reported by Bulté & Housen (2014, p. 51), which also came from 'controlled' essays. The Bulté & Housen (2014) AG statistics look much more like the measures taken from individual texts in the level 4 Korean students, some of which were very short (less than 250 words). This comparison would seem to confirm that length is an important methodological factor in the measurement of lexical sophistication using AG, which is a point that has not been clearly made before.

The pedagogical implication from these observations is that portfolios of written work may be a better way of assessment and determining 'academic readiness' is of course not new. (See Lam (2016) for a recent review of research and issues, including the relationship of portfolios to teaching and learning and issues of fairness and learner agency).

(3) *Is there an effect of proficiency at entry to the IEP in lexical development?*

The answer to this question is affirmative. Correlations with all measures of lexical development – both those for lexical diversity and those for lexical sophistication – correlate reliably with entry MTELP scores (Pearson's *r* correlations range reliably from 0.26 to 0.43). However, when MTELP is used as a co-variate, gains in AG are reliable, indicating that instruction is having a positive effect independently of proficiency on entry to the IEP. The data also suggest that learners who enter the IEP at level 3 are able to catch up and keep pace with learners who enter at a higher level.

(4) *Is there an effect of first language, such that students from one language group improve more than another?*

No interaction of L1 and level in the development of lexical diversity or sophistication were found. Although the Arabic-speaking learners began at a lower proficiency level, neither the improvement scores of vocD nor AG in their writing were reliably different from those of Chinese-speaking and Korean-speaking learners. However, a possibility exists that first language may not be a good enough way of distinguishing among L1 speakers. Although the majority of the Arabic-speaking participants were from Saudi Arabia, others were from Kuwait, Libya, and Lebanon. Similarly, the Chinese-speaking participants were from both Taiwan and mainland provinces of China. Differences in language training prior to the ELI, L1 literacy practices across language groups, and individual motivation may be more important factors than first language.

General discussion

The goal of the present edited volume is to look at empirical classroom studies and address advantages and disadvantages of different methodologies. In this paper, we have considered different types of corpora (structured/experimentally controlled vs.'less' structured and not experimentally controlled) and different measures of lexical development. The study found that measurement tools that are used in experimental studies can be used for less carefully controlled classroom data. In addition, the data suggest that studies that use formal tests, especially limited time and text length, may in fact underestimate learners' ability and knowledge. A methodological issue that could be a cause for concern is that AG in this study is in fact related to text length, which was not predicted by the SLA literature, but was noted by Baayen (2001) according to Daller, Turlik and Weir (2013). However, vocD also correlated with text length at level 4. These methodological concerns deserve more careful scrutiny, especially as Bulté and Housen (2014, p. 49) also point out that text length itself has been considered "a crude indicator of lexical complexity".

Another issue that the paper did not address in depth is the issue of word families in production data and usage (Nation, 2007, p. 39). However, the fact that word families are not useful in measuring vocabulary knowledge does not mean that they should be ignored. In fact, it could be the case that the development of knowledge of relationships among forms, because of the issues of semantic drift in derivation, can be an important indicator of mastery of lexis.

Examples of lack of knowledge of word families and other errors that are not caught by spell checkers abound in the output of the learners, especially at level 4.

> Arabic: Smoking addition
> A smoking is that person who cannot stop smoking cigarettes. A lot of people who smoking cigarettes cannot leave their feeling toward the smoking cigarettes and how they enjoy when you are doing smoke.

Here the learner seems to know one word 'smoking' but has not mastered the noun form, 'smoker'. In addition, coda cluster reduction likely leads to spelling of a word 'addition' instead of 'addiction' that is not flagged by spell check.

> Chinese: For example, you could eat row fish in Japan, wear their special clothes, signsee their beautiful temples.

This Chinese learner substitutes a real word 'row' for 'raw', likely based on pronunciation. The learner coins the word '*signsee', probably as the result of coda simplification of 'sightsee', and makes the verb transitive, whereas 'sightseeing' is usally intransitive.

Korean: (a) The most important thing is that we have different <u>politic</u> forms. The north is <u>communism</u> and the south is <u>democracy</u>.
(b) Over 30 month cow <u>is every probability of</u> mad cow disease.

In the first example from a Korean learner, the student has not mastered the appropriate adjective forms to be used predicatively. The use of 'probability' is completely wrong in the second example (b), where the learner most likely intended 'A cow which is over 30 months old has a high probability of (being infected with) mad cow disease'. (Use of Korean L1 head final relative clause).

The fact that some of these errors reflect properties of the interlanguage phonology suggest that the issue is not simply a matter of recognizing a form and using it, but a more complex issue of what Perfetti and Hart (2002) have called lexical quality – that is the robustness of the links among orthography, phonology, and meaning.

Pedagogical and methodological implications

Picking up on the common theme in the lexical diversity literature that no one measure will be satisfactory in all contexts, the data from this IEP support views that the construct of lexical development must rely on more than just one statistical approach (Jarvis, 2013; deBoer, 2014). This study confirmed previously reported experimental data that for very advanced learners, D is a statistic that cannot measure increases in lexical diversity, whereas AG does provide an indication of development based on the increased use of words in the bands that Schmidt and Schmidt (2014) suggest should be the focus of instruction at advanced levels.

In addition to diversity and sophistication, we should add robustness of lexical representation or lexical quality. To extend Jarvis' (2013) metaphor of the forest containing many types and sizes of tree, broad leaf and pine, spaced and contrasting in various ways (sophistication), we must add the health of the trees represented in the forest. It is no use for a student if her diverse forest of vocabulary consists imperfectly formed trees whose ecosystem of lexical links is compromised. Going forward, lexical growth must be gauged not only by automated measures of distribution of types among tokens, but also by the frequency bands that they occur in and how good the control of forms is. In other words, while correct usage and word families may be more difficult to measure automatically, they must be measured. Developing an automated measure of lexical quality may be a challenge, but a measure that calculates a score based on vocD, AG, and lexical quality might be goal worth pursuing.

It is well known that lengthy periods of in-class vocabulary instruction is not a good use of time because knowing a word requires many encounters, and there are simply too many words to learn (Nation, 2001, p. 156). Extensive reading is one way of increasing knowledge of lexis, but it would be inappropriate to suggest that this is the only way. Curriculum developers need to select words to focus on based on their utility. This study supports suggestions by Horst (2005) that a careful look at the 2000+ level words, which increase in these data by over 50% in types for all learners from level 4 to level 5, would be to focus some more instruction on this level. Even more specifically, the 3000 level contains many important verbs (or verbs that have zero derivation nouns) in academic English. Verbs are important because they are the core of the structure of a clause, vary cross-linguistically in their properties and are underrepresented in some basic ESL texts (Juffs, 1998) and have been identified as one area of special difficulty for learners (DeKeyser, 2005). The following words are a sample from the 537 verb types (with tokens used in brackets) from the Korean-speaking learners level 5 texts, those words beginning with the letters A-C only:

> abandon_[1] abuse_[3] accelerate_[1] accomplish_[8] accumulate_[2] achieve_ [21] acknowledge_[3] acquire_[4] addict_[1] adjust_[7] adopt_[2] advocate_[2] allocate_[1][analyse_[1] anticipate_[5] approximate_[7] assemble_[1] assert_[1] assess_[2] assign_[8] attribute_[6] ban_[7] behave_[1] bias_[7] blend_[2] budget_ [2] burden_[8] campaign_[4] cancel_[1] capture_[1] celebrate_[6] chart_[1] cite_[2] civilise_[3] clarify_[7] code_[3] coin_[1] collapse_[2] communicate_[8] compensate_[1] compete_[2] complex_[4] compose_[4] compromise_[3] concert_ [1] condemn_[1] conduct_[4] confer_[1] confirm_[1] conflict_[7] confront_[3] consent_[1] consist_[3] constitute_[1] construct_[2] consume_[13]] contrast_[14] convert_[3] convey_[6] cooperate_[2] counsel_[1] criticise_[4] curve_[1]

Such words form the basis of a more academic style and could be the focus on more intensive instruction, with word families and lexical quality being a focus. Thus, instruction on lexis will co-occur with instruction on derivational morphology and usage. The data here further suggest that as D reaches a high level (70+), instructional intervention with higher frequency band words such as those listed above remains useful. Thus, teachers can use word lists and diversity measures not only to evaluate writing but also to choose texts for students for input.

The study obviously has some limitations. One is that the role of individual differences based on motivation, outside reading, as well as social interaction outside the classroom was not controlled for. Second, we are also unable to control for the role of the teacher or topic choice, but these factors create the methodological counterpoint to controlled studies. Third, after skimming many of the texts during the analysis, the impression was that texts relating personal experience and opinion (even on 'academic' topics) contained fewer low frequency words than texts that required outside evidence/reference. In order to write about personal topics/opinion, students can rely on knowledge of a restricted code/vocabulary, while discussion of an unfamiliar topic will force the search for words (c.f. Hulstijn & Laufer's (2001) involvement load hypothesis). Thus, it may not be topic *per se*, but need and consulting outside resources that prompts the development of lexical diversity and sophistication. This impression should be followed up in future research. Finally, the analysis has not yet checked to see whether the 270 AWL list words that the students are exposed to in the IEP based on curriculum notes are used more frequently and more accurately in students' writing than other words.

Conclusion

This paper has considered lexical diversity in the writing of high intermediate to advanced learners of ESL in an IEP. The data showed that growth occurred between intermediate 4 and high intermediate 5, but this growth was best demonstrated based on a measure of lexical sophistication, rather than gains in a purely text-internal measure. The analysis strongly supports theories of lexical diversity that go beyond just one computerized metric (deBoer, 2014, p. 144), even though such computerized measures have been shown to be reliable in predicting human ratings of lexical features (Crossley et al., 2011; Daller, Turlik, & Weir, 2013). The role of text length in the assessment of vocD and AG also requires attention. I suggest that some metric of lexical quality be added to the construct of lexical diversity and sophistication. This move may make computation more difficult but would be a more valid measure of the development of lexical diversity that forces knowledge of word families into the picture rather than leaving them out because of problems with derivation and semantic drift.

References

Baayen, R. H. (2001). *Word frequency distributions* (Vol. 18). Springer Science & Business Media.

Bachman, L. F. (1990). *Fundamental considerations in language testing*. Oxford: Oxford University Press.

Booth, P. (2013). Vocabulary knowledge in relation to memory and analysis: An approximate replication of Milton's (2007) study on lexical profiles and learning style. *Language Teaching*, 46(3), 335–354. https://doi.org/10.1017/S0261444813000049

Brown, D. (2013). Types of words identified as unknown by L2 learners when reading. *System*, 41, 1043–1055. https://doi.org/10.1016/j.system.2013.10.013

Brown, J. D. (1988). *Understanding research in second language learning*. Cambridge: Cambridge University Press.

Bulté, B., & Housen, A. (2014). Conceptualizing and measuring short-term changes in L2 writing complexity. *Journal of Second Language Writing*, 26, 42–65. https://doi.org/10.1016/j.jslw.2014.09.005

Coxhead, A. (2000). A new academic word list. *TESOL Quarterly*, 34, 213–238. https://doi.org/10.2307/3587951

Crossley, S. A., Salsbury, T., McNamara, D. S., & Jarvis, S. (2011). Predicting lexical proficiency in language learner texts using computational indices. *Language Testing*, 28(4), 561–580. https://doi.org/10.1177/0265532210378031

Daller, H., Van Hout, R., & Treffers-Daller, J. (2003). Lexical richness in the spontaneous speech of bilinguals. *Applied linguistics*, 24(2), 197–222. https://doi.org/10.1093/applin/24.2.197

Daller, M., Turlik, J., & Weir, I. (2013). Vocabulary acquisition and the learning curve. In S. Jarvis & M. Daller (Eds.), *Vocabulary knowledge: Human ratings and automated measures* (pp. 185–218). Amsterdam: John Benjamins. https://doi.org/10.1075/sibil.47.09ch7

Duràn, P., Malvern, D., Richards, B., & Chipere, N. (2004). Developmental Trends in Lexical Diversity. *Applied Linguistics*, 25(2), 220–242. https://doi-org.pitt.idm.oclc.org/10.1093/applin/25.2.220.

deBoer, F. (2014). Evaluating the comparability of two measures of lexical diversity. *System*, 47, 139–145. https://doi.org/10.1016/j.system.2014.10.008

DeKeyser, R. M. (2005). What makes learning second-language grammar difficult? A review of issues. *Language learning*, 55(S1), 1–25. https://doi.org/10.1111/j.0023-8333.2005.00294.x

Duràn, P., Malvern, D., Richards, B., & Chipere, N. (2004). Developmental trends in lexical diversity. *Applied Linguistics*, 25(2), 220–242. https://doi.org/10.1093/applin/25.2.220

Ellis, N. C., & Simpson-Vlach, R. (2009). Formulaic language in native speakers: Triangulating psycholinguistics, corpus linguistics, and education. *Corpus Linguistics and Linguistic Theory*, 5(1), 61–78. https://doi.org/10.1515/CLLT.2009.003

Friedline, B. E. (2011). Challenges in the second language acquisition of derivational morphology: From theory to practice (Unpublished PhD dissertation), University of Pittsburgh, PA. <http://d-scholarship.pitt.edu/id/eprint/8351>

Gardner, D., & Davies, M. (2014). A new academic word list. *Applied Linguistics*, 35(3), 305–327. https://doi.org/10.1093/applin/amt015

Hamp-Lyons, L. (2007). The impact of testing practices on teaching: ideologies and alternatives. In J. Cummins & C. Davison (Eds.), *International handbook of English language teaching* (pp. 487–504). New York, NY: Springer. https://doi.org/10.1007/978-0-387-46301-8_35

Horst, M. (2005). Learning L2 vocabulary through extensive reading: A measurement study. *Canadian Modern Language Review*, 61(3), 355–382. https://doi.org/10.3138/cmlr.61.3.355

Hulstijn, J., & Laufer, B. (2001). Some empirical evidence for the involvement load hypothesis in vocabulary acquisition. *Language Learning*, 51, 539–558. https://doi.org/10.1111/0023-8333.00164

Hsu, W. (2014). The most frequent opaque formulaic sequences in English-medium college textbooks. *System*, 47, 146–161. https://doi.org/10.1016/j.system.2014.10.001

Jarvis, S. (2013). Defining and measuring lexical diversity. In S. Jarvis & M. Daller (Eds.), *Vocabulary knowledge: Human ratings and automated measures* (pp. 13–44). Amsterdam: John Benjamins. https://doi.org/10.1075/sibil.47.03ch1

Jarvis, S., & Daller, M. (Eds.). (2013). *Vocabulary knowledge. Human ratings and automated measures*. Amsterdam: John Benjamins. https://doi.org/10.1075/sibil.47

Juffs, A. (1998). The acquisition of semantics-syntax correspondences and verb frequencies in ESL materials. *Language Teaching Research*, 2, 93–123. https://doi.org/10.1177/136216889800200202

Lam, R. (2016). Taking stock of portfolio assessment scholarship: From research to practice. *Assessing Writing*. https://doi.org/10.1016/j.asw.2016.08.003

Laufer, B., & Nation, P. (1995). Vocabulary size and use: Lexical richness in L2 written production. *Applied linguistics*, 16(3), 307–322. https://doi.org/10.1093/applin/16.3.307

McCarthy, P. M., & Jarvis, S. (2007). vocd: A theoretical and empirical evaluation. *Language Testing*, 24(4), 459–488. https://doi.org/10.1177/0265532207080767

MacWhinney, B. (2000). *The CHILDES project: Tools for analyzing talk* (3rd ed.). Mahwah, NJ: Lawrence Erlbaum Associates.

Malvern, D., Richards, B., Chipere, N., & Duràn, P. (2004). *Lexical diversity and language development: Quantification and assessment*. Paulgrave: Palgrave MacMillan. https://doi.org/10.1057/9780230511804

McCarthy, P. M., & Jarvis, S. (2010). MTLD, vocd-D, and HD-D: A validation study of sophisticated approaches to lexical diversity assessment. *Behavior Research Methods*, 42(2), 381–392. https://doi.org/10.3758/BRM.42.2.381

Murakami, A., & Alexopoulou, T. (2016). L1 influence on the acquisition order of English grammatical morphemes. *Studies in Second Language Acquisition*, 38(3), 365–401. https://doi.org/10.1017/S0272263115000352

Nation, I. S. P. (2001). *Learning vocabulary in another language*. Cambridge: Cambridge University Press. https://doi.org/10.1017/CBO9781139524759

Nation, I. S. P. (2007). Fundamental issues in modelling and assessing vocabulary knowledge. *Modelling and assessing vocabulary knowledge*, 35–43. https://doi.org/10.1017/CBO9780511667268.004

Norouzian, R., & Plonsky, L. (2018). Eta- and partial eta-squared in L2 research: A cautionary review and guide to more appropriate usage. *Second Language Research*, 34(2), 257–271. https://doi.org/10.1177/0267658316684904

Penno, J. F., Wilkinson, I. A. G., & Moore, D. W. (2002). Vocabulary acquisition from teacher explanation and repeated listening to stories: do they overcome the Matthew effect. *Journal of Educational Psychology*, 94(1), 23–33. https://doi.org/10.1037/0022-0663.94.1.23

Perfetti, C. A., & Hart, L. (2002). The lexical quality hypothesis. In L. Verhoeven, C. Elbro, & P. Reitsma (Eds.), *Precursors of functional literacy* (pp. 189–214). Amsterdam: John Benjamins.

Schmitt, N., & Schmitt, D. (2014). A reassessment of frequency and vocabulary size in L2 vocabulary profiles and learning style. *Language Teaching*, 46(3), 335–354. https://doi.org/10.1017/S0261444813000049

Schmitt, N., & Schmitt, D. (2014). A reassessment of frequency and vocabulary size in L2 vocabulary teaching. *Language Teaching*, 47(4), 484–503. https://doi.org/10.1017/S0261444812000018.

Siskova, Z. (2012). Lexical richness in EFL students' narratives. *Language Studies Working Papers. University of Reading*, 4, 26–36.

Stanovich, K. E. (1986). Matthew effects in reading: some consequences of individual differences in the acquisition of literacy. *Reading Research Quarterly*, 21(4), 360–407. https://doi.org/10.1598/RRQ.21.4.1

Todd, R. W. (2017). An opaque engineering word list: which words should a teacher focus on? *English for Specific Purposes*, 45, 31–39. https://doi.org/10.1016/j.esp.2016.08.003

van Hout, R., & Vermeer, A. (2007). Comparing measures of lexical richness. In H. Daller, J. Milton, & J. Treffers-Daller (Eds.), *Modelling and assessing vocabulary knowledge* (pp. 93–115). Cambridge: Cambridge University Press. https://doi.org/10.1017/CBO9780511667268.008

West, M. (1953). *A general service list of English words: With semantic frequencies and a supple-mentary word list for the writing of popular science and technology.* London: Addison-Wesley Longman.

Yoon, H-J., & Polio, C. (2016). The linguistic development of students of English as a second lan-guage in two written genres. *TESOL Quarterly, First view.* https://doi.org/10.1002/tesq.296

Yu, G. (2010). Lexical diversity in writing and speaking task performances. *Applied Linguistics,* 31(2), 236–259. https://doi.org/10.1093/applin/amp024

CHAPTER 10

Discussion

Balancing methodological rigor and pedagogical relevance

Nina Spada
University of Toronto

In this chapter I reflect on the contributions to this volume with respect to two guiding criteria: Relevance to classroom applications and Advantages and challenges of methodology. I examine the goals, focus, and research questions investigated in the descriptive, quasi-experimental and experimental studies presented in this collection. I analyze their methodological characteristics in terms of cost, ethics, participant availability, experimental control, teacher collaboration, student motivation, and generalizability. I argue that all the ISLA studies presented in this volume are relevant to L2 pedagogy. Echoing the words of the editors, I also argue that placing experimental and descriptive research into a dichotomous relationship where the former is characterized as not relevant to the classroom and the latter as lacking validity is problematic. Such a categorization fails to acknowledge the different purposes of both types of research and the different contributions each can make to L2 pedagogy.

Keywords: research and L2 pedagogy, validity, generalizability, relevance

I am pleased to have the opportunity to comment on the contributions to this volume, which represent a range of methodological approaches to instructed second language acquisition (ISLA) research. In doing so, I will refer to the two criteria that the editors have provided as a framework for discussion and analysis: *Relevance to classroom applications* and *advantages and challenges of methodology*. The latter is further divided into the subcategories: (1) cost; (2) ethics; (3) participant availability; (4) experimental control; (5) teacher collaboration; (6) student motivation; (7) generalizability. In discussing the research within each section I will begin with the observational/descriptive studies followed by the quasi-experimental studies and the experimental studies.

https://doi.org/10.1075/lllt.52.10spa
© 2019 John Benjamins Publishing Company

Relevance to classroom applications

Descriptive research

In Chapter 2, the classroom observational study reported by Collins & White is a good example of research that has direct relevance to classrooms precisely because it took place in real classrooms with real teachers and learners. It focused on naturally occurring student-initiated language-related episodes (LRE) to investigate the effects of contextual factors on the type, frequency and resolution of LREs. The study took place in 3 intact elementary school classes with francophone EFL students in Canada. Typical teacher-selected classroom tasks were used as opposed to tasks designed for research purposes, and they were contextualized within regular classroom instruction. The study included observations and recordings of what was naturally occurring rather than introducing an instructional intervention. The descriptive research reported by Juffs in Chapter 9 also takes place in intact classrooms to investigate the development of vocabulary in the L2 writing of university students in an intensive English program (IEP). The data were produced in the course of the students' regular studies and are described as reflecting the real world behaviours of students and teachers in IEPs over time. Because both studies document naturally occurring practices rather than manipulate instructional variables, they represent a high level of ecological validity defined as "the degree of similarity between a research study and the authentic context that the study is purportedly investigating" (Loewen & Plonsky, 2016: 56). The exploratory nature of descriptive and observational studies means that there is a wide range of variables 'at play'. Indeed one of the strengths of descriptive/observational research is to identify key factors in the teaching/learning process and to formulate hypotheses that can be investigated in subsequent quasi-experimental or experimental studies. The process of using findings from descriptive research to set up experimental studies was discussed in an oft-cited research cycle proposed for first language (L1) education over 40 years ago by Rosenshine and Furst (1973), who identify three elements as a minimum requisite for research on teaching effectiveness: description, correlation and experimentation. They emphasize how research at each step in the cycle importantly influences the development and modification of research at other steps. Spada (1990) discusses this cycle in relation to process-product research in L2 learning and teaching. Thus, while the ecological validity is high in descriptive and observational research, there are limitations with respect to the kind of information it can provide (i.e. investigations of potential cause/effect relationships). Of course all research comes with strengths and limitations and these are discussed in more detail below.

Quasi-experimental research

Two quasi-experimental ISLA studies are described in Chapters 3 & 4. Sato & Loewen report on an investigation of the effects of two types of corrective feedback with/without metacognitive instruction on the grammatical development of university-level learners of English as a foreign language (EFL) in Chile. The study was undertaken in intact classes with the students' regular teachers providing the instructional intervention without researchers present. The teaching materials were imposed by the researchers but efforts were made to develop them in ways that approximated the regular classroom/textbook activities. Teachers were given extensive training in the corrective feedback treatments and assigned to instructional treatments that approximated their regular teaching styles. In the Bardovi-Harlig, Mossman, & Su quasi-experimental study adult learners in intact classes in an intensive English program at an American university received two types of corpus-based instruction for the teaching of pragmatics. The intervention, designed around authentic uses of pragmatic routines obtained in the Michigan Corpus of Academic Spoken English (MICASE), was delivered by the students' regular teachers. As with the Sato and Masatoshi study, the researchers made considerable efforts to ensure the fidelity of the instructional treatment. They met with the teachers several times before the intervention to go over the instructional strategies; they provided detailed lesson plans and scripts for teachers to follow; they also met with the teachers before each lesson to go over any questions and met with them afterwards to revise subsequent lessons based on teacher feedback.

In these quasi-experimental ISLA studies the ecological validity of the instructional intervention was increased through using intact classes and asking regular classroom teachers to provide the instructional intervention. These efforts to minimize the disruption of teacher/student interaction also meant that there was no systematic observation or audio/video recordings of how the instructional treatment was provided. This makes it difficult to know with certainty what actually occurred 'behind classroom doors' and to make direct connections between the instructional input and the learning outcomes. The tradeoff was between ecological validity and experimental control. In the words of Sato & Loewen, their research design "runs a risk of diminishing internal and external validity (generalizability) ... [but] increases ecological validity that helps link research and practice" (p. xx). These issues are discussed in more detail in the section Advantages and challenges of methodology.

Experimental research

The four experimental ISLA studies include the Prieto Botana & DeKeyser's re-search (Chapter 7) in which the contributions of explicit instruction to L2 learn-ing under task-essential and non-task essential learning conditions were explored with university learners of Spanish in the US. Also included is Nassaji's study (Chapter 6) examining the effects of different types of corrective feedback on short and long-term L2 learning with university students at different levels of proficiency in an intensive ESL program in Canada. In Chapter 5 Shintani reports on an exper-imental study in which she investigated the roles of metalinguistic information and guided production in the development of explicit and procedural knowledge. The only experimental study taking place within a computer-assisted language learning (CALL) environment is reported by Leow, Cerezo, Caras & Cruz (Chapter 8). In this curricular-based approach to CALL, the researchers explored, with a group of college-level students of beginning Spanish, whether guided versus direct instruc-tion delivered via videogames had differential effects on L2 grammatical develop-ment and the cognitive processes engaged in while learning.

In the experimental ISLA studies the instructional materials consisted of researcher-administered picture-cued oral production tasks (Nassaji); computer-delivered training and practice sessions (Prieto Botana & DeKeyser); computer-delivered story-reconstruction tasks (Shintani) and a computer-based video game (Leow et al.). While both researcher & computer-delivered formats are not typical of most instructional material, the use of technology and on-line learning compo-nents are increasingly available in educational contexts particularly for the majority of L2 learners who participated in the studies reported in this volume (i.e. students in North American universities). As stated by Prieto Botana and DeKeyser "in many of today's classrooms, the students will encounter presentation and practice very similar to the ones in this study" (p. 148). On the other hand, the nature of learner involvement in the dyadic researcher/learner interaction used in the Nassaji study differs more from typical whole class learner-teacher interaction as well as the kind of interaction that takes place between learners in classroom settings. It is also important to keep in mind that the participants in all the experimental studies were taken out of their classes and randomly assigned to treatment groups either in language laboratories, computer labs or quiet classrooms managed by the researchers. This renders this type of research less similar to the learning and teaching activities that occur in regular classrooms.

Not surprisingly, as we move from the descriptive/observational research to the quasi-experimental and experimental research there is a decrease in ecological validity and an increase in experimental control. Does this mean that findings from experimental ISLA research are not relevant for classroom instruction? I do not think so. It is my view that all the studies included in this volume have relevance for L2 teaching. To be sure, certain aspects of the research may be more or less relevant and there are limitations on the degree to which some elements of the research are directly applicable to L2 pedagogy. But to argue that experimental research has no relevance to classrooms or that descriptive research is methodologically weak and therefore not valid fails to recognize the diverse contributions that different types of ISLA research can make to L2 teaching and learning.

Certainly the research questions investigated in all the ISLA studies presented in this volume are relevant to L2 instruction. They may not be most urgent or pressing questions for all teachers in all contexts but I believe that most would agree that the questions listed below– representing a compilation of those investigated in the studies included here– are relevant to pedagogical practice.

1. Can L2 learners provide each other with accurate information about language?
2. What are the effects of different types of corrective feedback on L2 learning?
3. Does enhancing learners' awareness of language contribute to L2 development and to the process of learning?
4. Is explicit deductive information about the L2 beneficial for learning and for what kinds of L2 knowledge?
5. Are different types of explicit CALL instruction more effective than others?
6. How effective are corpus-based approaches for the teaching of vocabulary and pragmatics?

The instructional materials used in most of the studies are also pedagogically relevant in that they could be usefully employed with comparable populations of learners. This includes the online materials for Spanish L2 learners developed for the Prieto Botana and DeKeyser study and the user-friendly computer-based video games in the Leow et al. research. Because the linguistic features targeted in both studies are known to present challenges for English learners of Spanish, teachers and learners of Spanish in similar educational contexts could benefit from the availability of the instructional materials if they have access to similar online learning environments and the technical support for them. The materials used in the Sato and Loewen study were developed to reflect content and themes in the textbooks used by Spanish-speaking learners of English in their regular classes. Thus, they also have the potential to be of use for other teachers using similar textbooks and working with similar populations of learners in Chilean universities. The corpus-based materials used in the lexical and pragmatic studies could also be usefully employed with teachers and learners in similar programs. Bardovi-Harlig et al. point to the advantages of implementing the corpus-based pragmatics materials outside the constraints of a research design because teachers could "mix and match CM and

CS exercises in ways that they find most effective, at points where they are most needed." (p. 73). In Juffs' descriptive study the lexical corpus-based materials had in fact already been designed for and implemented in all classes in the IEP program.

When thinking about the relevance and applicability of the results of these ISLA studies to pedagogical practice I wondered how the research/practice relationship is being discussed in other professional disciplines (e.g. medicine, engineering, management). I discovered that there is an extensive and growing literature about this, which is undoubtedly related to increased pressure from funding agencies for researchers to demonstrate in concrete ways the relevance and impact of their work. In one publication from the field of management (Varadarajan, 2003), I came across no fewer than 11 different types of relevance that were proposed to result from research: direct versus indirect relevance, latent relevance, immediacy of relevance, first order versus second order relevance, breadth of relevance, conceptual versus instrumental relevance, duration of relevance and my favorite ... serendipitous relevance! Space does not permit a discussion of them here but it would be interesting to explore how these conceptualizations of relevance might map onto different types of L2 research and their applicability to pedagogy. For example, research that describes the use of a new L2 language assessment measure and makes it available to the broader L2 community could be argued to have instrumental relevance; a study that describes the conceptualization and validation phases of the development of the test could have conceptual relevance; a study that describes the use of the test with a group of learners to measure their knowledge of L2 grammar or vocabulary in relation to a particular type of instruction might have direct or indirect relevance depending on how similar/different the characteristics of learners, contexts, languages etc., are between the original study and another pedagogical setting.

As indicated above, it may be tempting to argue that because the descriptive studies are the most ecologically valid they are the most relevant to L2 pedagogy and the experimental studies with low levels of ecological validity are the least relevant. However, this is too simplistic given that there are other design features of ISLA research that need to be taken into consideration when making decisions about relevance and applicability. For example, if there is insufficient information and documentation about the type of instructional treatment provided in a quasi-experimental ISLA study this raises internal validity problems as well as questions about relevance. One cannot recommend a pedagogical approach based on research where there is incomplete information about it. In cases where systematic efforts are made to increase confidence about the precise nature and fidelity of the instructional treatment as in the Sato & Loewen and Bardovi-Harlig et al. studies one might consider the findings to be more relevant to classroom practice. With respect to experimental studies and the argument that the tight control of variables renders them less relevant, Prieto Botana and DeKeyser counter by stating that "adopting an experimental design did not come at the expense of ecological validity but rather, it increased the likelihood that our findings may actually be replicable in a regular classroom." (p. 143). Also related to relevance is the generalizability of findings from ISLA research. This is discussed below in *Advantages and challenges of methodology*.

Advantages and challenges of methodology

Cost

All ISLA research takes time and money. Either the time is front-loaded as in most experimental studies where considerable time is taken up in the preparation of materials and the development of procedures whereas the actual intervention takes comparatively less time. It tends to be the reverse with descriptive/observational studies where the preparation time is shorter than the data collection period. In the Bardovi-Harlig et al. quasi-experimental study the researchers comment on their surprise at how much time it took to design the supported corpus searches for the instructional intervention. It would be unrealistic to expect that teachers would have time to prepare such pedagogical materials on their own. Several ISLA researchers reporting in this volume discuss cost in terms of the time it took to get a sufficiently large pool of participants to meet their design requirements. The challenges of obtaining funds to compensate participation in experimental research are also considerable. Prieto Botano and DeKeyser discuss the costs that come with technology that is "not always user-friendly and may require an important time investment on the part of the researcher for stimulus preparation." (p. 145). In addition, software often requires expensive licensing. Leow et al., avoided technological expense by collaborating with another research team in the development of the videogame and in the collection of data and coding. Unfortunately, the platform they used ceased to exist, underscoring one of the potential risks of CALL, which is a reliance on free online platforms.

Ethics

One of the main advantages of descriptive/observational ISLA research is that it is minimally intrusive and disruptive to teachers and learners. Nonetheless, obtaining permission to observe classes is difficult and permission to video or audio record teacher-student interaction is challenging particularly when doing research with school-age children. Taking the appropriate steps to obtain parental consent in addition to that of school principals, and teachers can be very time consuming. In the Sato & Loewen quasi-experimental study, respecting the teachers' desire to deliver the instructional materials themselves to avoid a researcher presence in the classroom represented an ethical decision that came with methodological tradeoffs (i.e. the absence of an observational component). Also, as Collins & White remind us, even the most ethically sensitive and least disruptive classroom observation research leads to changes in the nature and rhythm of interaction between teachers and learners. This results in questions of validity such as whether the data are an accurate reflection of typically occurring pedagogical practice.

In experimental ISLA research the practice of random assignment of participants to treatment & control groups is highly intrusive because in order to accommodate the design and schedule, students miss out on classroom time. This is particularly the case with treatment groups because teachers are concerned that they will have less time to cover the content of the syllabus. Sometimes there are also concerns that students' negative attitudes about participating in research projects could be reflected in the course evaluations.

With respect to control groups, an ethical issue that has been raised is whether students who participate as controls may be missing out on an educational opportunity by not receiving any instructional treatment. An argument against this is that all education is an experiment and it is only unethical if we know for certain that one type of instruction is better than another. Not all research ethics boards agree with this and in fact are increasingly requiring that control groups are provided with experimental treatments *after* the study is completed. In their quasi-experimental study Sato & Loewen did not include a control group ostensibly because they had ethical concerns about not providing any corrective feedback to participants as reflected in their comment "knowing CF brings about positive learning effects regardless of its type, is it ethical to set up a control group that does not receive any CF?" (p. 49). In the Bardovi-Harlig et al. quasi-experimental study a control group was included. This was also the case with all the experimental studies. None of the researchers comment on this design aspect with respect to ethical issues presumably because there were no concerns that the participants in the control groups would be disadvantaged in any way.

Participant availability

Observational ISLA studies often yield larger numbers of participants, and this is partially due to their minimally intrusive nature. As discussed above, even here there are challenges that come with recruiting participants, particularly children and adolescents. One of the difficulties facing quasi-experimental ISLA studies is holding on to participants because of high rates of attrition. This was evidenced in Sato & Loewen where several students did not show up for class and others withdrew from the course. In their experimental study, Leow et al. lost 60% of their participants, which was partially due the timing of the experiment and its proximity to a major holiday.

Clearly, participant availability is facilitated when the research is compatible with the objectives of the educational context in which the research takes place. For example, Bardovi-Harlig et al. had no difficulty getting access to teachers and students, because their research was compatible with the curricular goals of the intensive English program. Indeed they were invited to come and do research on pragmatics in the classes. Low program enrolment, however, meant that it took a long time to collect data from enough participants in the experimental groups. In Juffs' descriptive study of lexical development they accessed a database of naturally occurring corpus data so recruiting participants was not an issue. (For a discussion of the importance and value of making research goals compatible with the goals of the research site, see Schachter & Gass, 1996).

As indicated above, access to participants in experimental research often involves financial remuneration and this can help to alleviate problems with attrition. Also, in educational contexts where research activity is encouraged and supported (e.g. university contexts), one often has access to a large pool of potential participants. This is likely one of the reasons why a disproportionate amount of ISLA research has taken place with university-level students (Collins & Muñoz, 2016; Ortega, 2005). Indeed of the eight studies reported in this volume, seven were conducted with this population of L2 learners. This does not mean that getting access to participants in such contexts is automatic or easy, particularly when large numbers are required.

Experimental control

Experimental control is not relevant to observational and descriptive ISLA research by definition. That is, both types of research take place in naturally occurring classroom settings, and the goal is to describe, not to manipulate variables. Because of this, there are often unexpected and uncontrollable factors that emerge in the course of the research. For example, Collins & White point to the poor quality of the audio recordings, the difficulty comparing across the naturally occurring tasks because of different lengths/demands, and coping with the sudden appearance of a student teacher. In Juffs' descriptive corpus-based vocabulary study it was revealed that not all the teachers provided the vocabulary instruction as requested and that, depending on the topic of the texts used, there were differences in the number of low-frequency words between the instructional groups.

Experimental control becomes more relevant in quasi-experimental research. Two critical components are equivalence of treatment conditions and fidelity in instruction. The most effective way of demonstrating both is via carefully documented descriptions of the instructional materials and verifiable records of the implementation of the instruction (i.e. audio and/or video recordings). As discussed above and reported in Sato and Loewen, it is not always possible to obtain permission to collect such data, and this limits the conclusions one can draw.

One of the advantages of experimental studies is the greater confidence in the delivery of the instructional intervention precisely because it is highly controlled and often delivered by the researchers themselves. However, learner and contextual variables can be difficult to control, even in experimental studies. For example, Prieto Botano and DeKeyser raise questions about whether all the participants were sufficiently engaged and focused on the tasks and how this might have interacted with the instructional treatment and their learning outcomes. Leow et al. wonder whether the cognitive demands of the tasks may have advantaged/disadvantaged learners with more/less rote memory capacity and language-analytic ability. Challenges with experimental control can also be technology-related, that is, programming computers to accurately and appropriately deliver the instructional treatment and testing. Other issues related to experimental control in ISLA research are discussed below.

Teacher collaboration

While the teachers in the Collins & White observational study selected their own tasks and delivered them in their own way, they collaborated by inviting researchers into their classrooms to observe learner and teacher behaviours. In Juffs' descriptive study all teachers in the intensive English program were encouraged to collaborate by providing enhanced vocabulary instruction over the course of the data-collection period even though not all of them did. In the Sato & Loewen quasi-experimental study the researchers describe the teachers as interested in the role of corrective feedback, and this motivated them to collaborate with the researchers. As indicated above, the teachers in the Bardovi-Harlig et al. research invited the researchers into their program because they were interested in the teaching of pragmatics. Some of the teachers also participated in the preparation of the instructional materials for the intervention. As is typical with most experimental studies, there was no teacher collaboration in the ones reported in this volume, apart from making their students available and revising their schedules to accommodate the research. The instruction was either researcher or computer delivered.

Student motivation

Collins and White speculate that in their observational ISLA research the existence of peer familiarity in intact classrooms could have contributed positively to
student motivation. On the other hand, they also point out that observers in the
classroom could disrupt learners and decrease motivation. In the Bardovi-Harlig
et al., quasi-experimental study the students were characterized as highly motivated
because of the novelty of pragmatics instruction and their desire for and appreci-
ation of the authentic language that the pragmatics instruction provided. Sato &
Loewen suggest that the high attrition rates in their research were related to low
levels of motivation. Prieto Botana & DeKeyser report that there was evidence that
some of their participants had "checked out" during the experiment leading them
to wonder what impact fluctuations in participant engagement and attention might
have had on their findings.

   It is important to note that no attempts were made to directly measure student
motivation or engagement in the research reported in this volume, making it impossible to know how this might have contributed to the results. Indeed there are a
number of individual learner variables that could have contributed to the findings
reported in these ISLA studies. For example, Sato and Loewen express concerns
about whether differences in learners' proficiency levels may have influenced their
results. While one might argue that selection criteria and random assignment to
treatment groups in experimental designs control for individual differences such
as these, it is difficult to be confident of this assumption when faced with the low
numbers of participants that are typical of ISLA research. Recent calls have been
made for more research to investigate how individual learner factors interact with
instructional input to produce differences in learning outcomes. One example of
this is aptitude-treatment-interaction research (DeKeyser, 2012; Li, 2013; Yalçin
& Spada, 2016).

Generalizability

While it is true that findings based on ISLA research can lead to important generalizations about L2 learning and teaching, one needs to keep in mind that generalizations are broad statements that apply to groups of learners but they do not
and cannot apply to all educational contexts, teachers, tasks, linguistic features,
languages and learners. As we know, the extent to which research findings are
relevant to classroom applications depends on the specific learning contexts in
which the research takes place. For example: Who are the learners (age, proficiency
level, first language background, motivation levels, aptitude); who are the teachers

(experience, pedagogical orientation, knowledge of learners' L1)? What is the nature of the educational context in which these teachers and learners are situated? What is the target language? What aspects of language are the focus of instruction? What is the nature of the broader social context in which the L2 teaching and learning takes place?

Given the wide range of factors that contribute to research outcomes, it is not surprising that the ISLA researchers reporting in this volume are reluctant to consider their findings as generalizable. In the observational study by Collins and White there is a high degree of similarity between the research study and the authentic context under investigation, but as the researchers point out, high ecological validity does not equal generalizability. This was partly due to the variation observed in individual teachers' pedagogical approaches that contributed to differences in learners' behaviour. Thus, as the authors point out, while the results of their study are close to being generalizable to other classrooms the question is *which* classrooms. Loewen and Sato state that the biggest challenge for generalizability in their study was the difficultly controlling for the instructional treatment – a common problem with quasi-experimental research. Thus, despite the compatibility of the experimental materials with regular classroom materials, extensive training with the teachers to implement the instruction as intended, the absence of a systematic record of what occurred in the classrooms makes it difficult to know whether it was the instruction or other factors that contributed to the results thus restricting applications to other contexts. Bardovi-Harlig et al., on the other hand, feel confident that the results of their quasi-experimental study can be extended to other contexts assuming that what they have in mind are similar populations of young educated adults learning English as a second language in intensive ESL programs at American universities.

The features of experimental research that are widely acknowledged to increase methodological quality and their potential for greater generalizability are: control/comparison groups, random assignment of participants, control over manipulation of independent variables, pre-testing and delayed post-testing. While all the researchers who conducted the experimental studies included these features in their designs, they were very careful when discussing the generalizability of findings. Because their study targeted only two linguistic features, Prieto Botana and DeKeyser state that "in truth, at this point we can only very cautiously suggest that our results may generalize to other semantically-based learnability problems such as the preterit/imperfect distinction, for example" (p. 147). Nassaji also comments on the limited applications of his findings given the focus on one linguistic feature as well as the dyadic nature of the research. The same concerns can be raised about Shintani's study that provided instruction on one feature through highly controlled computer-delivered teaching and testing tasks. The generalizability concerns that come with studies focused on one or two language structures are legitimate given the mixed empirical evidence for the effects of instruction on different grammatical features (Housen, 2014; Spada & Tomita, 2010).

With respect to the absence of delayed post-testing as a threat to generalizability, decades of educational research have demonstrated the importance of examining the durability of instructional effects. This was evident in Shintani's study where the benefits of only one of the experimental groups were maintained over time. In recent investigations of the methodological quality of ISLA research, Gass & Plonsky (2011) report that some of the largest effect sizes obtained in instructional intervention research are in studies that include delayed posttests in their design. As indicated above, however, problems with high levels of attrition in quasi-experimental research make delayed post-testing extremely challenging. This is also true of experimental research, but not to the same extent, particularly when participants are remunerated and/or if they represent a 'captive' population (i.e. recruited in contexts where research activity is encouraged, supported and expected).

Other independent variables that are identified as limits to generalizability in this volume include the ones pointed out by Leow et al.: the amount of practice, task-design considerations, and the learning environment. Juffs points to outside reading opportunities, social interaction outside the classroom and teacher or topic choices as limits to generalizability.

All of the above suggests that the concept of generalizability may not be a feasible or desirable goal in ISLA research. Instead it may be more appropriate to consider the concept of particularizability. a term that was introduced by Clarke (1994) when discussing the relationship between SLA research and L2 pedagogy over 20 years ago. The question that is typically asked with respect to generalizability is: Can inferences be made about the findings and their applicability to the larger population? The kinds of information used to make decisions about this are: sample size, selection procedures, reliability of data collection and analysis, confidence in the internal/external validity etc. On the other hand, the question that is typically asked with respect to particularizability is: Can the information from the research be made usable for particular teachers? The information that is relevant to responding to questions about particularizability are: details of the conditions of the classrooms studied, details of the characteristics of the learners, details of the materials and activities, description of teachers, description of institutional factors (Clarke, 1994). The argument is that if information like this is made available, teachers can better evaluate the research findings in light of their own situations and determine what is relevant and meaningful to them. In discussing the notion of particularizability, Larsen-Freeman (1996) argues that "we need to do more than give lip service to the research context ... and appreciate how this context significantly affects the outcomes of the teaching and learning processes"

(p. 169). In a review of the relationship between ISLA research and L2 pedagogy over several decades, Lightbown (2008) also calls for caution in the application of findings from one classroom context to another, emphasizing that teachers need to interpret the relevance of findings for their individual teaching situations. It is equally important for researchers to keep this in mind when making recommendations for pedagogical applications.

Finally, it is essential to remember that no one single piece of research, no matter how relevant and 'particularizable', will have a substantial impact on practice. Only cumulative findings obtained across multiple studies and examined in research syntheses have greater potential to inform questions about relevance to classroom applications.

Conclusion

The domain of ISLA research, a subfield of SLA, is intrinsically connected to L2 pedagogy because of its focus on the role of instruction in L2 learning. Thus, all types of ISLA research – descriptive, quasi-experimental and experimental – are relevant to L2 pedagogy. Some of the questions asked, materials used, procedures employed and findings obtained may be more (or less) directly relevant to L2 pedagogy depending on the nature of the research and the context in which it was carried out. Nonetheless, as Prieto Botana and DeKeyser argue in Chapter 7, placing experimental and descriptive research into a dichotomous relationship where the former is characterized as not relevant to the classroom and the latter as lacking validity is problematic. Such a categorization fails to acknowledge the different purposes of both types of research and the different contributions each can make to L2 pedagogy. What is important is that researchers working in the different traditions make concerted efforts to be as methodologically rigorous and as ecologically valid as possible within the constraints of their respective methodologies. There is ample evidence that such efforts have been made in the contributions to this volume.

References

Collins, L., & Muñoz, C. (2016). The foreign language classroom: Current perspectives and future considerations. *The Modern Language Journal*, 100(Supplement 2016), 134–147.

Clarke, M. (1994). Dysfunctions of the theory/practice discourse. *TESOL Quarterly*, 28, 9–26. https://doi.org/10.2307/3587196

DeKeyser, R. (2012). Interactions between individual differences, treatments, and structures in SLA. *Language Learning*, 62, 189–200. https://doi.org/10.1111/j.1467-9922.2012.00712.x

Housen, A. (2014). Difficulty and complexity of language features and second language instruction. In C. Chapelle (Ed.), *The encyclopedia of applied linguistics*. New York, NY: John Wiley & Sons. https://doi.org/10.1002/9781405198431.wbeal1443

Larsen-Freeman, D. (1996). The changing nature of second language classroom research. In S. Schachter & S. Gass (Eds.), *Second language classroom research: Issues and opportunities* (pp. 157–170). Mahwah, NJ: Erlbaum.

Lightbown, P. (2000). Classroom SLA research and second language teaching. *Applied Linguistics*, 21(4), 431–462.

Li, S. (2013). The interactions between the effects of implicit and explicit feedback and individual differences in language analytic ability and working memory. *The Modern Language Journal*, 97, 634–654. https://doi.org/10.1111/j.1540-4781.2013.12030.x

Loewen, S., & Plonsky, L. (2016). *An A-Z of applied linguistics research methods*. New York: Palgrave Macmillan.

Norris, J., & Ortega, L. (Eds.). (2006). *Synthesizing research on language learning and teaching* Amsterdam: John Benjamins.

Ortega, L. (2005). Methodology, epistemology, and ethics in instructed SLA research: An introduction. *The Modern Language Journal*, 89, 317–327. https://doi.org/10.1111/j.1540-4781.2005.00307.x

Plonsky, L., & Gass, S. (2011). Quantitative research methods, study quality, and outcomes: The case of interaction research. *Language Learning* 61, 325–366. https://doi.org/10.1111/j.1467-9922.2011.00640.x

Roshenshine, B., & Furst, N. (1973). The use of direct observation to study teaching. In R. Travers, (Ed.), *Second handbook of research on teaching* (pp. 122–183). Chicago, IL: Rand McNally.

Schachter, J., & Gass, S. (1996). *Second language classroom research: Issues and opportunities*. Mahwah, NJ: Lawrence Erlbaum Associates.

Spada, N. (1990). Observing classroom behaviours and learning outcomes in different second language programs. In J. C. Richards & D. Nunan (Eds.), *Second language teaching education: Content and processes* (pp. 293–310). New York, NY: Cambridge University Press.

Spada, N., & Tomita, Y. (2010). Interactions between type of instruction and type of language feature: A meta-analysis. *Language Learning*, 60, 1–46. https://doi.org/10.1111/j.1467-9922.2010.00562.x

Varadarajan, P. R. (2003). Musings on relevance and rigor of scholarly research in marketing. *Journal of the Academy of Marketing Science*, 31, 368–376.

Yalçın, S., & Spada, N. (2016). Language aptitude and grammatical difficulty: An EFL classroom-based study. *Studies in Second Language Acquisition*, 38, 239–263. https://doi.org/10.1017/S0272263115000509

Index